"Addressing the difficulty of speaking a[bout God], or
more broadly, Dr. Lim brings together a[ll these theological]
and philosophical issues. Around his central discussions of Wittgenstein
and Lindbeck he weaves an intricate tissue of references, drawing upon
thinkers from Aristotle to Augustine, Aquinas, Hume, Heidegger, Rorty,
and D. Z. Phillips. This is a deeply learned and profoundly knowing
discussion of the matter of 'God talk.'"
—David Jasper, University of Glasgow

"This is a clear, honest, and balanced study that explores with appropriate
scholarly depth the literature on Wittgenstein, Lindbeck, and their
significance for theology today. It promises to be a valuable resource for
others who wish to explore the nature of religious language."
—David Fergusson, University of Cambridge

"A theologian with a magisterial grasp of how traditions of religious
practice both connect and disconnect with one another, Dr. Lim finds
resources for serious ecumenical agreement by proposing how religious
believers may steer their conversations with one another along claims
either to inerrancy or infallibility. Both critical and reconstructive,
reading this book sharpens up our understanding of the interplay of
word and practice expressed in our differences, and consequently how
we may relish them in the hunt for truth in theology."
—Ann Loades, Durham University and University of St Andrews

"In shaping understanding of the nature of religious language, two
of the most important figures in the twentieth century were Ludwig
Wittgenstein (d. 1951) and George Lindbeck (d. 2018), the former
with his notion of language games, the latter with his idea of a cultural-
linguistic approach to doctrine. For some, though, their insights are seen
as unnecessarily restrictive, a threat to the objectivity of religious belief.
In a book which is a model of clarity in both argument and exposition,
Dr. Lim brilliantly advances the claim that the exact opposite is the
case. A wide range of potential contexts and allusiveness in metaphor
and symbol entail a richness of meaning even for centuries-old imagery,
while an inevitable lack of precision means only that God is never fully
contained by our words, not that truth fails to emerge. This is a work of
relevance to conservative and liberal Christians alike."
—David Brown, University of St Andrews

"Dr. Lim's attractively written book offers a thoughtful and convincing justification for the claim that it is possible to speak about God, despite God's transcendence. This is a topic that is of perennial concern to theologians and philosophers of religion. I particularly commend the author's detailed yet accessible account of Wittgenstein's contribution to the debate."

—JEFF ASTLEY, Durham University and Bishop Grosseteste University

Not Beyond Language

Not Beyond Language

Wittgenstein and Lindbeck
on the Problem of Speaking about God

Khay Tham Nehemiah Lim

FOREWORD BY *David Fergusson*

PICKWICK *Publications* · Eugene, Oregon

NOT BEYOND LANGUAGE
Wittgenstein and Lindbeck on the Problem of Speaking about God.

Pickwick Publications
An Imprint of Wipf and Stock Publishers
199 W. 8th Ave., Suite 3
Eugene, OR 97401

www.wipfandstock.com

PAPERBACK ISBN: 978-1-7252-7268-2
HARDCOVER ISBN: 978-1-7252-7266-8
EBOOK ISBN: 978-1-7252-7269-9

Cataloguing-in-Publication data:

Names: Lim, Khay Tham Nehemiah. | Foreword by David Fergusson.

Title: Not beyond language: Wittgenstein and Lindbeck on the problem of speaking about God / by Khay Tham Nehemiah Lim; foreword by David Fergusson.

Description: Eugene, OR: Pickwick Publications, 2021 | Includes bibliographical references and index.

Identifiers: ISBN 978-1-7252-7268-2 (paperback) | ISBN 978-1-7252-7266-8 (hardcover) | ISBN 978-1-7252-7269-9 (ebook)

Subjects: LCSH: Philosophical theology. | Language and languages—Religious aspects. | God (Christianity)—Knowableness—History of doctrines—20th century. | Wittgenstein, Ludwig, 1889–1951. | Lindbeck, George A. | Communication—Religious aspects.

Classification: BT103 L56 2021 (print) | BT103 (ebook)

For Jenise
to whom my gratitude is beyond language

Contents

Foreword

by
David Fergusson,
Regius Professor of Divinity, University of Cambridge

IN DISCUSSING THE TERM "persona" as a description of the Trinitarian distinctions, Augustine famously acknowledged his lack of understanding while pleading the impossibility of silence. The same dilemma has often been felt by Christian theologians who have tackled the question of religious language. How do we acquire a knowledge of "God talk"? What is the practical context of such words and statements as they are employed in faith communities shaped by Scripture and tradition? In what ways do they refer to a transcendent, infinite Other who is not of our making? How do we register divine mystery and human finitude without being reduced to an agnostic silence?

These questions lie at the heart of this fine study by Khay Tham Lim. Throughout his discussion, he wisely navigates a route between on the one side a naïve realism which assumes that religious statements timelessly mirror an extra-mental divine reality and its effects, and on the other a constructivist reduction of religious language to a process of human self-description through its shaping of liturgical and ethical action. His two protagonists are the philosopher Ludwig Wittgenstein (1889–1951) and the theologian George Lindbeck (1923–2018). From their different contexts, these two thinkers suggest ways in which we might properly understand the social context of meaning without abandoning a commitment to theological realism. What emerges is a nuanced set of proposals that draws our attention to the embeddedness of religious meaning in story and scripture, in forms of life, in church practice, and in Christian formation. At the same time, Dr. Lim resists non-cognitive views that seek to exhaust religious meaning by reference to who we are and what we do. He stresses the ways in which our language can bring genuine disclosure and understanding of the divine, and therefore of ourselves not as the creators of God but as creatures.

This is a clear, honest and balanced study that explores with appropriate scholarly depth the literature on Wittgenstein, Lindbeck, and their significance for theology today. It promises to be a valuable resource for others who wish to explore the nature of religious language.

Preface

THIS PRESENT BOOK IS a lightly edited version of my PhD dissertation (2019) which was submitted to the University of Edinburgh. I should like to record my grateful thanks to Professor Jeff Astley of the University of Durham and Professor David Jasper of the University of Glasgow, for examining me and for their constructive and encouraging comments on my work. To Professor David Fergusson, my academic supervisor, I owe a great debt of gratitude for writing the generous foreword to this book.

As reflected in its title *Not Beyond Language: Wittgenstein and Lindbeck on the Problem of Speaking about God*, the book's concern is with the problem of religious language. That problem is a longstanding one, having vexed philosophers and religious thinkers since the earliest times. It is a problem generated by the traditional doctrine that God is utterly transcendent and is "wholly other" from human or this-worldly existence. How can divine transcendence be talked about and expressed? Keenly felt and acknowledged by all was the inadequacy of their language. In traditional theology, the response opted by some was to keep silent.

The position I am putting forward is that it is possible to speak about God—he is *not* beyond language. However, while we may speak about God, the language we use cannot be pressed to yield precise definitions or complete explanations of the divine. This follows from the previously presumed notion of divine otherness. I must clarify that in saying that religious language is incapable of yielding precision or completion, I am neither denying the possibility of truth nor implying that "anything goes."

It is important to note the polarization of views regarding the religious use of language in modern theology. On one pole, there is a tendency to treat religious statements as having no factual content, or at best, as expressing moral or ethical intentions to follow a certain way of life. The consequence of this is that speech about God is rendered empty or even inauthentic, giving rise to skepticism. On the other pole, there is the tendency to assume that words are perfectly fitted to give believers precise explanations and render God (or, indeed, reality as a whole) completely intelligible. The consequence of the latter tendency is absolutism or idolatry.

What I am proposing is thus a *via media*. In support of my view, I draw on two protagonists—principally, the philosopher Ludwig Wittgenstein, and secondarily, the ecumenist theologian George A. Lindbeck. These thinkers were first suggested to me by Professor David Fergusson, and what rich stores of insights into the question of language they have opened up for me! Although Wittgenstein does not propose or develop what may be called a theory of language, his conception of language as more than a system of signs for stating facts or making truth-claims—even about God—is vitally instructive. To him, the speaking of language is grounded in the setting of everyday life. Meaning is thus bound up with "use"; that is to say, the meaning of a word or statement is dependent on how that word or statement is actually applied in relation to the conventions, practices and needs of a given community. Lindbeck's contribution is in appropriating language as an analogue for the understanding of religion and doctrine. Inspired by Wittgenstein's principles, Lindbeck suggests that religion be regarded as "similar to an idiom that makes possible the description of realities, the formulation of beliefs, and the expressing of inner attitudes, feelings and sentiments."[1] In his so-called "cultural-linguistic" approach to religion, the "inner" and the "outer" is reversed; which is another way of saying that it is language that shapes and structures inner experiences—especially religious ones— and not inner experiences that shape and structure articulation. His emphasis on language rightly situates the community as the location for theological exegesis.

The proposals that emerge from this study have, I believe, the potential to help us meet the challenge of how we are to speak appropriately of the divine who resists language, and to reach an understanding of religion that is much more than about the pursuit of objective facts and exhaustive conceptions about God. When religious believing is not fixated with inquiring or explaining "how things are in the world," as though religion were a science, doctrinal differences across religions as well as within a religion will become less intransigent and more reconcilable.

---

1 *ND*, 33.

Although I have written with a Christian audience in mind, I hope the appeal of this work will extend to readers who are of other faiths or of none.

Unless otherwise stated, quotations from the Bible are taken from the New Revised Standard Version (NRSV).

Khay Tham Nehemiah Lim
Singapore,
Feast of St Augustine of Hippo, 2020

Acknowledgements

IN UNDERTAKING THIS RESEARCH, I have been much helped and supported by many people. It is now my pleasure to record my gratitude.

Firstly, I would like to thank my supervisor, the Revd. Professor David Fergusson, for his comprehensive academic support and guidance. His penetrating critique at every stage of my research had been invaluable in furthering my thinking about what is presented in this study. I would also like to thank the Revd. Dr. Harriet Harris, my second supervisor, for her guidance and support. Thanks are also due to Ms. Karoline McLean, the Postgraduate Studies & Research administrator for assistance rendered.

I am deeply indebted to Professor Emeritus David Brown and Professor Emerita Ann L. Loades, both at the University of St Andrews. As my former teachers at the University of Durham where I earned my MA, they provided the recommendations for me to be accepted for this research project. In addition, David offered useful feedback on my work over several conversations, while Ann extended warm hospitality and encouragement.

Grateful thanks are due to the Revd. & Mrs. Jeremy-Joe Tan and their brilliant children (Joshua and Anna Joy), Andy and Mabel Lie (Newcastle-upon-Tyne), Jim and Rhona Dunn (Morpeth), Allan and Sue Percival (Durham), Eric Woodburn (Helensburgh) and the Revd. & Mrs. Jae-Hun Park (Edinburgh Japanese Church) for friendship, hospitality, and meals. Jeremy-Joe (a fellow doctoral student from Singapore) and Tricia not only provided a home for me in Edinburgh during the final stages of my writing-up, they gave me much support and encouragement. In spite of his busy schedule, Andy, whose enthusiasm greatly inspired me, proofread most of this thesis and saved me from numerous embarrassing errors. I hasten to add that the flaws remain my own.

I am also grateful to several fellow students at New College, the University of Edinburgh, who extended their hand of friendship as well as rendered help: Okky Chandra, E. R. Haire Jr., Anthony Haynes, Riyako Cecilia Hikota, IChun Kuo, Kazue Mino, Wen-Pei Shih, and Adam Trettel.

In my third year of study (2016–2017), I had the privilege of spending two semesters at the University of Tübingen, Germany under the Erasmus exchange programme offered by the University of Edinburgh. During my time there, I benefited from seminars at the *Evangelisch-Theologische Fakultät* as well as the community life at the *Evangelische Stift Tübingen* (EST) where I was housed. To the two universities involved and the EST, I record my sincere appreciation for an experience that had been enriching and worthwhile. To my fellow Tübingen students, namely, Matthias Keller, Calvin Urlich, and Elise Eckart, thank you for friendship and conversations. I must also thank a former Durham classmate, Ralf M. W. Stammberger of Limburg for making an effort to come down to Mainz to meet me shortly before I left Germany to return to Edinburgh.

I have been blessed with the best parents-in-law one can have. Mr. Lee Gee Chow and the late Mrs. Bebe Lee had been supportive from the start of my research. I give my utmost thanks to God for both of them, the latter in loving and fond memory.

My most heartfelt word of thanks is reserved for my beloved wife. Jenise borne the heaviest load throughout my long research journey. Yet, more than all other persons she was the one who kept me going: she was unfailing in praying, cheering, and encouraging me at every stage. This work is therefore affectionately dedicated to her in token of deep gratitude, and in acknowledgement that she has been very much part of its formulation and completion.

List of Abbreviations

THE FOLLOWING ABBREVIATIONS ARE used to refer to the works of Wittgenstein and Lindbeck.

BB	Ludwig Wittgenstein, *The Blue and Brown Books*
CV	Ludwig Wittgenstein, *Culture and Value*
LC	Ludwig Wittgenstein, *Lectures and Conversations on Aesthetics, Psychology and Religious Belief*
LE	Ludwig Wittgenstein, "Lecture on Ethics"
NB	Ludwig Wittgenstein, *Notebooks 1914–1916*
ND	George A. Lindbeck, *The Nature of Doctrine: Religion and Theology in a Postliberal Age*
OC	Ludwig Wittgenstein, *On Certainty*
PI	Ludwig Wittgenstein, *Philosophical Investigations*
PG	Ludwig Wittgenstein, *Philosophical Grammar*
TLP	Ludwig Wittgenstein, *Tractatus Logico-Philosophicus*
Z	Ludwig Wittgenstein, *Zettel*

Quotations from the main body of *TLP* and the first part of *PI* are indicated by referring to the proposition or paragraph number respectively. Quotations from the front material of *TLP* and the second part of *PI* (cited as *PI* II) are indicated by referring to the page number. Quotations from the *NB* are indicated by referring to the date of entry or, where applicable, the page number.

Introduction

Language is a labyrinth of paths. You approach from *one* side and know your way about; you approach the same place from another side and no longer know your way about.[1]

—Ludwig Wittgenstein

Language and Divine Transcendence

IN MOST OF THE world's religions and certainly in all the monotheistic ones, God is habitually spoken of, referred to, and reflected upon. Even God's ways, supposedly past finding out, are diligently searched and deliberated. Unsurprisingly, discourse centered on the divine or "God-talk" is most evident in the pages of the sacred scriptures (the Tanakh, the Bible and the Qur'an) belonging to the three Abrahamic religions—Judaism, Christianity, and Islam. Divine discourse also occurs in a wide variety of routine situations that are vital to the practice of religion, such as in confession, prayer and praise, thanksgiving, worship, preaching, theological reflection, and so on.

In all the diverse forms of God-talk just mentioned, the presupposition is that it is possible to say something about the divine by means of language, that is to say, language is a proper or even primary medium for portraying God or conveying truth(s) about God. There is plenty of support for attributing such a role to language, and the growing consensus that all experience of transcendence must come to language is, no doubt, a factor.[2] In the same vein, Jeff Astley (b. 1947) has averred that

---

1. *PI* 203.

2. See, e.g., Ricoeur, *Figuring the Sacred*, 35.

"there is no alternative to the medium of language."[3] To my mind, words are gifts to us; they are all we have for framing and fashioning what, for human, self-conscious existence, can only be called "our world." And if words can be used to do all sorts of work, it stands to reason that they can also be used to speak about the divine. We might thus say that God is not beyond words.

To be sure, most people of faith who talk about God are not unaware of the transcendence of the divine—that God is "wholly other" and radically different from human beings and what they ordinarily experience. Nevertheless, they seem to assume a good deal of knowledge about who God is and what his will and purpose for the world are. With Christians, for instance, it is believed that the gap between the divine and human has been bridged on account of the mediation and revelatory work of Jesus Christ, and, henceforth, God may be known and spoken of. One of Christianity's most influential theologians, Karl Barth (1886–1968), has declared, "We humans *cannot* speak of God, but because God has become human, we *may* speak of God."[4] Then there are the many other ordinary religious adherents who, unacquainted with the concept of divine alterity, go about believing that God, whom they trust is always close at hand, is in some dynamic mode of communication with them. The people I have here characterized could well be the ones Karen Armstrong (b. 1944) has in mind and identified with when she observes, "We are talking far too much about God these days, and what we say is often facile."[5] Whether that sentiment is fair or not, what we may note is how easily, in our attempt to speak about the transcendent God, we can overlook the absolute distance between our words and the divine reality.

Some Issues with God-Talk

Even if we have been respectful of the divine-human divide, we still should note that it is in the very realm of speaking that problems with different aspects of God-talk have arisen. For one thing, talking about God is very different from talking about people and things: the use of language in one case is different from the use of language in the other. In fact, the language that underlies talk about God is itself complicated, with its employment

3. Astley, *Exploring God-Talk,* 14–15.

4. Barth, *Word of God and Theology,* 191.

5. Armstrong, *Case for God,* ix.

of words for a reality that is said to be "beyond language" (and resisting all description). In making this observation about the underlay of language, I am referring not only to distinctively religious words like "incarnation," "justification," "sacrifice," "repentance," "predestination," and the rest, but *any* words that are appropriated to play a linguistic role within some religious context. For the most part, religious language uses ordinary words whose meaning is an adaptation of what has been fixed by their use outside religion. There are at least two pitfalls to watch out for when using religious language. The first is to want to take words at their face value. That would be too simple-minded, as words have "rough edges" and can have many meanings. The second pitfall concerns the incongruity of using human, and therefore materially derived and fallible, language for a subject who is presumed to be infinite, immaterial and beyond all human imaginings. One is reminded of the attempt of Eberhard Jüngel (b. 1934) at explaining this difficulty: "Our language is worldly language, and has only worldly words which refer to and are predicated of worldly beings."[6] Predictably, the result has been that God is sometimes spoken of as though he were a human person. Regular users of religious language are generally not very attentive to such an anomaly; indeed, they tend to regard God-talk as relatively unproblematic, and to just get on with it. However, I anticipate that once questions are raised about the meaning of particular words, statements or utterances in their religious context, or whether religious expressions are literally true or only symbolically so, the complaint that religious language is of the "oddest kind" will quickly emerge and become more keenly felt.[7]

Preliminary Considerations

Inquiring into the meaning of words and statements in religion seems almost required of us, for as language users we naturally presuppose that some kind of meaning must pertain to language about God. Certainly, most believers do assume that they know and understand—at least partially—what their religion teaches through its creeds and doctrinal statements. Still, we are never guaranteed easy or straightforward answers. Indeed, an inevitable circularity awaits us: for to ask about the meaning

6. Jüngel, *Theological Essays*, 59.

7. See Ramsey, *Religious Language*, 48, who has suggested the questions that concern us most demand the "oddest kind of language."

of words is to find ourselves entrapped within an almost endless round of other words, other signs. And if we ask for the meaning of these words which are meant to render the meaning of those earlier ones the response would still be in terms of words.[8] Be that as it may, we can do no better than recognize that words form "a complete system"[9] and try to make the best of it. Under the circumstances, all one can do is remain as reflective as one can be within language, resolutely resisting the temptation to embrace a nihilist view that "there is nothing except language in the world."[10] Here I should like to call attention to a confusion that is sometimes made in discussions about the use of religious language—that of collapsing knowing what a statement means with knowing the ways or conditions in which the statement is to be verified. While knowing the meaning of some statement must include knowing the conditions for its verification, the two forms of knowing are not the same. This has been made clear by Friedrich Waismann (1896–1959), a member of the famed Vienna Circle, who writes, "In the normal use of language the questions 'What does this sentence mean?' and 'How do I find out whether this sentence is true?' are two entirely different questions, and anyone will refuse to regard them as alike."[11] Thus, a statement like "a cat is a nocturnal animal" is false, and yet anyone who speaks English can easily understand it. If we are to attribute one single thing which the "linguistic turn" of the early twentieth century has reasonably established for us, it is that the question of meaning is prior to the question of truth: one must know what a statement means, or have an idea of its meaning, before one can even begin to discuss whether the statement is true or false. In the last example about cats being nocturnal, it is in virtue of the fact that we understand what is being claimed that we can say that the statement is not true. Further back in history, theology was concerned with a different set of questions, such as who God is, what the nature of God is, what the Trinity is, what the proofs of God's existence are, how did God become man, how God relates to the world and to us? The issues raised are largely

---

8. This is the basic idea of textualism. See Loughlin, *Telling God's Story*, 12–13; Cupitt, *Time Being*, 64.

9. Cupitt, *Long-Legged Fly*, 14.

10. Loughlin, *Telling God's Story*, 13, paraphrasing Derrida's famous line, "There is no outside-text."

11. Waismann, *Principles of Linguistic Philosophy*, 330, cited in High, *Language, Persons, and Belief*, 43.

metaphysical: they are about what "there is," and about the "how-to" of arriving at knowing what exists.[12]

The question of meaning with which we are concerned, is usually understood as a question about how words and statements refer or signify. This is the "word-object theory" of meaning, a theory that correlates words to their objects, where the latter could be thoughts, concepts, facts or even things. The root idea is that every word has a meaning and this meaning is "the object for which the word stands."[13] Most people, I imagine, would find this whole approach regarding the quest for meaning so intuitive as to be "commonsensical." It is because meaning here bears a correspondence to the word with which it is correlated, and is obtained by this correlation—it is the "hook" between word and object, as it were—this theory is also known by various designations, namely the "correspondentist," the "referential," and the "representationalist" theory of language. Designations aside, what matters is whether the theory is adequate as a system of communication facilitating the pursuit of meaning. If it is adequate, our research project can simply conclude by suggesting that we apply the theory and see how far it takes us, and how best it serves our purpose. Or, we can recommend consulting a standard dictionary or encyclopedia. But, as I shall argue, this theory is not so much outrightly false as it is deficient, for it seems to be oblivious to the complexity of issues surrounding the question of meaning. To give a foretaste of what I intend to claim, the theory seems woefully self-contained in a world of only word and object.[14] Is meaning simply a matter of establishing how the former relates or corresponds to the latter? Surely, the meaning of any religious utterance or expression cannot be detached from the matrix or "form of life" in which language functions and is embedded. Full details about the notion of "form of life" and the associated concept of "language-games," which are both borrowed from Ludwig Wittgenstein (1889–1951), will be provided later. For the moment, all that needs to be said here is that the application of these concepts to our research questions have thrown up important insights for our understanding of meaning. I have just mentioned that meaning cannot be fully arrived at, as if it is only the upshot of a two-term relationship between word and

12. See Murphy, *Beyond Liberalism and Fundamentalism*, 38.

13. *PI* 1.

14. We could say this is a concentration of a two-term relationship instead of a more holistic, three-term relationship among word, object, and the community or the wider world.

object; what has been overlooked—and which may matter for a fuller understanding of any word or statement—is the *context* in which such utterance is made. We shall have occasion to discuss "meaning" more fully, including the suggestion by Wittgenstein that language ought to be regarded as something we use in a variety of ways, for different ends and purposes.

Research Question and Thesis

Our enquiry into meaning, and what has been said about language, have prepared the ground for us to consider a longstanding puzzle, namely, the relation between "what is said" and "the way things are." In other words, we are concerned with how religious language functions. We might put the question: How do religious statements connect to or portray reality, or, rather, how do they *refer* to God? Religious believers have typically understood that there is a cognitive or factual dimension to religious language, and that theological statements reflect *content* which they take to be factual, if not also true. For example, the creedal statement, "Jesus Christ will come again in glory to judge the living and the dead" is read as entailing the factual claim that Jesus will return from heaven, and that he will sit in judgement over those who are still alive when he comes, as well as those who are not. It must be said that I have no issue with the contention that religious language is fact-stating or cognitive. Given that religion or theology deals with issues of supreme importance affecting human life (on both personal and communal levels), we can expect that what is said (or written) will include some measure of factual reference. To be sure, a good deal of religious language will be chiefly taken up with "second-order" discourse—discourse that goes beyond factual into the realm of the spirit and the immaterial. A case in point would be the Bible, the pages of which comprise a rich mix of statements of fact, metaphors, exhortations, prayers, imageries, parables, myths, and so forth. Still, "facts" are all-important for religious discourse, for what has no factual content cannot command serious interest or attention. Even so, what I think is problematic is the claim by some believers that words give them full or definitive access to the divine, as well as to reality as a whole. It would be too strong a charge to accuse those who think in this way of idolatry for identifying words with God.[15] A fairer assessment

15. See Cross, "Idolatry and Religious Language," 190–96. Cross thinks that the

would be to assign blame to a failure to take divine transcendence with sufficient seriousness. Or, it may all be a matter of mistakenly assuming that religious statements are the same sort of statements which we find or make in ordinary life and in the sciences. The thesis I am concerned to defend in this project is that although language about God can provide some factual (or cognitive) content, it cannot be pressed to yield precise definitions or complete comprehension of the divine. Again, while language about God can and does help us to know (more) about God, the sheer incommensurability between divine transcendence and its possible expression should leave us with ambiguities, gaps and even obscurities in our understanding. To quote Rowan Williams (b. 1950), "claims to be speaking truthfully about God can still be made even if we take it for granted that we cannot produce definitions of God or detailed descriptions of 'what it is like to be divine.'"[16] My claim is thus wedged between two extreme understandings of religious language. The first is one that regards religious statements as having no factual content, or at best, as expressing moral intentions or exhortations and attitudes toward the world. The second is one that tends toward treating language about God—especially the texts of sacred scripture—as the very Word of God from which one may obtain precise definitions and explanations about the divine or the world as a whole.[17]

To those familiar with modern linguistic theories, my contention would seem to go no further than to restate the arbitrariness of language.[18] Recall that Ferdinand de Saussure (1857–1913), who is widely regarded as the father of modern linguistics, had insisted that within any given linguistic structure, the sign is essentially arbitrary in relation to the

---

charge of idolatry (especially against those who uphold univocity) is often mistakenly made in theological literature.

16. Williams, *Edge of Words*, x.

17. For a case of religious statements being regarded as moral assertions, see Braithwaite, "Empiricist's View," 72–91. Braithwaite has famously suggested that to assert "God is love" is to express an intention to follow an agapeistic way of life (81). The passion of actress Joanna Lumley, who was brought up in the Christian tradition, to search for the remains of Noah's Ark offers a good illustration of the other approach towards religious text. She says, "It's so familiar to us all, from the animals going in two by two and the dove of peace, and the olive branch and the rainbow. But who was Noah, and what was the Ark and what was it made of? When and why did the flood happen? It has fascinated me all my life, and I'm going in search of the truth" (Lumley quoted in Tacey, *Religion as Metaphor*, xxii).

18. Saussure, *Course in General Linguistic*, 67.

signified. By "arbitrary," Saussure simply implies that sign actually "has no natural connection"[19] with that of which it signifies. He further notes, "Language is a system of interdependent terms in which the value of each term results solely from the simultaneous presence of the others."[20] A standard illustration of this linguistic principle, recalls Anthony Thiselton (b. 1937), is that of colorwords. "Where is the cut-off point between 'red' and 'yellow'?" Thiselton asks. The meanings of these colorwords depend on whether "orange" is part of the field of colorwords, and how other available terms contribute to that field.[21] Even so, we must underscore that such arbitrariness of language as is being raised should not be thought of as implying that the meaning of a word can be arbitrarily changed at an individual's whim or fancy.

My contention—not least in disclaiming the possibility of religious language to attain a precise definition of the divine—would also seem to echo the postmodern position that language cannot reflect reality, let alone deliver a complete explanation about the nature of God or the world. Whatever the famous postmodernist axiom "there is nothing outside the text"[22] may mean, some people who are sufficiently immersed in words and images have appealed to it as a sanction for imagining "themselves in a virtual reality, the sealed world of their own beliefs and sayings."[23] To be sure, it needs to be said that the view of reality being beyond language has occupied philosophers and thinkers long before the advent of postmodernism.[24] The view that language does not exactly fit reality has been demonstrated by the fact that the precise translation of one language to another is exceeding difficult, if not impossible. To quote David Brown (b. 1948), no one language "divides up the external world in precisely the same way as any other."[25] Nevertheless, I do not wish to disavow any pretention to being inspired by either the modern

19. Saussure, *Course in General Linguistic*, 69.

20. Saussure, *Course in General Linguistic*, 114.

21. Thiselton, *Two Horizons*, 119.

22. Or, "There is no outside-text; *iln 'y a pas de hors-texte*." See Derrida, *Of Grammatology*, 158.

23. Blackburn, *Truth*, 170.

24. E.g., Urban, *Language and Reality*, 49, who writes, "Reality is, in a sense, doubtless beyond language . . . and cannot be wholly grasped in its forms, but when in order to grasp reality we abandon linguistic forms, then reality, like quicksilver, runs through our fingers."

25. Brown, *God and Mystery in Words*, 44.

or the postmodern theories of language—or both. What I would strongly repudiate, however, is any suggestion that not much appears to be at stake here. For, as I hope to show, I am convinced that a discussion of the question of meaning and how religious statements are to be understood in the context of talk about God will take our theological reflection a good step forward.

What the Enquiry Might Yield

In undertaking this enquiry, I am concerned on the one hand to raise a caution against the extremes of a skepticism that denies language as having any epistemic relationship to reality, and of an absolutism that sees a one-to-one correspondence between words and reality, on the other. To assume the former position would be to succumb to the strict Cartesian separation between knowing-subject and knowing-object; while the latter position is hardly tenable given that the transcendent or the wholly other can never be exactly mirrored by or in language. According to the position that I propose to argue, religious terms and propositions can still have "factual significance" for the believer, even if their use involves our regarding them as having a certain level of ambiguity or incompleteness. In saying that language ought to be characterized in this way, I am not implying that religious truth claims should therefore be abandoned. Also, what is being proposed as an account of language most certainly does not mean "anything goes"—that we can make up whatever we want about the world. As we have sought and will have opportunity to stress, the language of religion does more than describe or represent "how things are"; it also orientates the user to what is central to life and thought. The "paradigm case" of religious expressions or utterances is not some fixed correspondence to a certain objective reality, rather, it is historically constructed out of the social framework within which it has arisen. This represents a key shift in our understanding of language—from looking at a word and then to the object it is said to stand for, to looking at how the word is actually used in its home context for its meaning.[26]

Besides seeking for a *via media* between skepticism and absolutism, I hope my argument will also steer us toward a better appreciation of the proper role of language. We might, for instance, begin to be more

---

26. Such a shift brings out the hermeneutic character of language. See Kerr, "Language as Hermeneutic," 491.

attentive to the depth of the problem faced in speaking about God, especially with respect to the way language must navigate between making claims about God that are literally true, and respecting the ontological difference between God and his creation. And seeing how the church and its theologians have sought to make creative use of metaphors, symbols, analogy, poetry and so on, to speak of the God whose ways are beyond complete discernment, we might also begin to be more sensitive to habits of language usage which have tended towards containment of the divine in words or, indeed, complete explanation. Here, I must again stress that neither the descriptive or representational role of language in portraying God in religious communication, in religious learning nor in theological reflection, is being denied. What I hope will be gained is an appreciation of the role of religious language in pointing allusively beyond itself—not unlike how a sacrament properly functions.[27] The key take-away is to be vigilant against the error of idolatry, that is, identifying what is intelligibly referred to in language at both the expressive and experiential levels of preaching, instruction, worship, prayer and so on, with the divine reality itself.

Another implication to draw from this study is that it might encourage greater caution in the explication of the meaning of particular statements in isolation from their larger *Sitz im Leben*, as well as healthy criticism in the evaluation of competing religious claims. Williams, who is well aware of the complicity involved in "making sense," has urged that we "question our clarity or truthfulness in the light of communications from others" and that we even "suspend judgement at certain points because we are aware of not having the conceptual or linguistic equipment to enable decisions."[28] Already, caution in deciding or assigning meaning to words and sentences should be a default response in light of the general rule in analytic philosophy that it is a "stretch of language" or a "speech-act" that is the bearer of meaning, rather than the atomic word, that is the word in isolation. I would take a step further to suggest that we should not be too quick to jump to the establishment of the meaning of propositions, statements, or even larger portions of text without

27. Brown is right to urge a "sacramental approach" in any attempt at using language to map reality (*God and Mystery in Words*, 44–74). Metaphor and sacrament are alike in being accused of much imprecision, yet both succeed in pointing allusively beyond themselves to the divine reality. They, so to speak, enable us to make "the jump to the divine." See also Brown, *Divine Generosity and Human Creativity*, 24–25.

28. Williams, *Edge of Words*, x.

relating them to other linguistic signs in our overall system of religious thought. As previously noted, meaning may not be adequately arrived at semantically, that is, it is not a matter of relation between word and object, but within a "syntactic" process in which it coheres with other signs. Connected with the issue of meaning is a crucial matter which has vexed most religions since their founding. It is the dissatisfaction with how disagreements and disputes over scripture, doctrine, teachings and even ethical conduct are managed.[29] A carefully nuanced de-emphasis on the cognitive/objective status of religious terms and statements may, hopefully, lead to less acrimony among the disputants, perhaps even to an enriched understanding of what truly divides them.

Finally, I hope my proposal can contribute to reaching a proper understanding of religion. What I think is erroneous with much current thinking about religion—especially in its popular or folk version—is that it is fixated with trying to enquire into "how things are in the world" and to explain them as though religion is some sort of a science with the necessary answers.[30] With their emphasis on the cognitive-propositional aspects of religion, religious practitioners[31] are often told by senior figures in their community to be ready to do intellectual battle with skeptics and atheists, staking out the claim that their particular religion can fill any explanatory gap that arises in the understanding of reality. The actual words of Norman Geisler (b. 1932), a conservative Christian, may illustrate what I have in mind here: "The challenge, then, is for the Christian to 'out-think' the non-Christian both in building a system of truth and in tearing down systems of error."[32] Never mind the Heideggerian criticism that the very question of being is thus left out of consideration, sacred texts are here being read as giving precise definitions and detailed explanations of God and his dealings with the world. The underlying conviction is that language, in having God as its original

---

29. This dissatisfaction is what prompted Lindbeck to write his landmark book, *The Nature of Doctrine*. See *ND*, 7.

30. Some scientists are careful to claim that "the necessary answers" from science are at best provisional. For example, Feynman (1918–1988) writes, "If you thought before that science was certain—well that is just an error on your part" (Feynman, *Character of Physical Law*, 77). Feynman was awarded the Nobel Prize for physics in 1965.

31. E.g., William Craig Lane and J. P. Moreland.

32. Geisler and Feinberg, *Introduction to Philosophy*, 73.

author, is fully "adequate for all religions and theological expression."[33] My unease with this stems from the fact that religion is put at risk of being reduced to an abstraction wholly concerned with explaining and mapping out external reality. The alternative kind of understanding of religion I wish to commend is significantly different. I would not be too anxious about spotting explanatory gaps, nor be overly preoccupied with the cognitive or factual content of religious expressions. I am emphatically not suggesting that religion is to be understood as being without objective content, or that we may just ascribe anything to the objective reality that religious language seeks to represent to us. Rather, I am simply acknowledging that we do not have the "extra descriptive resources" available to us in language to map out reality in absolute terms.[34] What is more vital and appropriate is for religious believers to attend to the truly spiritual and moral dimensions of faith, letting their "self" be molded and shaped by the "symbol system" of religion. The position I have in mind here is, I think, consonant with that which has recently emerged in the work of John Cottingham (b. 1943) on seeking a "new" model of religious understanding. Although Cottingham's claim to newness may be disputed, his proposal—that "we need to take seriously the possibility that understanding the world religiously is *not* an attempt to dissect and analyze and explain it . . . but rather a mode of engagement, or connection, with reality as a whole"[35]—is definitely not.

Why Wittgenstein and Lindbeck
Are Selected for Special Study

This study has been undertaken using resources mainly but not exclusively drawn from the philosopher, Wittgenstein and the ecumenist theologian George A. Lindbeck (1923–2018). I shall briefly explain in turn why I have chosen these two thinkers. The choice of Wittgenstein seems a natural one—by general consensus, Wittgenstein may well be regarded as the most creative and influential philosopher of language in modern times. His notions of "language-game," "form of life," and "meaning as use" (to name only a few), developed in his later philosophical phase, are

33. Clark, "Special Divine Revelation as Rational," 41. See also Clark, *Religion, Reason, and Revelation*, 146.

34. See Williams, *Edge of Words*, 8.

35. Cottingham, "Transcending Science," 31.

not only of relevance to our conceptual concerns, they lend themselves as tools for applying to our own enquiries. Even his "Tractarian" insight on the mystical has, I hope to show, useful bearings on any consideration of language in its relationship to the transcendent. As we proceed, I hope Wittgenstein's relevance will become clear. In the case of Lindbeck, he is selected primarily because he explicitly drew on Wittgenstein's work in developing his own ground-breaking postliberal approach to religion and doctrine. That the Wittgensteinian method is applied in that direction invites our keen interest, for it is rare that such a parallel is drawn. We might say that Lindbeck's foray represents a much welcome test case. Another reason for selecting Lindbeck as being of special importance for the present study is his ingenious use of the analogy of language for conceiving religion in terms of a cultural-linguistic framework that makes possible the following claimed outcomes: "the description of realities, the formulation of beliefs, and the experiencing of inner attitudes, feelings and sentiments."[36]

Organization of Material

The argument which I advance in this work is relatively uncomplicated. It is that although language about God can and does provide some cognitive content, it cannot be pressed to yield a precise definition or a complete description of the divine. The structure I have developed for establishing such a thesis is also a simple and straightforward one, comprising seven chapters, not including this introduction.

The opening chapter (chapter 1) entitled "'Discovery' of Language," is concerned with the general characteristics of language. It explores them by tracing the trajectory of how language has been understood in a variety of ways as the centuries advanced. My main purpose is to draw attention to the importance of language in the service of religion and the role of language in conveying meaning and cognition. I briefly touch on the so-called "linguistic turn," a development of great significance as far as the philosophy of language is concerned. That "turn" superseded the previous turn to epistemology and marked the beginning of a new epoch. Whereas attention had been focused first on epistemological and then metaphysical problems of philosophy, it was now to be focused on the linguistic categories of philosophical discourse itself. Philosophical

36. *ND*, 33.

problems came to be perceived as problems which may be solved either by understanding more about or reforming the language with which they are framed.

Against that backdrop, I proceed in chapters 2 and 3 to undertake an exploration of Wittgenstein's early and later phases of philosophizing with respect to language, picking out conceptual tools which may have a bearing on our argument. Both chapters serve as one long study on the philosopher, focusing on his two principal texts, namely, the *Tractatus Logico-Philosophicus* (henceforth referred to and cited as the *Tractatus* or *TLP*) and the *Philosophical Investigations* (henceforth referred to, and cited as *PI*). Attention is also given to Wittgenstein's shift from his earlier conception of language as merely a system of signs (*Zeichensprache*) for the explication or communication of ideas or things, to a later conception which regards language as reality-disclosing or world-disclosing (*Hermeneutik*).[37] Because, as was said before, Wittgenstein's new conception of language also represents the disavowal of the thought–language dualism which has been so prevalent throughout most of human history, some space will be devoted to a critique of René Descartes (1596–1650) and his dualist theory of mind and body as different kinds of thing. Other key concepts within the Wittgenstein corpus such as meaning-as-use, language-games, form-of-life, private-language, will also be discussed.

In chapter 4, I discuss Wittgenstein's thoughts on "the mystical," an element that is sometimes treated as an afterthought to his philosophic schema and thus one that might be conveniently ignored.[38] My view, on the contrary, is that *das Mystische* forms an integral part of *TLP*—it might even be considered a culmination of all that was said earlier in that work. But it is not difficult to understand why the concept of mystery is problematic: do most religious people not wish for clarity and intelligibility in matters of faith? Indeed, it is this drive for "clear and distinct ideas"—even certainty—that has fueled the "positivist" view about religious language that I am concerned to challenge. What I hope will emerge from my proposed discussion is the suggestion that the mystical cannot be exhaustively grasped by or contained within the categories of language.

---

37. Kerr, "Language as Hermeneutic," 491.

38. Bertrand Russell confesses to being left with "a sense of intellectual discomfort" by Wittgenstein's discussion of the mystical. See *TLP*, xxii.

In chapter 5 we turn our attention to the immensely complex issue of what "truth" itself might be. Besides engaging with the ancient question "what is truth?" and considering the Christian claim that Jesus Christ is himself the truth, we also attend to the assault on truth in the form of skepticism. The latter I find to be an ally of faith, not a foe. As the concept of truth is one of Wittgenstein's ongoing concerns, both his early and mature positions will be examined for the light they can shed on it. I aim to show that truth is not primarily an epistemic concept but a relational one, in the sense of being expressed in language. That is, we might say that we can have no account of it except by reference to language.

Our focus in chapter 6 will be on Lindbeck whose landmark book uses the language analogy to propose a new understanding of religion and doctrine. Lindbeck is unabashed about having drawn from Wittgenstein's work to support his "cultural-linguistic" model of religion and doctrine. For example, he makes good use of some of the philosopher's concepts like "language-games," "form of life," as well as his "private language" argument. Lindbeck's work thus provides a useful test case for our study.

Lastly, I provide a concluding chapter in which the key concepts from my two guiding lights—Wittgenstein and Lindbeck—are extracted and summarized. As suggestions for further research, I also indicate some of the important issues or questions that I may have either neglected or failed to discuss adequately or competently. This chapter ends with the affirmation that words are good enough to facilitate meaningful God-talk but that they cannot be pressed to render complete intelligibility and exact description of the divine reality.

Chapter 1

"Discovery" of Language

Man possesses the ability to construct languages capable of expressing every sense, without having any idea how each word has meaning or what its meaning is—just as people speak without knowing how the individual sounds are produced.[1]

—Ludwig Wittgenstein

Introduction

THE "DISCOVERY" OF LANGUAGE—BY which I mean the preoccupation with or the awareness of what language is and how it bears and conveys meaning—has been likened to a commonplace scenario portrayed by the British writer and philosopher Iris Murdoch (1919–1999). In her book about the "romantic rationalist" Jean-Paul Sartre who had repeatedly called attention to the crisis of language, Murdoch writes, "We can no longer take language for granted as a medium of communication. Its transparency has gone. We are like some people who for a long time looked out of a window without noticing the glass—and then one day began to notice this too."[2] The parallel drawn by Murdoch aptly illustrates how we have become more conscious that language is our window into reality and that instead of looking *through* words or signs as a matter of

1. *TLP* 4.002.
2. Murdoch, *Sartre*, 27.

1

routine, we are beginning to look *at* them. Naturally, such close attention to language itself has brought about a further awareness, the awareness that "the glass" through which we see may actually reduce or obscure our vision, should it become stained or smudged. This raises the question whether language is capable of accurately expressing reality or whether words can bear their semantic freight or cope with the use they are put to. For some of us, there is the further question posed by Wittgenstein, whose resources we have chosen to draw on for our present study: why has it never occurred to us to take off the "pair of glasses on our nose through which we see whatever we look at"?[3]

The discovery of language is, however, about much more than not taking language for granted. It is also not a recent phenomenon. Philosophers and other thinkers have long been preoccupied with the question of language—especially its epistemic primacy. Since early times, they have been beset by the perplexities that the use of words entails. Nor is the enduring concern with language an isolated movement. In this chapter, I will outline the key currents of thought on this subject-matter in the history of philosophy. As my objective is to set the stage for the larger argument of my project, I shall not be concerned to present a systematic or an exhaustive account of how language has evolved since the earliest years of human civilization; for such an undertaking would take us beyond the scope of our present study. What I wish to cover, namely the main outlines of the "story" at least up to the period of Wittgenstein, will for many be familiar territory; still I hope my recapitulation will help to generate a certain sensibility about how language has been perceived or understood as the centuries advanced, and serve to indicate how the fascination with language has impacted our present day understanding of this very human feature.

What has just been said about language in general applies naturally to the narrower phenomenon of "religious language," though the latter, in the sense in which I shall be using the term, does not refer to a natural language like English, French, or some other. The jibe, "Do you speak English, French, or religious?"[4] drives home this point for us. According to William Alston (1921–2009), whose jibe I have just used, "the term 'religious language' is a special case of the bad habit of philosophers to speak of a special language for each terminology or broad subject

---

3. *PI* 103.

4. Alston, "Religious Language," 220.

matter (the 'language of physics,' the 'language of ethics,' etc.)" in which the distinction between language and speech (or better, discourse) is neglected.[5] Alston further notes,

> The former is an abstract system that is employed primarily for communication, and the latter is that employment. What is erroneously called "religious language" is the use of language (any language) in connection with the practice of religion— in prayer, worship, praise, thanksgiving, confession, ritual, preaching, instruction, exhortation, theological reflection, and so on.[6]

So when we are engaged in speaking of God we are using the same concepts that we use in our social intercourse. Notwithstanding what was just said, however, we shall following Alston continue to use "religious language" because the term is now fully entrenched in popular parlance, as well as in academic literature.

In addition to what has been said, it may be helpful to distinguish the two ways in which the term "religious language" is used: one narrow, one broad. Narrowly, "religious language" occurs when a direct reference to God is made. Broadly and more widely, the term is used to cover ordinary religious reflection, and those religious activities noted by Alston above.

Historical Antecedents

Pythagoras (c. 570–490 BCE) may well have been the first of the Greek philosophers to have put forward a rudimentary theory of language— the idea that "the soul gives names to things."[7] Underlying Pythagoras's conviction is the belief that a name of a thing expresses or somehow identifies the true nature of a thing. So the names are not arbitrarily given by the soul, but are given "on the basis of the natural link between the name and the thing—a link somewhat like the correspondence between a mental image and the object represented by such an image."[8] In the *Cratylus*, Socrates (c. 470–399 BCE) who was Plato's teacher, is asked a question about language by two interlocutors. The question is whether words are just arbitrary signs, or whether they describe or resonate with

---

5. Alston, "Religious Language," 220.
6. Alston, "Religious Language," 220.
7. Brümmer, *Brümmer on Meaning and the Christian Faith*, 123.
8. Brümmer, *Brümmer on Meaning and the Christian Faith*, 123.

the things they signify. Socrates's response is one of support for the latter position—that words can disclose something about the world and so are more than conventional or arbitrary signs.[9] Accordingly, in asking after the meaning of justice in *The Republic* or the meaning of love in *The Symposium* what he aims for is to critically examine the way that these words are frequently used. Plato (c. 428–348 BCE) himself, in another work, tells us what his own view about language is—that when nouns or adjectives are applied to particular objects, "we assume them to have also a corresponding idea or form."[10] In short, words are instruments which reflect the structures within an unchanging and eternal world of forms. At the same time, though, Plato seems to be uneasy about the nature of language, not least with respect to the written word. What is rendered in written form, he suspects, could become "a vehicle of falsehood" if exploited by those who seek to fashion it (as something inert) into a permanent record of some understanding which is not corroborated by person-to-person discourse.[11] For Aristotle (c. 384–322 BCE), words, thought and things are related in a so-called "semantic triangle." In his *On Interpretation*, he writes,

> Words spoken are symbols or signs of affections or impressions of the soul; written words are the signs of words spoken. As writing, so also is speech not the same for all races of men. But the mental affections themselves, of which these words are primarily signs, are the same for the whole of mankind, as are also the objects of which those affections are representations or likenesses, images, copies.[12]

Aristotle's observation about the "mental affections" of words is undoubtedly astute. It seems that words as symbols or signs of objects do vary in their spoken and written forms across cultures, but not the "mental affections" to which the words refer. Indeed, as Aristotle had underscored, the mental affections themselves stay "the same for all races of men." Such a theory holds promise for boosting inter-faith relations, if religious people can similarly agree that though they use or have used different words to express the object of their ultimate concern—for example, "God," "Gott," "Dieu," "Dios," "Allah," "Tien," and so on—the

9. Plato, *Cratylus*, 433b–435b.

10. Plato, *Republic* X, 379.

11. Murdoch, *Metaphysics as a Guide to Morals*, 19.

12. Aristotle, *On Interpretation*, 115.

mental reference of these words is about the same entity. With respect to how Aristotle is able to arrive at his postulation about mental affections, no firm answer can be given except that thought has always been considered by him to have epistemic priority over speech.[13]

Given that language is of interest to theology in many varied and important ways—not least the part it plays in making divine revelation meaningful and more intelligible for believers—the question of language has been raised by religious thinkers from very early on in Western history. St. Augustine of Hippo (354–430), for instance, recognized the difficulty with language in speaking about God. After struggling to comprehend the mystery of the doctrine of the Trinity he wondered whether he should opt to be silent.[14]

Augustine's somewhat ambivalent view about language is shared by another figure whose writings wielded influence in the Middle Ages, early ascribed as Dionysius the Areopagite (he is better today known as Pseudo-Dionysius the Areopagite, whose writings date to the 6th c.). In *The Divine Names*, Pseudo-Dionysius calls attention to the radical transcendence, incomprehensibility and ineffability of God. In a particular passage, he elaborates:

> For even as things which are intellectually discerned cannot be comprehended or perceived. . . . by the same law of truth the boundless Super-Essence surpasses Essences, the Super-Intellectual Unity surpasses Intelligences, the One which is beyond thought surpasses the apprehension of thought, and the Good which is beyond utterance surpasses the reach of words. Yea, it is an [sic] Unity which is the unifying Source of all unity and a Super-Essential Essence, a Mind beyond the reach of mind and a Word beyond utterance, eluding Discourse, Intuition, Name, and every kind of being.[15]

Such portrayal of the Divine as beyond "the reach of words" naturally raises a vital question for those who believe that God is personal and that he can be known. The question as framed by Pseudo-Dionysius himself is this: can we speak or even form any conception concerning this hidden Super-Essential Godhead? As part of his response to the conundrum, Pseudo-Dionysius proposes a "naysaying" theological

---

13. Stiver, *Philosophy of Religious Language*, 11.

14. Augustine, *Trinity*, 197.

15. Pseudo-Dionysius, *On the Divine Names and the Mystical Theology*, 52–53.

system that proceeds by the negation or denial of words and concepts to "reach" God. Known technically as "apophatic" theology, this approach prescribes that in any attempt to speak of God the focus should be on what God is *not* (*apophasis*), rather than on what God *is*. The basic premise is that language is woefully inadequate in undertaking the task of God-talk. While on the one hand the strength of apophatic theology is in safeguarding the mystery of God, it is, on the other, beset by a self-contradiction—that of making the claim *in* human language about the very inadequacy of human language.

Another key figure who appealed to negation is the Jewish philosopher, Moses Maimonides (1135–1204). According to him, it is best that people should not apply any positive attributes to God, lest they misrepresent him. So extreme was Maimonides's view about negation, he even contended that negation itself is objectionable because it introduces complexity to our understanding of who God is. Well aware of the deficiencies of religious language, Maimonides held the view that claims about God are at best understood as us having merely come "one step nearer to the knowledge of God."[16]

A brief word may also be said about the contribution of John Duns Scotus (1266–1308) who had argued that since revelation has been given, language about God must be univocal. It is not that Scotus denies that God is transcendent but that he grounds the possibility of univocal talk in a univocal conception of "being." For Scotus, though divine being is different from created being, the same concept of "being" applies univocally to both. We need not discuss how this view of Scotus has been employed by certain modern theologians to support the case for the use of literal language about God, except to note that the conception of being as univocal is still very much alive and well.

Although St. Thomas Aquinas (1225–1274) finds the apophatic approach useful as a first step to understanding religious language, his own preference is for the *via analogia*—"a mean between pure equivocation and simple univocation." In what immediately follows, the "theory of analogy" will first be explained, then the two terms of extremes, namely "equivocation" and "univocation." According to St. Thomas, there exists a correspondence or an "analogy of being" (*analogia entis*) between the created order and its creator, God. The applicability of this idea extends as well to language we use. So, words like "wise," "good," "living," and so on

---

16. Maimonides, *Guide for the Perplexed*, 1.60.

when applied to God do bear a similar, though not identical, meaning to the meaning they normally carry when used within the human context. Following this line of reasoning, St. Thomas contends that we are entitled to use words *analogically* of God, that is, as a signpost to God. As he had expressed it more fully:

> Our knowledge of God is derived from the perfections which flow from him to creatures, which perfections are in God in a more eminent way than in creatures. Now our intellect apprehends them as they are in creatures, and as it apprehends them it signifies them by names. Therefore as to the names applied to God—viz., the perfections which they signify, such as goodness, life and the like, and their mode of signification. As regards what is signified by these names, they belong properly to God, and more properly than they belong to creatures, and are applied primarily to him. But as regards their mode of signification, they do not properly and strictly apply to God; for their mode of signification applies to creatures.[17]

What about "equivocation" and "univocation"? These are two other possible ways of applying human language to God, in contradistinction to the way of analogy favored by St. Thomas. Equivocation is perhaps better understood as doublespeak; thus, to speak equivocally of God is to use words which are the same but in completely different senses. The basis for speaking equivocally is the view that divinity and humanity are so distinct that they share no common ground. To apply a word univocally to God, we have noted, is to assume that God is exactly the same as us in some respect, and that the word means the same in its application to God and to the human user. Both ways of God-talk, however, have proven to be problematic: "If univocal, then language falls into anthropomorphism and cannot be about God; if equivocal, then language bereft of its meaning leads to agnosticism and cannot for us be about God."[18] Thus, the use of analogy in speaking of God provides a way out of these two opposite poles.

In the modern period, the debate on religious language may be said to have been initiated by David Hume (1711–1776). An empiricist, Hume was opposed to belief in God as well as any talk of God. True to form, he offered a mock-historical account of religious belief—that "the primary religion of mankind [sic] arises chiefly from an anxious fear of

17. Aquinas, *Summa Theologiae*, 1.13.3.
18. Ferrè, *Language, Logic and God*, 105.

future events."[19] His oft-quoted claim that any literary work, for instance, about divinity or metaphysics, which does not "contain any abstract reasoning concerning quantity or number" nor "any experimental reasoning concerning matter of fact and existence" should be consigned "to the flames: for it can contain nothing but sophistry and illusion" reveals not only the depth but the aggressiveness of his empiricism.[20] In his *Dialogues Concerning Natural Religion,* Hume likens talk about God to verbal disputes in which "the disputants may here agree in their sense, and differ in the terms, or vice versa; yet never be able to define their terms, so as to enter into each other's meaning: because the degrees of these qualities are not, like quantity or number, susceptible of any exact mensuration, which may be the standard in the controversy."[21] In other words, arguments about God are indeterminate and even meaningless. Given his ideas about the "perpetual ambiguity" of words and the radical otherness of God, Hume seems determined to press his readers to give up saying anything positive about God. Thus, we are left by him, in the words of Terrence W. Tilley, "with our feet firmly planted in mid-air, unable to touch down so as to make progress toward the goal of understanding any meaning for talk of God."[22]

Hume's rigid form of empiricism—that we can know the world around us or even the existence of the self *only* through observation by our senses—came to be embraced by A. J. Ayer (1910–1989) and others.[23] Ayer, in particular, appropriated Hume's distinction between "relations of ideas" (for example, propositions involving some contingent observation of the world, such as "the sun rises in the East") and "matters of fact" (such as mathematical and logical propositions) in the development of his own thesis.[24] Following Hume and members of the influential "Vienna Circle," Ayer posited that only two types of statements could be considered meaningful, or of literal significance. These are: (i) statements which are verifiable as true or false, and (ii) tautologies (i.e.,

19. Hume, *Natural History of Religion,* XIII.

20. Hume, *Enquiry Concerning Human Understanding,* XII, 164.

21. Hume, *Dialogues Concerning Natural Religion,* 217.

22. Tilley, *Talking of God,* 9.

23. We can count Bertrand Russell, Alfred North Whitehead, and G. E. Moore among the "others."

24. This distinction is famously called Hume's fork. The term has also been applied to a related distinction between "demonstrative" argument and "probable" reasoning. See Broackes, "Fork, Hume's," 285.

statements that define themselves such as "a novice at snow skiing has just begun to learn the sport" or those that are simply true in virtue of linguistic rules). To the first type belong statements of science as well as propositions which convey factual information about the empirical world; while statements of mathematics and logic belong to the second. Religious or metaphysical statements which do not fall under either type are dismissed as "meaningless" because they could not be verified (or falsified) empirically. Ethical statements too are adjudged meaningless, for the same reason that they could not be verified as true or false.[25] The central tenet in Ayer's thesis is what came to be known as the principle of verifiability and to which he offers the following formulation:

> We say that a sentence is factually significant to any given person, if, and only if, he knows how to verify the proposition which it purports to express—that is, if he knows what observations would lead him, under certain conditions, to accept the proposition as being true, or reject it as being false. If, on the other hand, the putative proposition is of such a character that the assumption of its truth, or falsehood, is consistent with any assumption whatsoever concerning the nature of his future experience, then, as far as he is concerned, it is, if not a tautology, a mere pseudo-proposition.[26]

It should thus occasion no surprise that objection against religion on the basis of the criterion of verifiability is much more unanswerable than that which ensues from a traditional assault on religion that its beliefs are not true. The believer's proposition, for instance, that "God exists" may be dismissed by his or her opponents as lacking evidential support, but at least it is admitted as meaningful. By Ayer's criterion of verifiability, religious beliefs are not even within the realm of truth and falsity, nor do they possess any literal significance.[27] "In other words," so notes Dan Stiver, "they have not achieved the merit of being meaningful, albeit false; they are simply cognitive nonsense."[28] Discussing the question of verifiability and its challenge to religious language further would take us much too far afield. It should suffice to note that the verification principle

25. Ayer, *Language, Truth and Logic*, 107–9. Ayer, however, grants that ethical statements have emotive meaning.

26. Ayer, *Language, Truth and Logic*, 35.

27. Ayer, *Language, Truth and Logic*, 115.

28. Stiver, *Philosophy of Religious Language*, 44.

was eventually discredited, having "dissolved in its own acids."[29] The main reason for its dissolution is that on applying the very criterion to itself the principle was shown to have failed the test of verifiability—it too was as metaphysical as any religious statement or proposition. It remains for me to point out that though many aspects of Hume's empiricism had echoes in logical positivism, he should not be simply assimilated into that twentieth-century school of thought. There are important divergences.[30] For one thing, Hume was not primarily interested in language or logic, nor was he concerned about the meaningfulness and verifiability of propositions. And though he was "skeptical about the power of reason to determine what we believe"[31] he did not reject presuppositions of an external world, causation, and nature.

Now it must be pointed out that Wittgenstein had also argued for the disavowal of metaphysical and religious propositions. That was during an early positivistic phase of his philosophizing when he bought into the "logical atomism" of his teacher, Bertrand Russell (1872–1970). Russell's theory presupposes that the world is made up of irreducible particulars which he labelled "atoms" and that there is a perfect one-to-one correspondence between an "atom" of language and reality. John Macquarrie (1919–2007) tells us that underlying Russell's account of language is a naturalistic assumption that because language—and thus knowledge—is confined to the physical world, all statements which seek to deal with concerns beyond this world are logically invalid, meaningless, or nonsensical.[32] Out of the exposure to these ideas and having imbibed their logic, Wittgenstein wrote his first book, *TLP*, with the self-confessed aim of drawing a limit to "the expression of thoughts," that is, language.[33] He purported to show that "what lies on the other side of the limit will simply be nonsense,"[34] a reference to metaphysics, aesthetics and religion. On the basis of what he had written about, the philosophers comprising the Vienna Circle, as well as Ayer, were inspired to rule out anything except empirical and analytic statements as cognitively meaningful. In good time, however, Wittgenstein came to believe that such positivistic

29. Soskice, "Religious Language," 351.

30. For a useful discussion on how the logical positivists have misread Hume, see Winters, "Hume's Naturalism and Logical Positivism," 40–60.

31. Blackburn, "Happy 300th Birthday, David Hume!"

32. Macquarrie, *God-Talk*, 57.

33. *TLP*, p3.

34. *TLP*, p3.

views were mistaken. In *PI*, Wittgenstein espouses an entirely new approach to considering language, not in terms of *whether* language refers, but in terms of *the way* it refers. His contention that "the meaning of a word is its use in the language"[35] compels a rethink on the part of those who recognize only certain kind of language as meaningful while rejecting other kinds as nonsense. In introducing the analogy of language-games, one of Wittgenstein's purposes must surely be to indicate that a multiplicity of languages is the order of the day. As his work had been of inestimable influence on the study and understanding of language it deserves a more detailed consideration which we shall undertake in the next chapter. There is more to the history of the development of thought on language than what is covered above. As I mentioned at the outset, my chief concern has been to offer only a sketch of developments leading up to Wittgenstein. Continental philosophers who developed structuralism, post-structuralism and deconstructionism have therefore been put to one side in order to limit the scope of inquiry. For our present purposes, we shall turn next to a significant development in twentieth-century philosophy—the so-called "linguistic turn."[36]

The Linguistic Turn

The expression "linguistic turn" is said to have been introduced by Gustav Bergmann (1906–1987), although it is Richard Rorty (1931–2007) who gave it currency by using it in a collection of essays entitled *The Linguistic Turn: Recent Essays in Philosophical Method.*[37] Naturally what concerns us here is not the provenance of the term[38] but what the "turn" is about. To get to an understanding of the phenomenon we must first note that the word "turn" can mean more than a change of direction or course. It can also imply a revolution or reformation of sorts. Indeed in explaining why

35. *PI* 43.

36. In Milbank, *Word Made Strange*, 85–87, the author has argued that it is Christian thinkers like Berkeley, Hamann, Herder, and Vico who first brought about a "modern" linguistic turn into Western thought.

37. So Hacker, "Linguistic Turn in Analytic Philosophy," 928.

38. For a narrative of how the term has developed, see Surkis, "When Was the Linguistic Turn?," 700–722. Surkis draws a controversial conclusion: "The evidence, when examined closely, suggests that the 'linguistic turn' was not a coherent moment. It cannot be conceived as the intellectual property of a single historiographical generation or consigned to a collective past" (719).

he put together the said collection of essays, Rorty fittingly speaks of "the most recent philosophical revolution, that of 'linguistic philosophy'"—the term "linguistic philosophy" being his parlance for the "linguistic turn."[39] That the two terminologies he uses are identical is not in doubt: consider the following statement that he pens immediately thereafter: "I shall mean by 'linguistic philosophy' the view that philosophical problems are problems which may be solved (or dissolved) either by reforming language, or by understanding more about the language we presently use."[40] The last remark is certainly striking for the claim it makes—that philosophical problems could be solved by simply but closely attending to language. In the history of human thought, no such role has ever been ascribed to language. Bergman had himself given a brief description of the "turn" when he wrote, "All linguistic philosophers talk about the world by means of talking about a suitable language. This is the linguistic turn, the fundamental gambit as to method, on which ordinary and ideal language philosophies agree."[41] A recent writer has usefully expressed the essential feature of the linguistic turn:

> [It represents] a decidedly modernist redirecting of philosophical attention from an outward focus on the perennial problems of philosophy (such as the problem of evil, the mind-body problem, the nature of the good, etc.) toward a reflexive, inward focusing on the normative vocabulary of philosophical discourse itself (asking, rather, what we can coherently *mean* by using the term "evil" and "good," indeed, what it means to mean anything at all; or how to understand and analyze utterances about what is better than what, and, indeed, what it means to understand and analyze any utterance at all).[42]

It may be useful to review how the linguistic turn has come to be adapted in analytic philosophical thought. We have already indicated that Wittgenstein's ideas are contributory to the shift; what follows is a brief elaboration of his argument. Here I borrow from Carl A. Raschke (b. 1944) who tells us that Wittgenstein first sought "to resolve the plethora of 'conceptual muddles' and 'pseudo-problems' rife in metaphysics and neo-idealism by exposing them as confusions of language."[43] The

39. Rorty, *Linguistic Turn*, 3.
40. Rorty, *Linguistic Turn*, 3.
41. Rorty, *Linguistic Turn*, 8.
42. Fisch, "Taking the Linguistic Turn Seriously," 607.
43. Raschke, *Alchemy of the Word*, 2.

strategy provided is one which sees problems of philosophy as problems concerning language, after which they would be easier to overcome. Wittgenstein also argues that the grounds of certainty can be found in language, and not (necessarily) in metaphysics. His answer according to Raschke, is simply astute: "Ordinary language had its own built-in certitude because *that was the way one spoke.*"[44] To illustrate this, we recall Wittgenstein's famous remarks:

> When philosophers use a word—"knowledge," "being," "object," "I," "proposition," "name"—and try to grasp the *essence* of the thing, one must always ask oneself: is the word ever actually used in this way in the language-game which is its original home?— What *we* do is to bring words back from their metaphysical to their everyday use.[45]

Two further suggestions in accounting for the turn to language may be briefly noted. The first attributes the shift to language to the general awareness that "we cannot understand knowing or thought apart from the language in which it is expressed."[46] Few would disagree with such logic, especially as articulated by Immanuel Kant (1724–1804), who insisted that one must first understand knowing before one can be sure of what one knows. The second suggestion by Stiver is somewhat speculative. Stiver thinks that the traditional epistemological turn was supplanted by the linguistic turn because to attend to language seemed to have the advantage of a "detour" or perhaps even a short cut. This argument is best quoted in its entirety to be appreciated:

> Therefore, to put it perhaps too simply, we must understand speaking in order to understand knowing, and perhaps in the end we can return to the issue of understanding reality or being. It is true, however, that the long road back has appeared too treacherous to many thinkers, so that in the meantime the purpose of philosophy has often taken a permanent detour from metaphysics in the grand style to more chastened and limited enterprises of analyzing language.[47]

It should occasion little surprise to state that the linguistic turn has left quite an imprint on the philosophy of religion and theology. For one

44. Raschke, *Alchemy of the Word*, 2.

45. *PI* 116.

46. Stiver, *Philosophy of Religious Language*, 5.

47. Stiver, *Philosophy of Religious Language*, 6.

thing, a great deal of attention has been directed toward theories about language with the welcome result that we have become more aware of how our thought, our experience and indeed our lives are shaped by language, and not just by historical context. For another, philosophers and theologians can no longer be concerned only with questions about *what* reality is or *how* it can be known; they must now raise a further question, namely, what do we *mean* by what we say in the assumptions, claims and even conclusions we make or draw? It would seem that the question of *meaning* is prior to the question of *truth* or *validity*[48] and this is not illogical since one must have some idea of the meaning of a statement or utterance in question before one can properly enter into a discussion as to its truth or falsity.

What Is Language?

From our brief sketch of developments that have arisen in language, we must now pause to attempt an investigation into the nature of language itself. If language has indeed been discovered—as we have claimed—the question, "What is language?" ought to be a straightforward one. Yet, it is not the case, because the inquiry into language is one that presupposes a circularity—that of using the very language to inquire about language. As Paul Matthew van Buren (1924–1998) points out, using Murdoch's analogy, "this means we are in a position like that of a man who wishes to examine the lenses of his eyes, yet must have those lenses in place in order to carry out his examination."[49] Needless to say, there seems to be no way out of this circle, except by a "phenomenological" recourse as has been proposed by Macquarrie. Macquarrie's proposed analysis of language comprises the following action steps: (i) that we take developed language as we find it; (ii) that we examine the various phenomena that go to constitute language, and (iii) that we endeavor to understand the inner workings of language.[50] This scheme, Macquarrie further elaborates, may "amount to no more than making explicit and clarifying as far as possible the understanding of language which we already have."[51] In what follows,

---

48. See Gilkey, *Naming the Whirlwind*, 13.

49. Buren, *Edges of Language*, 45.

50. Macquarrie, *God-Talk*, 63. For a critical assessment of the "phenomenological method" of investigation, see Putnam, "Language and Philosophy," 6.

51. Macquarrie, *God-Talk*, 63.

we shall attempt something of a phenomenological investigation into the use of words, using words to do so. Some views from other sources about language will be introduced for good measure.

Origin of Language

We begin with the "curious" question of the genesis of language: is language of divine or human origin? Admittedly, this question belongs to the realm of speculation, and it is one that may never be resolved agreeably by all. Macquarrie, we read, had anticipated that "the study of this particular question would turn out to be a blind alley for any investigation into the nature of language."[52] Then there are those who are quite quick to return a definite answer to the question. In his *Treatise on the Origin of Language* published in 1772, the philosopher Johann Gottfried von Herder (1744–1803) forthrightly dismissed the hypothesis of the divine origin of language as "groundless" and therefore not worth pursuing. Interestingly, his argument is said to be based on "the fact that in order to understand the language of the gods on Olympus the human being must already have reason and consequently must already have language."[53] It is, however, useful to note that John Milbank (b. 1952) has recently contended that Christian orthodoxy has always encouraged a similar point of view.[54] He cites St. Gregory of Nyssa (c. 335–395) and Richard Simon (1638–1712) (the latter, a priest of the Oratory) as attributing the invention of language to Adam rather than God, and adds that "this was exactly what the eighteenth century tried to see as clear and self-evident—the origins of language, its natural foundation and rational succession, and thus the true character of humanity and culture, and the belonging of both within nature."[55] Even so, the issue that matters (here, anyway) is not whether language has come from God or from Adam; rather it is the question of whether one is able to see and accept language as a "gift" from God. To make the affirmation that language is a divine gift is not to suggest that language is therefore to be accorded a special status that sets it apart from the regular activities which we as humans do and are concerned about. Rather, the affirmation is intended to disabuse

---

52. Macquarrie, *God-Talk*, 56–57.
53. Macquarrie, *God-Talk*, 56–57.
54. Milbank, *Word Made Strange*, 85.
55. Milbank, *Word Made Strange*, 85–86.

the "naturalistic" view, made popular by Russell, that language is wholly restricted to describing our physical world, with human knowledge confined to material reality. In the following passage, Russell's reductive naturalism about language is all too clear:

> A spoken sentence consists of a temporal series of events; a written sentence is a spatial series of bits of matter. Thus it is not surprising that language can represent the course of events in the physical world; it can, in fact, make a map of the physical world, preserving its structure in a more manageable form, and it can do this because it consists of physical events. But if there were such a world as the mystic postulates, it would have a structure different from that of language, and would therefore be incapable of being verbally described.[56]

The weakness of this sort of view, it will be clear to us, is its refusal or inability to consider that words and sentences are more than physical entities which can also "stretch" beyond our world. Russell's view rests on a certain assumption, namely, that the real is (and can only be) physical. I am, however, not suggesting that it can be challenged simply by claiming that language is a gift from God.

The Ubiquity of Language

That language is everywhere is well attested by ordinary, casual observation: anyone can easily see for themselves that words are used in every context of human life, and one can find them in all forms of media, from print media (books, magazines, etc.) to video games. Words are indispensable means or tools by which people communicate with each other. For the eminent philosopher of meaning, Maurice Merleau-Ponty (1908–1961), "the whole landscape is overrun with words as in an invasion."[57] It is, however, important to mention that words can also be thought of as acts. In much of our conversation we do more than just speak words: we make promises, declare intentions, issue commands and warnings, pronounce judgements or benedictory blessings, and so on. In his ground-breaking William James Lectures, John L. Austin (1911–1960) takes issue with the then popular assumption that "the business of a statement can only be to *describe* some state of affairs, or to *state some*

---

56. Russell, *Outline of Philosophy*, 275.
57. Merleau-Ponty, *Visible and the Invisible*, 155.

fact."[58] Austin points out that there are utterances (or "performatives" as he labels them) which can actually do things—hence the title of his lectures, *How to Do Things with Words*. The following are some examples of "performative utterances" from his writings:

1. "I do (sc. take this woman to be my lawful wedded wife)"—as uttered in the course of the marriage ceremony.

2. "I name this ship the *Queen Elizabeth*"—as uttered when smashing the bottle against the stem.

3. "I give and bequeath my watch to my brother"—as occurring in a will.[59]

One welcome benefit of the notion of "performative utterances" (or the "speech-act" theory) has been that language users are enabled to recognize what the later Wittgenstein has sought to show, namely, that language is behavior, indeed a distinctively human behavior. People can sit easy with thinking that language is tied to everyday activities of human life, such as "commanding, questioning, recounting, chatting," and that it belongs "as much to our natural history as walking, eating, drinking or playing."[60]

The Embeddedness of Language

To theologians who have been labelled "narrativists" the ubiquity of language implies more than the affirmation that words are everywhere present. They have insisted upon a further claim—that the way we think, feel and sense, indeed our whole awareness of reality have been formed and shaped by the language which inheres or circumscribes our everyday lives, including the stories, myths, narratives, propositions and sentences which we hear or which we ourselves tell or produce. As linguistic beings, we are embedded in language as language is embedded in us. Gerard Loughlin has offered a helpful explanation of the narrativist understanding of language, as follows:

> There is a reciprocal relation between story and story-teller. As I recount my life-story, my story produces the "I" which recounts it. I tell the story by which I am told. And since I am part of a

58. Austin, *How to Do Things with Words*, 1.

59. Austin, *How to Do Things with Words*, 5.

60. *PI* 25.

larger community—one in which others tell stories about me, just as I tell stories about them—I am the product of many inter-related narratives, as is everyone else.[61]

The validity of the narrativist analysis has been demonstrated by recent studies. According to Lera Boroditsky, writing in *The Wall Street Journal*, "If you change how people talk, that changes how they think."[62] It seems that learning a new language or switching to another can also cause a person's way of looking at life to change. More alarming is the finding by Boroditsky that "if you take away people's ability to use language in what should be a simple non-linguistic task, their performance can change dramatically, sometimes making them look no smarter than rats or infants."[63] To be sure, the narrativist position on language and the findings of recent times cited above are nothing new: early linguists like Johann Herder, Wilhem von Humboldt (1767–1835) and others had in the eighteenth century already espoused similar views.[64] Wittgenstein, too, appears to hint of us being shaped by the language within which we are embedded. Consider these fascinating words of his:

A *picture* held us captive. And we could not get outside it, for it lay in our language and language seemed to repeat it to us inexorably.[65]

Naturally, the view of language just presented will raise questions for those concerned about truth. Given that our perception is shaped by language how can truth be attained without any contribution from the words used in stating it? If language is so central to thought, and everything we know we know in and through language, are we then cut off from any direct access to the divine reality? Is there an objective reality outside language or is it the case that stories "go all the way down"? Indeed, can we find meaning in the vastness of the maze of words?

---

61. Loughlin, *Telling God's Story*, 18.

62. Boroditsky, "Lost in Translation."

63. Boroditsky, "Lost in Translation."

64. Hallett summarizes, "A people's language, it is suggested, shapes their *Weltanschauung*, their worldview" (*Theology within the Bounds of Language*, 23).

65. *PI* 115.

Meaning

This leads us to the question of meaning and the reminder that it is a question that must precede the question of truth. For until some meaning is found in a statement or an utterance, there can be no discussion as to whether what is stated or uttered is true or false. As we have put it before, meaning is prior to verifiability. Perhaps it is just such a recognition that has prompted the quest for meaning to begin from the earliest times in Western history, with Socrates's keen interest in the meaning of concepts like "justice," "knowledge," and "good." Most certainly, the search for meaning has also led to a corresponding and abiding interest in language, given that language is believed to be the bearer of meaning. Even the close attention that philosophers have paid to religious language has grown out of the controversies over how words and statements in religion are to be understood. For, many words when they are used of God do not fully share the same meaning as when they are applied to human beings. Take the statement that God is good or wise or loving but that he is not good or wise or loving in the same sense that human beings are.[66] Such statements are clearly problematic and will invite analysis by both philosophers and casual critics.

In dealing with the question of meaning, a distinction is sometimes made between meaning as a "mental fact"[67] (as in "I mean to read Heidegger's *Time and Being*") and meaning as logical meaningfulness. Naturally we shall not be concerned with the former, which is really an expression of intent. Confusion often occurs when we are not careful to differentiate between the various uses of the word "mean." Here we cite, borrowing from Alston, a few more examples in which "mean" is used in a sense that is other than logical meaningfulness:

- That is no mean accomplishment. (insignificant)
- The passage of this bill will mean the end of second class citizenship for vast areas of our population. (result in)

---

66. When one says that God is good, one does not mean that God must abide by a set of moral values to be judged good, or that he is subject to temptations and is deemed good if he succeeds in overcoming them. As Hick has observed, there has been a long shift of meaning from the original use of these words to their present use in religion. See Hick, *Philosophy of Religion*, 82–83.

67. Ferré, *Language, Logic and God*, 19.

- He just lost his job. That means that he will have to start writing
  letters of application all over again. (implies)[68]

We have still to ask: what is meaning? Or, even better, what is the
meaning of meaning? In Wittgenstein's *Blue Book*, the question "What
is the meaning of a word?" appears as its opening line, and it is believed
that his entire corpus of writing is engaged upon the same question. The
usual response is to think of meaning as an object or an entity awaiting
to be analyzed, and so words get their meaning from the facts or state of
affairs they represent. In this so-called "picture of language," Wittgenstein
remarks, "We find the roots of the following idea: Every word has a
meaning. This meaning is correlated with the word. It is the object for
which the word stands."[69] Admittedly, this "picture" theory does seem to
fit our own understanding of how language operates: words do seem to
label things, and a collection of words seem to describe states of affairs.
It is an understanding that has the backing of the philosopher Russell, no
less, whose thesis about atomic words being in perfect correspondence
with reality we have briefly touched upon. Even Augustine may be cited
as a proponent. The picture theory, however, encourages the form of
logical positivism which we saw in Ayer and others, with its dismissal
of whole realms of religious and metaphysical discourse as meaningless.
The theory is also unable to incorporate some other important functions
of language; indeed, it only appears adequate when applied to a limited
pool of examples, such as nouns and certain verbs. So here we find
Wittgenstein distancing himself from it, and also debunking the claim
that there is a correspondence between words and objects. He writes,

> It is important to note that the word "meaning" is being used
> illicitly if it is used to signify the thing that "corresponds" to
> the word. That is to confound the meaning of a name with the
> bearer of the name. When Mr. N. N. dies one says that the bearer
> of the name dies, not that the meaning dies. And it would be
> nonsensical to say that, for if the name ceased to have meaning
> it would make no sense to say "Mr. N. N. is dead."[70]

Let us defer further discussion on Wittgenstein's idea of meaning to
a later stage in order to return to our attempt to get a working definition

---

68. For additional examples of uses of "mean" that are not within the realm of
linguistic signification, see Alston, *Philosophy of Language*, 10–11.

69. *PI* 1.

70. *PI* 40.

of meaning. A helpful approach has been to call the kind of meaning that belongs to a word its "signification," reserving the term "meaning" for whole sentences.[71] The usefulness of this approach is in the express caution that any single word can be understood only within the context of a given discourse. As Gerhard Ebeling (1912–2001) has argued, one may well understand each and every individual word comprising a sentence but still not understand its overall message.[72] It is thus sound advice that one should attend to the context of words in order to understand the context of meaning. Yet, attention to the context of meaning may well overlook the fact that meaning is "an event constituted by the dialectic between sense and reference."[73] By "sense" is meant "the propositional integrity" of the sentence or linguistic expression;[74] sometimes simply equated with meaning.[75] By "reference" is meant "naming"; it is "the proposition's claim to reach reality."[76] Perhaps a quick example may help to clarify the distinction: The statement, "Santa Claus will be distributing gifts to those attending the party" makes sense and anyone who speaks English can understand it. So even though the Santa referred to is fictitious, the sense of the statement is not compromised. In general, then, the sense of what is said does not depend on its truth or falsity, whether or not it refers. In his discussion of a certain philosopher's view of language, as well as that of Plato's, Alston has observed "a confused assimilation of meaning [read "sense"] and reference" on the part of these thinkers, an assimilation he hopes he would later straighten out.[77] It is still a temptation for us to pursue meaning as primarily informational, overlooking the need to attend to the dialectic between the sense of the text and its reference.

A final point before we bring these initial and tentative thoughts on meaning to a close is that it would be wrongheaded to think of meaning as some "acts that take place in the realm of the mind,"[78] stored away privately inside our heads. The reason? If such were the case, we shall be looking for meaning as if it were a thing or object that awaits to be

71. Macquarrie, *God-Talk*, 85.
72. Ebeling, *Nature of Faith*, 16.
73. Schneiders, *Revelatory Text*, 15.
74. Schneiders, *Revelatory Text*, 15.
75. Tilley, *Talking of God*, 2.
76. Schneiders, *Revelatory Text*, 15.
77. Alston, *Philosophy of Language*, 2.
78. Kerr, *Theology after Wittgenstein*, 55.

categorized. This tendency to think of meaning as a mental activity entrenches us in a picture of the self as very much "the autonomous bearer of mental or spiritual properties."[79] The assumption that thoughts have an existence and function independent of language is also questionable. Thinking is not prior to language; indeed, as van Buren explains, "although we can think without speaking . . . we cannot think without language."[80] The sum of what we are driving at is the location of meaning within a proper social dimension. As Fergus Kerr (b. 1931) so aptly puts it, "the locus of meanings is not the epistemological solitude of the individual consciousness but the practical exchanges that constitute the public world which we inhabit together."[81]

Concluding Remarks

The preceding account is not intended to give a detailed or complete story of the phenomenon of language. I am aware of gaps and omissions in what I have written. Still, I hope my survey has called attention to the fact that religion has always been concerned about language, for the simple reason that language gives religion a form and a means of expression in order that it can survive, spread and flourish. I also hope that my brief treatment of the past movements affecting language and the later currents of thought about language has shown us that there has been a definite shift in how language is understood. Despite voices to the contrary, the epochal "turn" to language is far from over; indeed, in my view, it is a development that must still be given due attention. Given that language is of interest to theology, or rather, that language is *needed* by theology, the very first task of theology must be to seek for the necessary understanding of the nature and character of language. In the following chapters, we shall be looking to both Wittgenstein and Lindbeck for insights and resources with which they may be able to assist us.

79. Kerr, *Theology after Wittgenstein*, 56.
80. Buren, *Edges of Language*, 50.
81. Kerr, *Theology after Wittgenstein*, 58.

Chapter 2

Wittgenstein's Relevance for Theology

If God had looked into our minds he would not have been able
to see there whom we were speaking of.[1]

—Ludwig Wittgenstein

Introduction

LUDWIG WITTGENSTEIN IS UNDOUBTEDLY among the most important
and influential philosophers of the last century. Whether by consent or
dissent, whether through understanding or even misunderstanding, his
works on philosophy are thought to have revolutionized the subject.[2]
In point of fact, they have inspired the development of two major
but differing movements of thought, namely logical positivism and
so-called "ordinary language philosophy." These movements usually
associated with the two phases of his philosophical life—the early and
later Wittgenstein—have had a profound influence on many succeeding
generations of philosophers. Beyond the field of philosophy, Wittgenstein's
insights have also made an impact on areas of human endeavor as diverse
as culture, politics, ethics, aesthetics, epistemology, psychology, law and
theology.[3] In each and every of the disciplines where his influence has

1. *PI* II, 185.

2. See Strawson, "Review of Wittgenstein's Philosophical Investigations," 64. See
also Ayer et al., *Revolution in Philosophy*, 88, for the view that Wittgenstein had "quite
changed [his] philosophy."

3. While the overwhelming majority of scholars acknowledge Wittgenstein's

been felt, his ideas are acknowledged to be original, unconventional, and full of subtlety. Wittgenstein's iconic status has been given a further boost by his being named among the one hundred "most important people of the century" by *Time*.[4]

In this chapter, we shall be concerned to pursue a narrow compass of inquiry on Wittgenstein, namely the significance of his philosophy for religious discourse. We shall not be concerned with all of his philosophy which means that not all aspects of his work will be touched on. What I propose to do, however, is to consider his early and later works and pick out the issues that, as I see them, have a bearing on theology. I will then attempt to interpret and elucidate the thoughts or ideas that he expresses as accurately and clearly as I can. Finally, I will also attempt, where applicable, to indicate the connection between Wittgenstein's insights with the question of the nature of religious language.

Our intended task here may seem quite straightforward, but it is by no means a simple one. The reason has to do with the rather terse style and unsystematic form in which Wittgenstein has written his philosophy. The text of *PI* is saturated with aphorism, wit and paradox which are hard to comprehend; moreover, the content often reflects a multiplicity of voices and perspectives which can be rather confusing to the reader. Wittgenstein was well aware that he had written a difficult book that few would understand. In a conversation with his friend Norman Malcolm (1911–1990) after they had both read the book's typescript, he remarked, "The reason I am doing this is so there will be at least one person who will understand my book when it is published."[5] Another difficulty that assails us when we attempt to apply Wittgenstein is that although *PI* is concerned with "the concepts of meaning, of understanding, of a proposition, of logic, . . . and other things,"[6] we are never given a complete theory of language. Wittgenstein has famously said that he seeks neither to advance any sort of theory, nor to give explanations or new information.[7] He avers that "description alone must take its place," which is an approach that

---

influence on theology, there are some dissenters who do not think that he has made any impact. See, for instance, Labron, *Wittgenstein and Theology*, 3; Glock, *Wittgenstein Dictionary*, 28–29.

4. Dennett, "Ludwig Wittgenstein," 88–90. See also Stern, *Wittgenstein's Philosophical Investigations*, 1.

5. Malcolm, *Ludwig Wittgenstein*, 44.

6. *PI*, ix.

7. *PI* 109.

aims to solve philosophical problems "by arranging what we have always known."[8] Following Wittgenstein, I shall not attempt to seek a theory of language. Instead, I shall focus on insights and perspectives that may be drawn from his works with a view to applying them to the use of religious language.

A Biographical Sketch

One's personal life and one's thinking are profoundly bound together. This is certainly true of Wittgenstein. Before his ideas are explored, it is useful to know and understand something about the man himself.[9] Since our concern is with how his philosophy impinges on religious belief, of particular interest to us will be his personal attitude to religion.

Ludwig Wittgenstein was born on 26 April 1889 into a wealthy family in Austria and baptized into the Roman Catholic Church. He was the youngest of eight children, but three of his brothers would later commit suicide, with Wittgenstein himself contemplating to do so, too. As a very young man, he came to Manchester, England, initially to study mechanical engineering. By 1912, his interest having switched to philosophy, he went to Cambridge upon the advice of Gottlob Frege (1848–1925) to work under Bertrand Russell. He did well in his studies and received high praise from Russell and G. E. Moore (1873–1958). Moore, a leading philosopher in his own right, testified: "I soon came to feel that he [Wittgenstein] was much cleverer at philosophy than I was . . . with a much better insight into the sort of inquiry which was really important and best worth pursuing, and into the best method of pursuing such inquiries."[10] When war broke out, Wittgenstein volunteered for the Austrian army and fought on the Russian and Italian fronts. It was while on active duty, and presumably while a prisoner-of-war for some months, that he wrote the notes and drafts of his first book, *TLP*, which saw publication after the war.

From 1920 to 1926, Wittgenstein worked as a teacher before spending two years supervising the building of a mansion for his sister

---

8. *PI* 109.

9. The following are a few good sources for biographical information on Wittgenstein: Ayer, *Ludwig Wittgenstein*; Kenny, *Wittgenstein*; Malcolm, *Ludwig Wittgenstein*; Ray Monk, *Ludwig Wittgenstein*; Hacker, "Wittgenstein, Ludwig Josef Johann," 912–16.

10. Hudson, *Wittgenstein and Religious Belief*, 2.

in Vienna. These were years spent divorced from philosophy because he thought he had solved every philosophical problem there was to solve. In the preface to *TLP* he had written: "The truth of the thoughts that are here communicated seems to me unassailable and definitive. I therefore believe myself to have found, on all essential points, the final solution of the problems."[11] By 1929, however, he was drawn back to philosophy after disputes with members of the Vienna Circle over the theory of logical positivism, which his *Tractatus* had, ironically, inspired to a considerable extent.[12] In remarks made around that time, he seemed already more conciliatory towards religion, though the view of religion he proffered could still be regarded as somewhat positivistic: "Is speech essential for religion? I can quite well imagine a religion in which there are no doctrines and hence nothing is said. . . . Therefore nothing turns on whether the words are true, false or nonsensical."[13]

Wittgenstein returned to Cambridge in January 1929 as a research student and, on completing his PhD the following year, was made a research fellow in philosophy. Moore thought that he had chosen Cambridge "for the sake of having the opportunity of frequent discussion with F. P. Ramsey."[14] Be that as it may, for the next few years until the outbreak of Second World War, Wittgenstein threw himself wholly to working through his new notions of language in classroom lectures, but without publishing them. In 1939 just before war broke out, he succeeded Moore as professor of philosophy. During the war years (1939–1945) he worked as a porter in London and later as a laboratory assistant in a hospital in Newcastle-upon-Tyne. He returned to his academic post in Cambridge when the war ended but resigned in 1947. Two years later, he was diagnosed with cancer and died in 1951. It was during the last years of his life that he completed his mature work, *PI*.

In his lifetime, Wittgenstein published only two short works. The first is *Logisch-Philosophische Abhandlung* which appeared in 1921. It was translated a year later into English under the better-known title of *Tractatus Logico-Philosophicus*. His second publication was entitled *Some Remarks on Logical Form* which he had prepared in 1929 for the joint session of the Mind Association and Aristotelian Society. His later work,

---

11. *TLP, p4.*

12. For a fuller account of the Vienna Circle—its membership, activities, and views—see Ayer et al., *Revolution in Philosophy*, 70–87.

13. Waismann, "Notes on Talks with Wittgenstein," 1.

14. Moore, "Wittgenstein's Lectures in 1930–33," 1.

i.e., *PI*, was published posthumously in 1953; it has remained one of the most important works of philosophy of the twentieth century. Several other publications comprising either unfinished books or lecture notes dictated to his students had since appeared under the following titles: *Remarks on the Foundations of Mathematics* (1956, revised 1978), *The Blue and Brown Books* (1958), *Zettel* (1967), and *On Certainty* (1969).

Question of Religion

The question whether Wittgenstein was a believer in the Christian faith has often been raised by those concerned with the significance of his philosophical reflections for religion. The matter, however, cannot be easily settled, as he did not make any profession of faith, nor was he formally linked to any church.[15] It seems that in his youth he was contemptuous of the Christian faith, though this attitude soon changed. We are given an impression of the change in his religious outlook by one of his closest friends who relates,

> Throughout his adult life Wittgenstein's attitude to religion was anything but that of a hostile positivist critic. He always gave his own religion during his wartime service as "Roman Catholic." Amongst his closest friends and most appreciated pupils he happily numbered many christians [sic]. It is said that when he encountered the rituals of organized religion he observed them without demur. He never spoke derisorily about Christianity, or its priests and pastors. When other philosophers expressed contempt for religious beliefs, Wittgenstein on occasion rebuked them.[16]

W. Donald Hudson (1920–2003), who provided this account, also concluded that Wittgenstein was not a religious believer.[17] The views of other friends of Wittgenstein's, namely, Norman Malcolm, Georg von Wright (1916–2003), and G. E. M. Anscombe (1919–2001)—all of whom were eminent philosophers in their own right—are not dissimilar; Malcolm for instance, was "confident enough about the matter to deny that he was a religious man."[18]

15. Hudson, *Ludwig Wittgenstein*, 6.

16. Hudson, *Wittgenstein and Religious Belief*, 9.

17. Hudson, *Wittgenstein and Religious Belief*, 9.

18. Kerr, *Theology after Wittgenstein*, 32.

Yet, religion does receive a great deal of mention in Wittgenstein's writings. Even if we agree with Alan Keightley that one has to tread very warily with respect to those direct references to religion in Wittgenstein's corpus, one must still grant that their preponderance does cast doubt on the view that he was not religious or that he had no interest in religion.[19] Norman Malcolm, faced with the vast amount of remarks about religion found in the *Nachlass* (the collection of notes made by Wittgenstein) and in *Culture and Value,* has since modified his judgment about Wittgenstein's religiosity.[20] He now thinks Wittgenstein "was more deeply religious than are many people who correctly regard themselves as religious believers."[21]

We must also consider the following enigmatic disclosure which Wittgenstein is said to have made to his friend Maurice O'Connor Drury (1907–1976): "I am not a religious man but I cannot help seeing every problem from a religious point of view."[22] What does being in such a state tell us about the person himself? We may draw several conclusions here. Although not outwardly religious, religion did matter to him. He was concerned to reflect often and deeply about its relevance and outworking in his everyday life. Discerning the depth and persistence of Wittgenstein's thoughts about religion in his notes from 1937 onwards, Kerr avers that they "disclose a sympathetic and penetrating understanding of the matter that few Christians, never mind professed non-believers, could match."[23]

Whether Wittgenstein's religiosity has anything to do with his attack on logical positivism we shall never know, though we think it is his discrediting of this "old Adam" of analytic philosophy that makes many people think he was an ally of religion.[24] There is an interesting record of his conversation with Moritz Schlick (1882–1936), the leader of the Vienna Circle, which seems to indicate that even in the early days of the logical positivist movement, his attitude towards religious belief was different from that of Schlick and the other logical positivists. Wittgenstein did agree that doctrines of religion had no theoretical content, but he was not with them in consigning religion to a childhood

19. Keightley, *Wittgenstein, Grammar and God,* 14.

20. Kerr, *Theology after Wittgenstein,* 32.

21. Malcolm, *Wittgenstein: A Religious Point of View?,* 22.

22. Drury, "Conversations with Wittgenstein," 79.

23. Kerr, *Theology after Wittgenstein,* 36.

24. See Sherry, *Religion, Truth and Language-Games,* 2; Keightley, *Wittgenstein, Grammar and God,* 11.

phase of humanity or oblivion. At one stage in the conversation he even defended the admissibility of a metaphysical statement made by some philosopher.[25]

Wittgenstein's Early and Later Phases

Wittgenstein's philosophical life, we have noted, comprises an "early" phase, exemplified by *TLP*, and a "later" phase, articulated in *PI*. Separating the two periods is an interval of several years, during which Wittgenstein even gave up philosophizing altogether. Whatever view one takes on such a periodization of the philosopher's career, it is clear that there are marked differences between the "two" Wittgensteins. For a start, the two books that Wittgenstein wrote could not have been more different in terms of style and presentation, and we are told in his preface to *PI* that there are "grave mistakes" in his first book.[26] To be sure, we are not suggesting that the books simply negate one another, as some have claimed.[27] If that had been the case, Wittgenstein would not have expressed the wish to publish them together, nor would he have said that the new ideas in his later work "could be seen in the right light only by contrast with and against the background of [his] old way of thinking."[28]

Still, several commentators have questioned whether a strict division in Wittgenstein's thought can be made and cautioned against an exaggeration of the differences between the earlier and later works. Their main contention is that the fundamental issue which engages Wittgenstein remained unchanged throughout. Duncan J. Richter writing for the *Internet Encyclopedia of Philosophy*, for instance, contends that Wittgenstein's writings spanning the two periods "attack much the same problems, [although] they just do so in different ways."[29] While acknowledging marked differences of style and content between the works in question, Anthony Kenny (b. 1931) detects many connections and common assumptions between them.[30] Given that "there are both continuities and discontinuities in Wittgenstein's thought," adds yet

25. See Carnap, *Philosophy of Rudolf Carnap*, 26–27.

26. *PI*, x.

27. E.g., Hartnack, *Wittgenstein and Modern Philosophy*, 49.

28. *PI*, x.

29. Richter, "Ludwig Wittgenstein (1889–1951)."

30. Kenny, *Wittgenstein*, 173.

another commentator, "we would be better off acknowledging that his writings are 'related to one another in different ways' (*PI* 65) and turning to the more productive task of investigating those relations in greater detail."[31] These remarks are certainly valid, prompting us to pick out not only the discontinuities between Wittgenstein's early and later philosophy, but the continuities as well.

In both periods of Wittgenstein's philosophical career, his preoccupation has been the task of attending to the question of meaning and its implication for connecting thought, language, and the world. As Hudson maintains, "one of his main concerns throughout was to clarify the nature of reality from a consideration of language."[32] In *TLP*, Wittgenstein exudes confidence in explaining the nature of language, drawing what he terms "a limit to thinking" or more carefully put, a limit "to the expression of thoughts."[33] He divides language between what makes sense and what does not, and between what can and what cannot be said. In the preface to this work, he expresses the view that the problems of philosophy are due to the misunderstanding of the logic of language.[34] In *PI*, the same aim of understanding the structure and limit of thought is pursued, as is the attempt to provide a critique of language. Evidently, some of the ideas and insights developed and arrived at in *TLP* continued to serve as a leading thread in his later work.

Of the discontinuities between the two periods in question the most basic is that which relates to the methodology of inquiry employed by Wittgenstein. In the preface to *PI*, Wittgenstein has asked us to contrast his later work with his "old way of thinking"—that is, his former method of doing philosophy. The implication is difficult to miss—it is that his old way and his new way of thinking are in opposition. Indeed, the two ways or methods are, as K. T. Fann (b. 1937) puts it, "poles apart."[35] Fann further elaborates, "The *Tractatus* follows the methods of traditional theoretic construction (even though to construct only a 'ladder' to be abandoned at the end) while the *Investigations* employs what can best be described as the method of dialectic."[36]

---

31. Stern, "How Many Wittgensteins?," 205–6.
32. Hudson, *Wittgenstein and Religious Belief*, 15.
33. *TLP*, p3.
34. *TLP*, p3.
35. Fann, *Wittgenstein's Conception of Philosophy*, xiii.
36. Fann, *Wittgenstein's Conception of Philosophy*, xiii.

Wittgensteinian Fideism

It has sometimes been suggested that Wittgenstein should be more widely read and appropriated by theologians than has been the case. Kerr, whose work we have earlier referenced, thinks that the charge of "Wittgensteinian fideism" against the philosopher may have deterred theologians from taking him seriously. This repugnant label with which Wittgenstein's name is linked owes its genesis to the atheist philosopher, Kai Nielsen (b. 1926) the author of a widely-circulated article of that title.[37] Fideism takes the view that religion is "self-contained," as being in a class of its own, and therefore is immune from any criticisms that are based on criteria of meaning or truth drawn from any other domain or enterprise. According to this view, the concepts and tenets of faith are intelligible only to the insider, and so unless one is a believer, one cannot understand the faith or have any right to criticize it.

Certain strands in the later work of Wittgenstein do seem to license a fideistic approach to religion. The most common is that of a "language-game," with its specific rules, applicable and intelligible only to the players. Another strand is that of the notion of a "form of life," which illustrates that language is bound up with the community within which it is used and is subject to its own particular "grammar." A third strand is that Wittgenstein seems to think that it is not the business of philosophy to play the master adjudicator in questions about God, recalling his insistence that philosophy should leave everything as it is. These strands do render a good description of an innocuous form of fideism: that religion is a form of life which has to be simply accepted; or, that religious discourse, like a language-game, has its own rules and goals; that people should let religion be, and not try to criticize it or interfere with it. More will have to be said about Wittgenstein's notions of a "form of life" and a "language-game." In the meantime, let us simply note that there is little agreement on what Wittgenstein really means by these phrases. For instance, Norman Malcolm, whose work we have already referenced, is said to have understood religion as a "form of life." If this is correct, his remark in which the two phrases in question appear, gives us a perfect illustration of fideism: "Religion is a form of life; it is language embedded

---

37. Kerr, *Theology after Wittgenstein*, 28, 31; Nielsen, "Wittgenstein's Fideism," 191–209.

in action—what Wittgenstein calls a 'language-game.' Science is another. Neither stands in need of justification, the one no more than the other."[38]

To be sure, the attempt to infer that by "form of life" Wittgenstein means religion has been found wanting by Kerr, citing textual grounds. Based on his reading of *PI*, Kerr points out that when Wittgenstein uses this particular phrase, he has only small-scale activities in mind. The list of activities that can be considered "forms of life" runs as follows: giving and obeying orders, describing, surmising, forming a hypothesis, telling a story, joking, counting, thanking, cursing, greeting and praying.[39] Clearly, only the "very elementary patterns of social interaction" are meant, so it is wide of the mark to equate "forms of life" with something as vast and both internally and externally diverse as religion.[40] Nevertheless, Kerr concedes that Wittgenstein may have been a fideist.[41] Kerr notes,

> There are no grounds in Wittgenstein's text for the version of Fideism (so-called) which makes great play with his notions of "form of life" and "language game." This doesn't mean, on the other hand, that much of what he is reported to have said specifically about religion might not be reasonably held to move in the direction of a certain Fideism.[42]

The problems produced by fideism have been well-rehearsed and so may be passed over. It is, however, useful to note how fideism itself emerges as a problem. There must first be the domains of reason and faith to begin with, for if either one is not present there can be no fideism. Fideism emerges once reason and faith are divided into distinct domains without any traffic whatsoever between them, or when one domain is reduced to the other. For our purposes here, we are only concerned with the fideist who interprets religion as a self-contained enterprise and who urges reliance on faith rather than reason. This sort of fideist operates as though the domain of faith is all that mattered, such that reason is disparaged or denigrated. They make the further claim that because the language of faith they use is *sui generis* and private, they can have no public accountability whatsoever. What follows from such a fideistic

---

38. Malcolm, *Thought and Knowledge*, 212, cited in Kerr, *Theology after Wittgenstein*, 31.

39. *PI* 23.

40. Kerr, *Theology after Wittgenstein*, 30.

41. Kerr, *Theology after Wittgenstein*, 29.

42. Kerr, "Wittgenstein and Theological Studies," 502.

stance is well anticipated by D. Stephen Long (b. 1960), whose invective equally applies to the fideist who privileges and uses "pure" reason to displace faith:

> A putative "public" reason seeks to force people of faith into an arational space where they can have their faith in private. Some people accept that "invitation" and act accordingly, refusing to be policed by a putative universal reason. . . . If the language of faith is nothing but the assertion of our will to power, it can have no public accessibility. Likewise if we have no public accessibility for our languages and practices, then the only way to adjudicate differences is through force, power, and coercion. This is why fideism can be a serious political problem. We see "fideism" among those persons and religious movements who cling to a faith devoid of all reason and allow it to guide their actions without any rational accountability to the consequences of their actions.[43]

In spite of possible shortcomings, much about fideism is well worth commending. We may briefly note two of its merits. One is its recognition that religion is not a hypothesis about how or what the world is and, moreover, that belief in God is not a matter of intellectual demonstration. Religion is rather a way of life, to be embraced and lived out in daily practice. To apply the canons of the sciences to prove or disprove religious beliefs such as the existence of God is simply wrongheaded. The second merit is the relief it affords the believer who is weary of justifying his or her religious convictions to those who are unbelievers. While it is not defensible to claim immunity from external criticism, a fideistic believer confronted by unbelievers may well be warranted to question whether his or her critics know what they are talking about.

A return to or an unquestioning embrace of fideism is not likely; nor should one press for it. We have no quarrels with the church's past rejection of fideism—for pitting faith against reason. However, the self-confident, anti-fideist believer should guard against mischaracterizing the nature of the Christian religion by turning religion, as we have earlier remarked, into a hypothesis to be debated or examined in abstraction. Wittgenstein has sounded a cautionary note:

> Christianity is not a doctrine, not, I mean, a theory about what has happened and will happen to the human soul, but a description of something that actually takes place in human life.

43. Long, *Speaking of God*, 25.

> For "consciousness of sin" is a real event and so are despair and salvation through faith. Those who speak of such things . . . are simply describing what has happened to them.[44]

The best counter to fideism is, perhaps, to draw on Wittgenstein's argument that no private language exists. As more will be said about this argument later in the chapter, here we shall briefly remark that if we grant that there is no private language, it follows that language must always bear within itself a public accessibility and be publicly answerable to a considerable extent.

Wittgenstein's Anti-Cartesianism

It may come as a surprise to read a remark by David Pole that though Wittgenstein initiated the study of language, his interest "was not in language itself taken as a field of inquiry in its own right [but] in the roots of philosophical perplexity which he located there."[45] The truth of this disclosure is not to be gainsaid given Wittgenstein's tendency to be concerned with what underlies the way language is viewed and understood. Recall, for instance, his characterization of philosophy as "a battle against the bewitchment of our intelligence by means of language."[46] Or, when he famously says the aim of philosophy is "To shew [sic] the fly the way out of the fly-bottle."[47]

One of the philosophical assumptions that greatly bothers Wittgenstein is the Cartesian paradigm of the self. According to which, the self—famously known in the literature as the Cartesian "I"—is the "thing that thinks" or *res cogitans*. The body, on the other hand, is not a thing that thinks. Descartes further insists that the "I" that is him *is* the mind, not the human body with its physical parts. Descartes's own words cannot be clearer about such a dualist conception:

> At last I have discovered it—thought; this alone is inseparable from me. I am, I exist—that is certain. But for how long? For as long as I am thinking. For it could be that were I totally to cease from thinking, I should totally cease to exist. . . . I am, then, in the strict sense only a thing that thinks; that is, I am a mind,

44. *CV*, 28.
45. Pole, *Later Philosophy of Wittgenstein*, 2.
46. *PI* 109.
47. *PI* 309.

or intelligence, or intellect, or reason—words whose meaning I have been ignorant of until now. But for all that I am a thing which is real and which truly exists. But what kind of a thing? As I have just said—a thinking thing.... I am not that structure of limbs which is called a human body.[48]

In the same "foundationalist" vein, Descartes can even argue from the "clear and distinct ideas" in his mind to the existence of God, but that is another story.[49] What concerns us here is his view of the mind in relation to the body. Having posited that the mind is the thinking substance he is led to relegate the body—considered also a "thing"—to the status of a mere automaton. Thus, the mind and the body are both separate and different to each other, the former having no extension in space and is immaterial, whereas the latter like other physical objects, occupies space and is material. Puzzled by the strict division he has thus fashioned, and being unable to explain the causal nexus between the two, Descartes further postulates that the mind, being a bodiless thing, is housed in a material body. With such a dualistic conception of the human person, Wittgenstein is clearly not altogether comfortable as his comments below reveal:

We feel then that in the cases in which "I" is used as subject, we don't use it because we recognize a particular person by his bodily characteristics; and this creates the illusion that we use this word to refer to something bodiless, which, however, has its seat in our body. In fact this seems to be the real ego, the one of which it was said, "Cognito, ergo sum."—"Is there then no mind, but only a body?" Answer: The word "mind" has meaning, i.e., it has a use in our language; but saying this doesn't yet say what kind of use we make of it.[50]

One result of Descartes's notion of the *res cogitans* is the emergence of a picture of the fully self-conscious, autonomous and disembodied individual. It is a picture of the self that, according to Kerr, many philosophers including Wittgenstein have striven to revise, if not

---

48. Descartes, *Meditations on First Philosophy*, 37.

49. See Descartes, *Meditations on First Philosophy*, 49–73. Descartes avows, "Altogether then, it must be concluded that the mere fact that I exist and have within me an idea of a most perfect being, that is, God, provides a very clear proof that God does indeed exist" (71).

50. *BB*, 69–70.

obliterate altogether.[51] This is because the "worldless ego" thus created is individualistic to the point of being isolated from and totally impenetrable to other selves. Furthermore, the perspective of this Cartesian "I" is so completely egocentric that the individual cannot be sure if other bodies surrounding him or her are real or not. The following scenario in Descartes's Second Meditation illustrates just how egocentric the "I" can be:

> But then if I look out of the window and see men crossing the square, as I just happen to have done, I normally say that I see the men themselves just as I say I see the wax. Yet do I see any more than hats and coats which could conceal automatons? I *judge* that they are men. And so something which I thought I was seeing with my eyes is in fact grasped solely by the faculty of judgement which is in my mind.[52]

Descartes makes the point that he judges the hats and cloaks he has seen beyond his window as covering human beings and not machines; presumably *he* could have judged otherwise. Clearly, he is claiming that the "I" is in a position to decide what to make of the surrounding world, perhaps giving it a God-like status. The resultant picture of an individual who is self-conscious, autonomous, and all-responsible is still very much with us today. It is a picture that Wittgenstein finds difficulty with. In a lecture delivered in the 1930s, Wittgenstein had already expressed his opposition to such an emphasis on the Cartesian "I."[53] That word "I"— the first-person pronoun—is one among others he proposes should be brought back from its metaphysical misuse to its home in everyday conversation:

> When philosophers use a word—"knowledge," "being," "object," "I," "proposition," "name"—and try to grasp the essence of the thing, one must always ask oneself: is the word ever actually used in this way in the language which is its original home?— What we do is to bring words back from their metaphysical to their everyday use.[54]

Yet, the idea of the Cartesian ego dies hard; and modern theology seems very much saturated with it. Kerr, who is concerned to alert Christians

51. Kerr, *Theology after Wittgenstein*, 5.

52. Descartes, *Meditations on First Philosophy*, 43, 45.

53. Kerr, *Theology after Wittgenstein*, 43.

54. *PI* 116.

to the rise of human subjectivity, counts many major contemporary theologians among those who are decidedly Cartesian dualist in mode of thought, especially in terms of their epistemological assumptions about the individual.[55] One of those named has even affirmed that "there must be no going back on 'the transcendental-anthropological turn in philosophy since Descartes.'"[56] What they had inadvertently brought on—so Kerr charges—is an "inverted theology," the type of theology in which the individual (ego) is at the center of theological reflection as well as the starting point.[57]

What is relevant to our study is that the Cartesian paradigm of the solipsistic self has also fostered an inclination "to think of meaning as some essentially occult state or act inside one's consciousness, radically inaccessible to anyone else."[58] This follows from the belief that the self, concealed inside the person exists and thinks, while matter merely extends in space, whose existence could even be doubted. Now mind and matter are distinguished by the theory of knowledge into a distinction of subject and object, for the subject is what knows, and matter is the object of thought and knowledge. What enters the mind as content are ideas such as mental images, sensations, thoughts and even pain. Following an ancient principle, Descartes had held that "there must be at least as much [reality] in the efficient and total cause as in the effect of that cause."[59] In virtue of this conception of ideas—and by extension, meaning—as being in the mind and therefore radically private has become assimilated into our epistemologies, most people today do still think of thinking as a private mental activity. It follows that knowledge of material objects is gained by one's inspection of the ideas inside one's mind that correspond to or represent the reality outside one's mind—an "inside/outside picture of knowledge,"[60] as Charles Taylor (b. 1931) calls it. Yet, it is a picture which does not sit well with Wittgenstein—or should not with us,

55. He names Karl Rahner, Hans Kung, Don Cupitt, Schubert Ogden, and others. See Kerr, *Theology after Wittgenstein*, 7–23.

56. Rahner, *Theological Investigations*, 9:38, cited in Kerr, *Theology after Wittgenstein*, 7.

57. Kerr, *Theology after Wittgenstein*, 23.

58. Kerr, *Theology after Wittgenstein*, 42.

59. Descartes, *Meditations on First Philosophy*, 57.

60. Taylor, "Merleau-Ponty and the Epistemological Picture," 26, cited in Smith, *Who's Afraid of Relativism?*, 24.

either—because the assumption is still that of the self who is concealed as well as imprisoned inside the person.

> This simile of "inside" or "outside" the mind is pernicious. It is derived from "in the head" when we think of ourselves as looking out from our heads and of thinking as something going on "in our head." But we then forget the picture and go on using language derived from it.[61]

Two uncanny trends are the upshot of the inside/outside epistemological framework, namely the aspiration to seek a representation of reality by means of language, and a disregard for the mediation of the community in one's quest for an absolute conception of reality. Wittgenstein would counter that language is not always representational, and that the role of the community cannot ever be downplayed since one cannot step outside a community to gain any objective perspective of things. I would further add the concern that the inside/outside paradigm encourages one to be rather skeptical since one is in doubt as to whether language can ever grasp the external world and God. That paradigm assumes that what is "inside" and what is "outside" are two regions of being. Knowledge, as James K. A. Smith (b. 1970) puts it, becomes "a matter of getting something 'inside' our minds to hook onto things 'outside' our minds."[62] If language is the means by which external things are represented or copied, one is still entitled to question whether our perception matches these objects, which is the ground for the radical epistemological skepticism exhibited by Descartes at the beginning of the *Meditations*. But if religious language is given a full Wittgenstein treatment of rehabilitation from such dualist assumptions, and is rid of its representational role, one would be able to worry less about not getting "what are out there" right.

Resources for Theology

We must now turn to consider how some of Wittgenstein's thoughts and ideas have been or could be relevant for theology.

---

61. Wittgenstein, *Wittgenstein's Lectures, Cambridge, 1930–1932*, 25.

62. Smith, *Who's Afraid of Relativism?*, 24.

1. Meaning

Wittgenstein has always been concerned about the question of meaning; indeed, as we have noted, all his works revolve around this particular topic. Much of his first book, *TLP*, is devoted to what scholars have called the "picture theory" of meaning. Briefly stated, this theory maintains that propositions reflect the nature of what they represent. In the *Blue Book* (so named because its content comprises Wittgenstein's lecture notes for students bound in blue cloth) the question "What is the meaning of a word?" is not only raised, it even appears at the very beginning of the book.[63] In *PI*, the concept of meaning is a key concern.[64]

The question of meaning in religious discourse is now widely held to be prior to the question of truth or falsity. This is an entirely logical and sound position: in order to verify whether an assertion is true or false, one must first be clear about its meaning. As Hudson puts it, "Any proposition, say, 'John loves Mary,' must (logically) be known to be meaningful before it can be known to be true or false."[65] In her insightful study, *Beyond Liberalism and Fundamentalism*, Nancey C. Murphy has provided a helpful illustration of how the judgement that philosophical problems could best be addressed by first attending to language has supplanted the concern over epistemological issues:

> We might say that whereas ancient and medieval philosophers asked metaphysical questions about what there is, early modern philosophers recognized a prior question: how can we know what exists? Late modern philosophers ask: what do we mean when we say that we know something? (or, what are the linguistic categories needed to give a complete account of what there is?). It should not be surprising, then, that a great deal of attention has been given . . . to the development of explicit theories about language, answering especially the question: how does language get its meaning? Or, better: what is the meaning of meaning?[66]

---

63. *BB*, 1.
64. *PI*, vii.
65. Hudson, *Wittgenstein and Religious Belief*, 24.
66. Murphy, *Beyond Liberalism & Fundamentalism*, 38.

Wittgenstein's Early Theory

Since Wittgenstein's later views can only be understood against the background of his old way of thinking, let us now return to the "picture theory" of meaning that we find in *TLP*. According to this theory, language consists of propositions, with each proposition standing for— or "picturing"—a definite state of affairs in the world. "In a proposition," Wittgenstein posits, "a thought can be expressed in such a way that elements of the propositional sign correspond to the objects of the thought."[67] In other words, there is an unambiguous correspondence between language and reality, such that individual words in language are labels for objects or things other than themselves, and sentences are combinations of such labels or names.[68] The supposition, derived from logical atomism, is that the world is a "totality of facts" comprising states of affairs,[69] which, in turn, can be reduced to a collection of *objects or simples*.[70] Language can likewise be reduced, with each level of the structure of language matching a level of structure in the world. What language reduces to is a collection of "elementary" propositions—so-called as they cannot be further analyzed—which match facts in the world. Thus, the early Wittgenstein comes to view language as a perfect mirror of the world: there is a one-to-one correspondence between a proposition and the situation it describes. Anticipating possible objection to such a schema, Wittgenstein proffers the following comparison:

> At first sight a proposition—one set out on the printed page, for example—does not seem to be a picture of the reality with which it is concerned. But neither do written notes seem at first sight to be a picture of a piece of music, nor our phonetic notion (the alphabet) to be a picture of speech. And yet these sign-languages prove to be pictures, even in the ordinary sense, of what they represent.[71]

---

67. *TLP* 3.2.

68. *PI* 1.

69. *TLP* 1.1.

70. It is important to note that in the early Wittgenstein's scheme of things, "objects" are the ultimate "simples" of reality, not further divisible or reducible into parts. As they "make up the substance of the world" (*TLP* 2.021), they must therefore exist necessarily.

71. *TLP* 4.011.

Apparently, he does seem to have made a strong case for insisting upon the correlation between "name" and "object." His reasoning is robust, though as will be shown, such correlation is valid only within a narrow range of words:

> The word "Excalibur," say, is a proper name in the ordinary sense. The sword Excalibur consists of parts combined in a particular way. If they are combined differently Excalibur does not exist. But it is clear that the sentence "Excalibur has a sharp blade" makes *sense* whether Excalibur is still whole or is broken up. But if "Excalibur" is the name of an object, this object no longer exists when Excalibur is broken in pieces; and as no object would then correspond to the name it would have no meaning. But then the sentence "Excalibur has a sharp blade" would contain a word that had no meaning, and hence the sentence would be nonsense. But it does make sense; so there must always be something corresponding to the words of which it consists.[72]

So convinced was Wittgenstein that the picture theory (also known as the referential theory) he has formulated is valid and that he had consequently solved the central problem of philosophy, he quit the practice of philosophy.[73]

Wittgenstein's Later Theory

When Wittgenstein returned to philosophy many years later, he questioned the assumptions upon which the theory of meaning espoused in *TLP* was based. Some of the issues he has problems with may be briefly reviewed. Firstly, he rejects the notion that elementary propositions are logically independent of each other. He counters that they can be logically related to one another within systems, and that if we are to understand any single proposition, we must take into account the whole system to which it belongs. Wittgenstein also challenges the idea that the simples in a proposition must have a one-to-one correspondence with the basic blocks making up reality. His critique of this assumption comprises two parts, namely, that it makes no sense to think of reality as comprising simples because the attempt to distinguish between simple

72. *PI* 39.
73. See *TLP*, p4.

and composite is bound to fail; and that the one-to-one correspondence between language and reality fails to maintain a separation between meaning and the signified object.

Wittgenstein, we have noted, admitted "grave mistakes" in *TLP*. Accordingly, in *PI*, he devoted much attention to refuting and correcting many of the assumptions and doctrines of the picture theory. However, he never presented his later work as an absolute repudiation of the earlier work. We recall again his express desire for both works to be published within a single cover. Unsurprisingly, we find in *PI* the same quest for answers to essentially the same question about how language is related to the world. The key difference is that whereas in *TLP* Wittgenstein had turned to logic for answers to questions about language and meaning, he now placed the problems of logic within the wider, and much more complicated, nexus of human existence. As Anthony Thiselton has rightly perceived, in the later Wittgenstein "language was now grounded not in a single comprehensive abstract calculus of formal logic, but in the varied and particular activities of human life."[74]

PI opens with a passage from Augustine's *Confessions* (I:8) in which the saint recounts his experience as a child learning a language. The narrative clearly reveals the epistemological predicament of the infant Augustine.[75] Wittgenstein uses it to summarize a "particular picture of the essence of human language" that he (Wittgenstein) would distance himself from. He imputes the following idea of language to Augustine:

> The individual words in language name objects—sentences are combinations of such names.—In this picture of language we find the roots of the following idea: Every word has a meaning. This meaning is correlated with the word. It is the object for which the word stands.[76]

This summary will sound familiar for it is much like the confused theory of language espoused in *TLP*. The view of language correlating a word and an object may seem "natural" or "commonsensical" to us, but Wittgenstein has identified problems with this view, namely, (i) locating meaning in atomized words rather than in their use, and (ii)

---

74. Thiselton, *Two Horizons*, 357.

75. Kerr, *Theology after Wittgenstein*, 40.

76. *PI* 1. Wilson has observed that "this picture promised to satisfy the Fregean requirement that any proposition that has meaning must have an exact meaning" (*Wittgenstein's Philosophical Investigations*, 1).

learning words by ostensive definition rather than from a wider context. The issues are closely related, as one leads to another: if the meaning of a word is located in the object that the word stands for, then meaning is obtained by us pointing to the object. The assumption behind this so-called "ostensive teaching of words" should not escape us: "Meaning is *reference*: a word refers to a thing and the 'hook' between the two is 'meaning.'"[77]

While Wittgenstein does not say that Augustine's theory is entirely wrong, he considers the saint's conception of how language works "primitive."[78] He thinks that as a system of communication it is only appropriate within a narrow range of words. He explains,

> Augustine, we might say, does describe a system of communication; only not everything that we call language is this system. And one has to say this in many cases where the question arises "Is this an appropriate description or not?" The answer is: "Yes it is appropriate, but only for this narrowly circumscribed region, not for the whole of what you were claiming to describe."[79]

We need to remember that Wittgenstein is here correcting himself as well, for he has once held the same "representational" theory that a language functions only to name objects. It seems that he had been so focused on finding solutions to the philosophical problems about the nature of propositions that the perspective of how everyday language actually functions escapes him.[80] If Wittgenstein had been able to see the contrast between what his theory leads him to claim and the workings of ordinary language, he would have seen far earlier that naming objects is far from the only function of words.

The inclusion of Augustine's story also enables Wittgenstein to make the point that meaning is not just a "mental activity."[81] The inclination to think of meaning as being in the head is, as we have noted, a legacy of the Cartesian dualist bent to cast a divide between the mental and the physical, tempting us to picture the self as fully autonomous and solitary, locked within a private world inaccessible to other persons. Having thus

77. Smith, *Who's Afraid of Relativism?*, 41.

78. *PI* 2.

79. *PI* 3.

80. McGinn, *Wittgenstein and the Philosophical Investigations*, 34.

81. *PI* 693.

argued that the meaning of words is located neither in the object with which they are associated nor in one's head, Wittgenstein arrives at the brilliant notion of defining meaning in terms of use. The meaning of words, he decides, is to be understood by the way in which words are used within their context.

In the course of his investigation, Wittgenstein would propose a new image to convey the nature of language along the following lines:

> Our language may be seen as an ancient city: a maze of little streets and squares, of old and new houses, and of houses with additions from various periods; and this surrounded by a multitude of new boroughs with straight regular streets and uniform houses.[82]

In this picture of language, one sees language in an entirely new and dynamic way. Language is shaped and built up over time; its growth is historical, not a construction built according to some plan and completed all at once. Also, as no uniform plan forms the basis of an ancient city; similarly, no uniform logic or grammar forms the basis of our language. The additions to the city refer to new terminologies and vocabularies which are added to deal with change. Most importantly, just as we think of a city as having a population of people, language too is at the center of all social interactions. This manner of conceiving language, I should add, is important for the direction of my present project. Closely linked to this analogy are the concepts of language-games and form of life. To these we shall now turn.

2. "Language-Games" (*Sprachspiel*)

Wittgenstein introduces the highly influential notion of "language-games" at the beginning of *PI* with the intention of encompassing the whole of language, and all the actions and performances woven into it.[83] Whatever the subsequent understandings given to "language-games," the term has evolved into common parlance. In what follows, I shall be concerned with two questions. The first is: what does Wittgenstein mean by the concept of language-games? The second question is: why does he

82. *PI* 18.
83. *PI* 7.

introduce it? These questions should prepare us in inquiring into how "language-games" apply to religious language.

With respect to the first question, the term is first applied by Wittgenstein to simple activities such as his imaginary builders, children's games with words such as "ring-a-ring-a-roses," and the way children learn their native language.[84] Later, he includes many more examples, including giving orders and obeying them, reporting an event, making up a story and reading it, making a joke, asking, cursing, greeting, praying, and so on.[85] Wittgenstein does not tell us what a language-game actually is, or how one is to be identified.[86] Instead, he stresses that there are countless different kinds of words and sentences which make up language-games, and that there are countless different uses of such utterances.[87] "This multiplicity," he underscores, "is not something fixed, given once for all; but new types of language, new language-games, as we may say, come into existence, and others become obsolete and get forgotten."[88] If the last remark is true it will bear on how we understand religious language. We will consider this issue in the next chapter.

It may be useful if I mention here that the notion of language-games is intended by Wittgenstein to be no more than an analogy. In his own words, "language-games are rather set up as *objects of comparison* which are meant to throw light on the facts of our language by way not only of similarities, but also of dissimilarities."[89] If so, it can hardly be justifiably claimed by anyone that Wittgenstein had intended to construe language in general as a "mere game."[90] Nor should the concept be misconceived as a sanction for fideism, a charge with which, we have noted, Wittgenstein's name has been linked. In defense of Wittgenstein, we need only point out that of the language-games he exemplified, most are not exclusively associated with particular practices. For by "language-games," Wittgenstein does not have in mind complete domains of discourse (scientific, religious, political, and so forth). Moreover, he asks

84. *PI* 7.

85. *PI* 23.

86. *PI* 65.

87. *PI* 65.

88. *PI* 65.

89. *PI* 130.

90. Macquarrie, *Thinking of God*, 6, questions whether the game-analogy is appropriate.

us always to look out for "similarities" or "family resemblances" between language-games.[91] That Wittgenstein does not wish "to draw strict boundaries between language-games"[92] and even admits to similarities between them must be read as a negation of any fideistic inference that there is no commonality at all. We can see again an obvious application here—that those who use the religious language-game are not to suppose that they are hermitically sealed against overtures and inputs from other types of discourse.

The question of why the expression "language-game" was introduced is a natural one to raise. I propose that it is to refute the view in *TLP* that language is "an object or independent entity, all above-board and open for detached inquiry and analysis."[93] At bottom, what Wittgenstein wants to show is one's behavior and the language one uses are very closely woven together. Thiselton is thus correct to understand the language-game analogy as seeking to highlight "the fact that language-uses are grounded in the *particular surroundings* of situations in human life."[94] Like games, language or the speaking of language is a social and rule-guided activity, and it is embedded in life. He further notes that the analogy also illustrates that language is not to be used in a singular and uniform way.[95] As we have been informed by Wittgenstein himself, there are "many kinds of sentence" and "countless different kinds of use of what we call 'symbols', 'words', 'sentences.'"[96]

We may perhaps advance another reason why the concept of language-games was created. What it is will have an obvious application to religious language which will be taken up in the next chapter. Let us draw a parallel between the two. Games are usually played according to rules, but the rules that have force in one game may not apply in another. In a similar vein, certain terms and concepts which are meaningful for a game for the part they play within it, may have no relevance in another. There is, for instance, no such thing as "targeting a bull's eye" in a game of chess. In the case of religious language, some of its terms and concerns will simply not make sense if they are uttered outside their

91. *PI* 66.

92. D'hert, *Wittgenstein's Relevance for Theology*, 47.

93. High, *Language, Persons, and Belief*, 28.

94. Thiselton, *Two Horizons*, 373.

95. Thiselton, *Two Horizons*, 373.

96. *PI* 23.

original context. The question "Is Jesus the Messiah?" will not interest or fully make sense to those who are not familiar with or part of a religious tradition in which messiahship has significance. By means of language-games, what Wittgenstein has done is recognize that language can be conceived as having different "concrete entities."[97] Within its own "entity" the religious language-game is properly played, under the circumstances and terms in which it is set.

3. "Form of Life" (*Lebensform*)

What does Wittgenstein mean when he uses the phrase "form of life"? As in the case of "language-game," we are not offered any precise definition of the term. Opinions are thus not only divided about its meaning but also as to whether it is a useful concept at all. A close reading of the passages where the phrase appears in *PI* will confirm how difficult it is to know precisely what is meant:

- "To imagine a language means to imagine a form of life."[98]

- "The term 'language-game' is meant to bring into prominence the fact that the speaking of language is part of an activity or of a form of life."[99]

- "It is what human beings say that is true and false; and they agree in the language they use. That is not agreement in opinions but in form of life."[100]

- "Can only those hope who can talk? Only those who have mastered the use of a language. That is to say, the phenomena of hope are modes of this complicated form of life."[101]

- "What has to be accepted, the given, is—so one could *say—forms of life.*"[102]

Yet, from these expressions it is possible to deduce a number of ways in which the notion "form of life" may be understood: "transcendentally

97. Specht, *Foundations of Wittgenstein's Late Philosophy*, 53.

98. *PI* 19.

99. *PI* 23.

100. *PI* 241.

101. *PI* II, 148.

102. *PI* II, 192.

(e.g., as a necessary condition for the possibility of communication); biologically (e.g., an evolutionary account of how practice is possible); and culturally (e.g., a sociological or anthropological account of what members of a particular social group have in common)."[103]

In a recent study, Steven Knowles reveals an understanding of "form of life" that I think is reached by the very approach just enunciated. For instance, he takes the use of the phrase to illustrate "that language is intrinsically bound up with communities who evolve and change through the process of ongoing dialogue and activity."[104] He further suggests that the idea of "form of life" is a reference to the cultural phenomena of language, all of which is valid because the term in question is certainly linked to language and its use. The phrase seems also intended by Wittgenstein to remind us that language is embedded in daily human life, and that it is within the social context that the meaningfulness of language is located. Perhaps Ignace D'hert is correct in saying that the notion of "form of life" is "simply a deepening of the concept of language-game" and that it does not add anything new to our knowledge.[105]

However, if the concept of "form of life" is anything like what we have said, the implications for understanding the nature of language are immense. For one thing, the process of understanding a language will require more than an understanding of its rules of grammar and its vocabulary. It would entail an interaction with the culture, the environment and, not least, the people who are the users of that particular language. As has been widely acknowledged, we cannot understand language except by being "part of an activity which is not simply oral."[106] This point is subtly driven home in a remark by Wittgenstein: "If a lion could talk, we could not understand him."[107] We can see why this should be the case: it is because a lion does not share our forms of life so that even if he could utter words we would still not be able to tell what he communicated.

As the notions of "form of life" and "language-games" seem for most purposes to come to much the same thing, I shall henceforth subsume the former into the latter in my subsequent discussion.

103. Stern, *Wittgenstein's Philosophical Investigations*, 161.

104. Knowles, *Beyond Evangelicalism*, 43.

105. D'hert, *Wittgenstein's Relevance for Theology*, 51.

106. Hudson, *Wittgenstein and Religious Belief*, 54.

107. *PI* II, 190.

4. Argument against Private Language

Wittgenstein's argument against private language is introduced and contained in *PI* 244–71. Though highly significant in philosophical discussion, it is often misunderstood.[108] Let us briefly clarify that he is not denying that people cannot have such a language in which they can describe their inner thoughts and feelings; nor is he denying that people cannot formulate their own expressions to represent how they feel or think. Indeed, he even grants that people can coin individual words that refer to private sensations which only they themselves can understand. To affirm that language has a public nature is not to deny that words and utterances can be used "privately" by or within specific groups of people, such as a church or a fellowship.

What Wittgenstein is chiefly concerned to point out is this: if a word—"red," say—is made to refer to a private sensation, it ceases to function as a word within the repertoire of our everyday speech. For it is possible that under such a condition of use, the word may refer to something different in every case. In contradiction, our whole system of language has developed on the basis that there is a distinction between "correct" and "mistaken" applications of words, a distinction arrived at by the community of language users. An essential feature for meaning is the level of constancy. Thus, the word "red" in the earlier example must mean something that is generally understood. Otherwise, what obtains is "that one section of mankind had one sensation of red and another section another."[109] Concisely put, Wittgenstein's argument against private language is not that it is not possible to devise one, but that it is useless for establishing communicable content. He writes, "When I talk about language (words, sentences, etc.) I must speak the language of every day."[110]

The significance of this issue for theological language is immense. Firstly, Wittgenstein's rejection of private language helps to undermine the view that one can have a strictly fideistic language. As noted above, fideism is countered once it is denied a private language by which it can

108. Wittgenstein explains what a private language is: "The individual words of this language are to refer to what can only be known to the person speaking; to his immediate private sensations. So another person cannot understand the language" (*PI* 243).

109. *PI* 272.

110. *PI* 120.

shield itself from public accountability. Secondly, Wittgenstein refutes the view that religious terms are merely non-objective symbolizations of experience, and thereby "helps us to discern false accounts of 'inwardness' in religion."[111] Lastly, at the heart of Wittgenstein's argument is his insistence that religious language cannot be abstracted from the community that uses it—by which the determinants of its content are located.

Concluding Remarks

This chapter has served to introduce Wittgenstein and sketch out a little of his background, career, and achievements. We have also explored what he thinks about religion and seen how his philosophy has developed or changed. Although it is difficult to determine the precise degree of his sympathy with Christianity, I do not think that what he was in terms of his religious affiliation matters as far as his logic of language is concerned. It would be wrongheaded of us to embrace or reject his philosophical insights on the grounds that he was religious or even a Christian. But there can be little doubt that religious beliefs played a big role in how his thought took shape.

Our consideration of his philosophical development has led us to question the common view that Wittgenstein's early and later philosophies are totally disparate. I am inclined to think that his philosophical interest has remained consistent throughout his career, while the changes and corrections of the later phase have been the result of a continuous and maturing process on his part. Still, it would be a serious lapse of judgement to fail to recognize that the atomism of *TLP* is poles apart from the mature view in *PI* that language is grounded in the varied and particular situations of everyday life. There are several ways of accounting for the contrast between the two views respecting language. Thiselton's has already been noted, namely, that the ground of language has moved from logic as an abstract calculus to the varied and particular activities of human life. The contrast can also be seen as a shift from an understanding of logic as being separated from the use of language and thus hidden in language in the early Wittgenstein, to an understanding of logic as being shown in our use of language in the later Wittgenstein. Quite clearly, the atomism of *TLP* is based on a dualist assumption of an external/internal

---

111. Sherry, *Religion, Truth and Language-Games*, 8.

distinction, a distinction that the later Wittgenstein seeks to eliminate. Once the dualism is overcome, we would see that language is available for a diversity of use, and that more importantly, it is grounded in the setting of human life. Wittgenstein's later manner of conceiving language, together with other aspects and terms of his philosophy, are relevant to our argument about how language about God is to be regarded.

In the next chapter we will look at how insights from Wittgenstein's philosophy may be appropriated in our conception and use of language in religion.

Chapter 3

Applying Wittgenstein

What we are destroying is nothing but houses of cards and we are clearing up the ground of language on which they stood.[1]

—Ludwig Wittgenstein

Introduction

IN THE PREVIOUS CHAPTER we have considered the work of Wittgenstein and identified several of his ideas which are of theological relevance. In particular, we looked at his notions of meaning-as-use, language-games, form of life, and his private language argument. We also considered the Cartesian paradigm of the "worldless self" which Wittgenstein has sought to revise, and the form of fideism with which his name is now linked. In the present chapter, I shall attempt to go beyond what has been raised and say more about how these themes could be constructively appropriated in our conception and use of language in religion. In order to be in a position to realize this aim, we shall need to look again at the main features of both the early and later phases of his philosophy.

On Appropriating Wittgenstein

First, however, I would like to indicate where I stand regarding my own approach to Wittgenstein. Although I have explained my reasons

1. *PI* 118.

for choosing to consider him, I should specify the two insights of his philosophy that have hugely appealed to me. The first is that the philosophical problems which confront us have arisen "through a misinterpretation of our forms of language"[2] arising from the fact that "we do not *command a clear view* of the use of our words."[3] The second is that because meaning does not have an absolutely determinate sense, the quest for absolute exactness in language is bound to fail.[4] These thoughts appear to cohere very much with the concerns of my work. While I do not claim to have "mastered" Wittgenstein's corpus, I believe that there are useful resources to be mined for my project. In recent years, theologians[5] have become more open to appropriating Wittgenstein's insights. Standing squarely in that philosopher's shadow is Rowan Williams who has urged that "there are things which we must learn from Wittgenstein if we are to avoid paralysing or simply confusing ourselves as theologians, things that have to do with language as sheer practice rather than 'simple' naming."[6] However, there are also those who have been hesitant to consider Wittgenstein, or found his writings of little value for their enterprise.[7] Some who did draw on him are bashful that they had done so. A case in point is Anthony Thiselton's appropriation of Wittgenstein for his celebrated work on hermeneutics. In that tome, Thiselton writes,

> In our use of Wittgenstein, our concern is only to borrow from this thinker certain *conceptual tools* for the various tasks which we shall undertake in formulating hermeneutical theory and in expounding the text of the New Testament. To make a constructive use of a particular philosopher's conceptual tools is not necessarily to subscribe to his view of the world.[8]

For whatever reason, Thiselton is clearly being unnecessarily cautious here. In my opinion, one need not be defensive about applying Wittgenstein's

2. *PI* 111.

3. *PI* 122.

4. See *PI* 88.

5. To name a few: Paul Holmer, George Lindbeck, D. Z. Phillips, Stanley Hauerwas, Fergus Kerr. See Ashford, "Wittgenstein's Theologians?," 357–75.

6. Williams, "Response to Kerr," 631.

7. See, e.g., Ward, "*Theology after Wittgenstein* (Book Review)," 267; Creegan, "*Theology after Wittgenstein* by Fergus Kerr (Book Review)," 122; Moore, *Realism and Christian Faith*, 73.

8. Thiselton, *Two Horizons*, 9–10.

insights. As a philosopher, Wittgenstein is not at all concerned to convert anyone to his beliefs; his aim is strictly to stimulate thoughts.[9] Recall his comments to his students, "What I should like to get at is for you not to agree with me in particular opinions, but to investigate the matter in the right way."[10] What Wittgenstein offers is more a method of understanding, and it is this that we shall seek to apply. For what matters is whether his "way" works, and whether we can learn how to use his ideas.

Early Phase of Wittgenstein's Philosophy

Key Elements

We begin with the views articulated in Wittgenstein's earliest work, *TLP* with its theme about the nature of the world and its representation in thought and language. I shall first expand the key elements in his position that continue to be relevant to my discussion before turning to specific applications.

Wittgenstein's concern with language first merged within a metaphysics of wanting to determine "the character of the world."[11] He was not primarily concerned with language *per se*. In his very first statement in *TLP,* Wittgenstein declares, "The world is all that is the case."[12] The world, he further postulates, is a totality—comprising not things or objects but *facts;* and as such, the world is represented by propositions of language.[13] One may ask: why facts? It is because, to quote one of his interpreters, "facts are the way things *are*; they are even more fundamental than objects, because the latter are contingent."[14] To be sure, objects are "simples" of reality: they "make up the substance of the world"[15] and can be referred to only by being named. But facts, as Wittgenstein clarifies, determine "what is the case, and also whatever is not the case,"[16] and are themselves described by propositions, which as he

9. *PI*, x.

10. Rhees, *Discussions of Wittgenstein*, 42–43.

11. Fogelin, *Wittgenstein*, 3.

12. *TLP* 1.

13. *TLP* 1.1.

14. Klein, *How Things Are in the World*, 21.

15. *TLP* 2.02; 2.021.

16. *TLP* 1.12.

said, represent reality. The implication he would have us note is that "the stuff of the Universe does not consist of entities describable by nouns, but of objective counterparts of whole grammatical sentences."[17]

Admittedly, Wittgenstein's account of language is not a simple matter to understand or explain or even grasp. And, it is not only because of his use of a special terminology or aphorisms. It is also the fact that the numerous things that are said to be admitted to reality must seem odd to the common person who would not have dreamt of seeing them as constituents of the world. Perhaps, Norman Malcolm's account of "a hierarchy of ordered structures" in *TLP* may help. He explains:

> A state of affairs in the world is a structure of simple objects. A thought is a structure of mental elements. A proposition of language is a structure of signs. If a particular proposition is *true* there are three structures which, in a sense, are equivalent. There is a configuration of simple objects which *constitutes* a state of affairs. There is a configuration of mental elements which *depicts* that state of affairs. There is a configuration of signs, which also depicts that state of affairs. These are three parallel structures in the three different domains of reality, thought and language.[18]

It is important that we understand what Wittgenstein means by "the world" since he uses the term throughout the text. The world of *TLP* is neither the world of science, nor the world of sensible objects or things. It is rather the world *conceptually* viewed and analyzed as "it funnels through the dynamism of the human mind."[19] This explains why Wittgenstein has insisted that the world is not the totality of things, but of facts. Being of facts, the world can both be encountered and represented in language. But most importantly, as Terrance W. Klein points out, "a synthesis is presupposed as existing in the world and in language; through the latter we have access to the former."[20] Such a conception of the world is nothing new or original as philosophers have long been known to get at the fundamental facts about the world by considering the fundamental features of language. Plato, for instance, teaches that a given term such as "tree" or "sharp" can be truly applied to a large number of individual things—even different ones—in more or less the same sense;

17. Cleobury, "Wittgenstein and the Philosophy of Religion," 175.

18. Malcolm, *Wittgenstein: A Religious Point of View?*, 32–33.

19. Klein, *How Things Are in the World*, 21.

20. Klein, *How Things Are in the World*, 30.

this is possible only because there really exists some one entity named by the term in question, namely, treeness or sharpness.

Wittgenstein's investigation into the nature of the world is strictly an exercise in logic which he believes "is prior to every experience."[21] Thus, he seems indifferent to defining or providing any actual examples of objects or propositions, making no appeal to empirical facts. Most of his claims, including the one that reality is represented by propositions, are *a priori*. "It is," he contends, "as impossible to represent in language anything that 'contradicts logic' as it is in geometry to represent by its co-ordinates a figure that contradicts the laws of space, or to give the co-ordinates of a point that does not exist."[22] In "Notes on Logic," Wittgenstein remarks, "Philosophy gives no pictures of reality, and can neither confirm nor confute scientific investigations. It consists of logic and metaphysics, the former its basis."[23] Given such a conviction, what occupies him intensely is the question of how the world as it is, relates to the world known through the language he uses. Quite clearly, Wittgenstein's order of investigation is in such manner: from the nature of logic to the nature of language and then to the nature of the world. At this stage of his philosophical development, he is clearly committed to the view that language has a basic and rational form, a form in which there is a correspondence between atomic propositions and atomic facts.

The conclusion at which his early investigation arrived, we have said, is called the "picture theory of language." Why such a theory is rejected and abandoned by Wittgenstein himself may now be briefly noted. Firstly, it has wrongly assumed that the "simples" in a proposition and the world must correspond absolutely. The reality, as Wittgenstein comes to appreciate is: there is no such thing as a "logical form" that can or must be held to identify once and for all the essence of language with the world. The other reason for jettisoning the picture theory is his recognition that a proposition need not have an absolutely determinate sense. A further reason is his recognition of the limits of analysis.[24] It is, however, necessary to clarify that Wittgenstein does not repudiate *every* insight in *TLP*. Otherwise, why would he be keen to have that book and

21. *TLP* 5.552. For our purposes, we shall interpret "logic" as a science that is concerned with correct reasoning, and that is attentive to the intelligibility of what a person says or thinks.

22. *TLP* 3.032.

23. *NB*, 93.

24. Hudson, *Wittgenstein and Religious Belief*, 36.

PI published in a single volume and say that "the latter could be seen in the right light only by contrast with and against the background of my old way of thinking"?[25] It would therefore be wrongheaded to consign *TLP* to oblivion; it is certainly not "like a bag of junk professing to be a clock, but like a clock that did not tell you the right time."[26] Indeed, there are a number of "achievements" which one can identify in the book that have provided the foundations for the development of a new dimension about human speaking, thinking and understanding.

This brings us to the final sections of *TLP* where Wittgenstein makes the celebrated point that there are things which cannot be put into words but nevertheless show themselves.[27] These things are, he adds, "what is mystical."[28] It is not disputed that "the mystical" is used by Wittgenstein to refer to God. To be sure, the term is also spoken of as having to do with "the sense of the world," ethics, aesthetics, meaning of life, and so forth.[29] But the most famous sentence that ends *TLP*, "What we cannot speak about we must pass over in silence"[30] is still mired in controversy. One interpretation is that these words are an injunction against an over-confident and uncritical approach to doing philosophy.

Applications

In what follows, we shall be concerned to consider specific applications arising from some of the insights or themes gleaned from *TLP* as they relate to the use of religious language. Our discussion can be brought under three headings: (1) Language and metaphysics, (2) Meaning and truth, and (3) Reference(s) to God.

1. Language and Metaphysics

In *TLP*, we have noted, Wittgenstein is primarily concerned to arrive at an understanding of the nature of reality. His book is therefore properly a work of metaphysics, but with an important difference—the

25. *PI*, x.

26. Anscombe, *Introduction to Wittgenstein's Tractatus*, 78.

27. *TLP* 6.522.

28. *TLP* 6.522.

29. See *TLP* 6.4–6.522.

30. *TLP* 7.

introduction of language to the undertaking. In the earlier philosophy held by Descartes, Locke and others, language had little or no role to play in how material objects were represented to the human subject.[31] The belief was that reality was directly represented by ideas in the mind, not by words which functioned only to stand for ideas. Locke had held that "words in their primacy or immediate signification, stand for nothing but the ideas in the mind of him that uses them."[32] Thus, if we look at, say, a square table from any position other than directly above it, we would not see square but trapezoidal. The mismatch between what we see and what the real object is, is said to be because we are not seeing the table but a representation of it. On this way of thinking, language simply "interfered" with the old schema of thought and representation. Admittedly, such a distinction can be quite useful, though to avoid confusion the tendency to regard thought, idea and sign as separate entities should be resisted. In his formulation of a proposition, Wittgenstein steers a balanced course, drawing a distinction between proposition, thought and sign, yet not treating them as different entities.[33] The upshot of such an interpretative approach makes possible "the insight into the internal relations between thought, language and reality, construed . . . as intra-grammatical relations between concepts," enabling the work of analysis of language to begin.[34] If thought and language are one and the same thing, it follows that what can be known about the world arising from thought must find expression in language.

For his part, Wittgenstein has long been convinced that there is always a connection between his analysis of language and his conception of reality. The natural question is: how are the two entities—reality and language—related? Wittgenstein, we have noted, has presupposed that a synthesis exists between the world and language, and that consequently, one is able to access the former by a consideration of the latter. In this connection, Felicity McCutcheon is certainly right to suggest that "the assumption on which Wittgenstein's method is based is that language matches the world at the deeper level of meaning and essence and it is this fundamental match that makes it possible for language to match the

---

31. Bolton, *Approach to Wittgenstein's Philosophy*, 88.

32. Locke, *Essay Concerning Human Understanding* 3.2.2.

33. Barrett notes, "A *distinction* can be made between proposition, thought and sign, but the idea they are *separate entities* was anathema to Wittgenstein" (*Wittgenstein on Ethics and Religious Belief*, 8).

34. Hacker, *Wittgenstein's Place*, 32.

world at the empirical level of truth and facts."[35] At all events, language for him is a cipher, pointing beyond itself to what reality is. Wittgenstein errs, however, in positing that "a proposition is a picture of reality."[36] This so-called "picture theory" is a plain but mistaken case of drawing ontological conclusions from premises based on logic. As we have already noted, the theory was later jettisoned by Wittgenstein himself. But in an important sense, Wittgenstein was right to perceive the world as a linguistic one.

This brings us to his insistence: "What *can* be shown, *cannot* be said,"[37] which is stated in the context of his discussion about the roles of propositions as pictures of reality. Let us first review what he has written:

> Propositions can represent the whole of reality, but they cannot represent what they must have in common with reality in order to be able to represent it—logical form. In order to be able to represent logical form, we should have to be able to station ourselves with propositions somewhere outside logic, that is to say outside the world.[38]

Here an important point is being made. It is not so much that language is limited (though in a sense, it is) but that we as language users cannot jump out of our own skin and talk about language from some neutral Archimedean point of view. The following illustration is frequently drawn to help us see our constraint: a map depicting a certain terrain cannot thereby depict its own method of depiction; a supplementary insert is needed to do that. Language is all that we have and we can use it to depict states of affairs and to speak about God, but we cannot assume a position outside it that would allow us to gain a pre- or extra-linguistic access to these realities. "There is no outside; outside you cannot breathe."[39] For this reason, Wittgenstein will later admonish us to bring language back from its metaphysical to its everyday use.[40] The insight which is relevant to our study is that the problem of language about God is inevitably bound up with the limitation that we can never get at "languageless

35. McCutcheon, *Religion within the Limits of Language Alone*, 10.

36. *TLP* 4.01.

37. *TLP* 4.1212.

38. *TLP* 4.12.

39. *PI* 103.

40. *PI* 116.

things-in-themselves," to use Kerr's phrase.[41] That should also lead us to an admission of our human finitude, especially in relation to the use of language to speak of God.

It therefore behoves those of us who reflect on theology or religion to undertake as a first task the analysis of the language we use. Broadly speaking, theology is the study of God, his nature and his dealing with humankind—among other things. Such a study is wholly dependent on the use of language in its formulation, development and communication. It is now widely recognized that theology not only involves the use of language, it even creates and reveals itself as language. As George Tavard (1922–2007) puts it well, "just as the thought is never separate from the word, just as one does not reflect save to the extent that one uses a language from which to draw the symbols of one's reflection, so theology is inconceivable save in the measure that it is language."[42] We can thus expect that the careful analysis of theological language will also reveal a great deal about "the nature of all being" and the experiences that give rise to theology. In applicable terms, the following are what we can expect the analysis of language to accomplish for the language user: the elimination of misunderstandings, the resolution of unclarities, and the dissolution of philosophical problems that arise out of confusing features of the surface grammar of natural language.[43]

Wittgenstein's remark, "what can be shown cannot be said," draws more than a fine line between "showing" and "saying"; it further suggests that certain matters relating to human existence are of the sort that can be said, while others can only be shown. For Wittgenstein, matters pertaining to religion, ethics, and aesthetics belong to the latter category. The question for us is how are those matters which "lie outside the world" shown, if they cannot be (adequately) spoken? One answer is by indirect means such as stories, literature and even plays. I suggest that in addition to language-use, we express these things in action and in our lives.

2. Meaning and Truth

In the preface to *TLP*, Wittgenstein provides a generous acknowledgement which reads, "I am indebted to Frege's great works and to the writings

---

41. Kerr, "Language as Hermeneutic," 508.

42. Tavard cited in Hallett, *Theology within the Bounds of Language*, 194.

43. See Hacker, *Wittgenstein's Place*, 36.

of my friend Mr Bertrand Russell for much of the stimulation of my thoughts."[44] Under the influence of the two named philosophers, the young Wittgenstein had imbibed a number of suppositions, some of which were to have an influence in the development of his own thoughts. For example, he embraced a version of what he would later call "Augustine's picture of language." According to this view of language, the fundamental role of words is to name, and of sentences to describe; and the meaning of a simple name is the object for which it stands. All this is familiar enough. Now Wittgenstein, however, differed from Frege and Russell with regard to the relation between language and logic. The senior philosophers were of the opinion that natural languages are logically defective and so fail to adequately represent the subject-matter of the truths of logic. Russell had held that the grammatical form of a proposition regularly causes the logical form to be hidden. To illustrate, he used the following example:

> The *is* of "Socrates is human" expresses the relation of subject
> and predicate; the *is* of "Socrates is a man" expresses identity. It
> is a disgrace to the human race that it has chosen to employ the
> same word "is" for these two entirely different ideas—which a
> symbolic logical language of course remedies.[45]

Thus, according to Russell, a logically perfect or ideal language, namely the language of *Begriffsschrift* or *Principia* is needed to replace them.[46] Wittgenstein, on his part, espoused the contrary view that "all the propositions of our everyday language, just as they stand, are in perfect logical order."[47] In a letter to his friend, C. K. Ogden (1889–1957) recalling the differences he has had with Frege and Russell, Wittgenstein insists that "the propositions of our ordinary language are not in any way logically *less correct* or less exact or *more confused* than propositions written down, say, in Russell's symbolism or any other 'Begriffsschrift.'"[48] In other words, our everyday ordinary language will do nicely, even if usually the words and propositions of such language are too complex or vague. For Wittgenstein, language and logic are closely related; indeed,

---

44. *TLP*, p3.

45. Russell, *Classics of Analytic Philosophy*, 19.

46. See Hacker, *Wittgenstein's Place*, 26.

47. *TLP* 5.5563.

48. Wittgenstein, *Letters to C. K. Ogden*, 50, cited in Hacker, *Wittgenstein's Place*, 26.

the latter, he claims, is a "condition of sense."[49] Logic is even *prior* to every experience.[50] Accordingly, "if a sign expresses a sense at all, then it is in good logical order; if it does not, then it is just a meaningless mark, and says nothing."[51] Against the views of Frege and Russell on the nature of the proposition, Wittgenstein maintains that a proposition is *essentially* either true or false; indeed, it must be bipolar. Frege has conceived of propositions as either of the true or false variety, and that there is no essential connection between the pair. The axiom: "Some propositions are true and some false, just as some roses are red and some white" encapsulates Russell's view—as if "true" and "false" signified two properties among others. Both philosophers, according to P. M. S. Hacker (b. 1939), have thus failed "to apprehend the essential connection between the concept of a proposition and truth and falsity."[52]

I have consciously belabored the point espoused by Wittgenstein that a proposition is capable of being true, and capable of being false. A proposition can either assert that a state of affairs exists, or that it does not.[53] In any event, it still has sense, for sense does not depend on its correspondence with a particular existing state of affairs. The following quotation may clarify what is being emphasized here:

> What corresponds in reality to a proposition depends upon whether it is true or false. But we must be able to understand a proposition without knowing if it is true or false. What we know when we understand a proposition is this: we know what is the case if it is true and what is the case if it is false. But we do not necessarily know whether it is actually true or false. Every proposition is essentially true-false. Thus a proposition has two poles (corresponding to case of its truth and case of its falsity). We call this the *sense* of a proposition. The *meaning* of a proposition is the fact which actually corresponds to it.[54]

The distinction between the sense (*Sinn*) of a proposition and its meaning or more properly, its referent (*Bedeutung*)—a distinction borrowed from Frege—is skillfully drawn. Wittgenstein further elaborates, "A proposition

49. Hacker, *Wittgenstein's Place*, 27.

50. *TLP* 5.552.

51. Hacker, *Wittgenstein's Place*, 27.

52. Hacker, *Wittgenstein's Place*, 28.

53. See *TLP* 4.1.

54. *NB*, 93–94.

shows its sense. A proposition shows how things stand if it is true."[55] Hence, "to understand a proposition means to know what is the case if it is true. (One can understand it, therefore, without knowing whether it is true.)"[56] What Wittgenstein is expressing echoes the ground-breaking work of Frege whose elucidation of the distinction between sense and referent is worth recalling:

> It may perhaps be granted that every grammatically well-formed expression representing a proper name always has a sense. But this is not to say that to the sense there also corresponds a referent. The words "the celestial body most distant from the earth" have a sense, but it is very doubtful if they also have a referent. The expression "the least rapidly convergent series" has a sense; but it is known to have no referent, since for every given convergent series, another convergent, but less rapidly convergent, series can be found. In grasping a sense, one is not certainly assured of a referent.[57]

For our immediate purposes, there is an instructive way of regarding these considerations about the *Sinn* and *Bedeutung* distinction. This is simply to adopt the direction taken at the "linguistic turn" of the early part of last century, namely, to move from a concern with the question of truth to the question of meaning. We are not saying that the question of truth is unimportant: it is, but it cannot be *prior* to that of sense. The obvious reason being that any statement or proposition, say, "all the disciples deserted him and fled" (Matt 26:56) must be understood for what it is claiming or asserting before it can be shown to be true or false. We are to ask what we mean by what we say before we can be concerned with questions about *what* reality is or *how* it can be known. As we have earlier maintained, questions of *meaning* have overtaken questions of *validity* in priority.

3. Reference(s) to God

In *TLP*, God is mentioned four times but only the last of the references is not incidental to the subject of religion. Even then, it is a negative proposition that reads, "*How* things are in the world is a matter of

55. *TLP* 4.022.

56. *TLP* 4.024.

57. Frege, "Sense and Reference," 211.

complete indifference for what is higher. God does not reveal himself *in* the world."[58] The spatial expression "what is higher"[59] should be especially noted as it is a reference to the realm in which—at least in Wittgenstein's own ontology—ethics, aesthetics, religion, and God are located.[60] The emphasis on the word "in" is clearly deliberate on the part of Wittgenstein, the significance of which comes to light in his next remark but one, "It is not *how* things are in the world that is mystical, but *that* it exists."[61] Thus, Wittgenstein may be clarifying that he is *not* saying that God does not reveal himself, but rather that God is not like any fact, item, or thing we know. Or, he might be intimating "that God reveals himself in the fact that the world exists, the fact that 'there is what there is.'"[62] In any event, we must remember that the term "world" is used by Wittgenstein in a special way: it is, as we noted, what is conceptually viewed or portrayed. A theologically significant point thus becomes apparent, namely, that God is transcendent, being like no other. This markedly contrasts with the approach adopted by the so-called "militant atheists" of our time who interpret belief in God as somewhat "analogous to belief in extra-terrestrials, the Loch Ness monster, or wild cats in the Scottish highlands."[63] For these atheists, God is just another object, albeit much more powerful, knowledgeable and moral, among others in our system. To be sure, that is also how many people, including religious believers, still think of their deity.

It is, of course, open to us to draw the inference that given God's transcendence and the gap that exists between him and us, the importance we attach to speaking about God may be the result of an illusion. That Wittgenstein continued to give attention to religion and engage in theological discussions is an indication that such an inference cannot have been intended by him. For years after writing *TLP*, he was still doing

---

58. *TLP* 6.432.

59. The use of spatial terms like "world," "outside/inside," and "what is higher" presupposes a synthesis between the world and language, that we have access to the former through the latter. Also, Wittgenstein might be applying the Kantian's concept of space which he accepts as an *a priori* intuition.

60. It is not difficult to see why Wittgenstein classified ethics, aesthetics, and religion under one category. "They all have similar concerns; their concepts and contexts of use frequently overlap" (Bell, "Wittgenstein and Descriptive Theology," 9).

61. *TLP* 6.44.

62. Hyman, "Gospel According to Wittgenstein," 3.

63. Fergusson, *Faith and Its Critics*, 34.

philosophy. In connection with what Wittgenstein is saying about God in the remarks cited, Klein perceptively notes, "*a way of speaking* is being censured here, not a subject matter."[64] A more persuasive alternative is perhaps to recognize that what we can talk about is measly compared with what we cannot. While we have learned from Wittgenstein that the concept of the world is a linguistic one, we must be mindful that "propositions cannot express anything higher."[65] Our ability to speak about God as Klein points out, "depends upon God as the unlimited horizon of each world's limited horizon."[66] The reality to be faced and accepted is that language is self-contained and that it can only go so far; there are limits to what can be said about God. Perhaps all we can aim for and work hard to ensure, is that our words are clear and adequate enough to point to what can only show itself.

Later Phase of Wittgenstein's Philosophy

Key Elements

The later phase of Wittgenstein's philosophical life is exemplified by his *PI*. Although the work deals with a wide range of subject-matter, namely the nature of philosophy, logic, the inner/outer relation, consciousness, and so on, it is almost wholly attentive to one central theme and its ramifications, namely language and meaning. That is perhaps why Wittgenstein writes, "Our investigation is therefore a grammatical one."[67] In *TLP*, language and meaning had also been a key focus, but, as we have noted, Wittgenstein's earlier concern was with *whether* language refers rather than with the *way* it refers. His primary interest was in what could or could not be stated in words. Although the discontinuities—as well as the continuities—between the two masterpieces are not our present concern, it is useful to keep the contrast in mind when reading the Wittgenstein corpus and when seeking to understand the material aright. On this point, I have found Hacker's juxtaposition of the doctrines of *TLP* with those of *PI* helpful not only in revealing essential differences,

---

64. Klein, *How Things Are in the World*, 36.

65. *TLP* 6.42.

66. Klein, *How Things Are in the World*, 45.

67. *PI* 90.

but especially in showing up key innovations (or "achievements") that mark the later work:

> (i) The one [*Tractatus*] characterized by a striving for a sublime *Wesensschau*, the other [*PI*] by "a quiet weighing of linguistic facts" (*Z* 447) in order to disentangle the knots in our understanding;

> (ii) The one possessed by a vision of the crystalline purity of the logical forms of thought, language and the world, the other imbued with a heightened awareness of the motley of spatial and temporal phenomena of language (*PI* 108), the deceptive forms of which lead us into conceptual confusion;

> (iii) The one obsessed by a craving for the revelation of the hidden essences of things, placing its faith in depth analysis, the other demanding for the purposes of philosophical elucidation no more than the description and arrangement of what is simple and familiar, "hidden" only because it is always before one's eyes and so goes unnoticed (*PI* 129).[68]

These themes of *PI*, so skillfully detected, echo the author's declared intention to make "a radical break with the idea that language always functions in one way, always serves the same purpose: to convey thoughts—which may be about houses, pains, good and evil, or anything else you please."[69] Admittedly, it had been a mistake to insist that a single theory of language operates to define "how things stand,"[70] or "to look for something in common to all entities which we commonly subsume under a general term."[71] As a corrective, Wittgenstein proposes that we consider an alternative way of using words which recognizes that they are of very different kinds and have different uses. He urges, "Think of the tools in a tool-box: there is a hammer, pliers, a saw, a screw-driver, a rule, a glue-pot, glue, nails and screws.—The functions of words are as diverse as the functions of these objects."[72]

In *TLP*, logic is all-embracing, standing over and even making possible all forms of human discourse. The mature Wittgenstein,

---

68. Hacker, *Wittgenstein's Place*, 98 (the tabulation is mine).

69. *PI* 304.

70. *TLP* 4.022.

71. *BB*, 17.

72. *PI* 11.

however, comes to think otherwise: logic stands within language, and it is the latter that makes the former possible.[73] For that reason, he turns away from logic's univocity to embrace a "descriptive" approach. His celebrated line is, "We must do away with all *explanation,* and description alone must take its place."[74] Whereas he has assumed that the workings of language can be logically thought out *a priori,* he now stresses the need to "look and see how propositions really work."[75] He also dismisses "a one-sided diet" in which "one nourishes one's thinking with only one kind of example."[76] What is done by the positivist in defining a word like "meaning" or "truth" according to a given formulation and insisting that such a word must always correspond to this definition is an example of a one-sided diet.

To better account for the varied and, in his view, confusing ways in which language is used, Wittgenstein makes use of the notions of "language-games" and "form of life." As both terms had been discussed in the previous chapter, they need not detain us here, though we shall shortly return to them to consider how they may be applied.

Applications

We shall now proceed to take up some of the themes mentioned above and explore their ramifications in so far as religious language-use is concerned. The discussion to follow will fall under the following headings: (1) Diversity of functions of language, (2) Meaning as use, and (3) Language-games.

1. Diversity of Functions of Language

In dismissing religious language as cognitive nonsense, the logical positivists had assumed a certain "logic," namely, that a sentence is meaningful only if it is analytic or can be verified through sense

---

73. Klein, *How Things Are in the World,* 49.

74. *PI* 109. It is important to clarify that "description" in philosophy is not the attempt at a detached analysis of language *per se,* rather it is concerned to "serve the end of helping to determine what is being said." See Bell, "Wittgenstein and Descriptive Theology," 5.

75. *PI* 93.

76. *PI* 593

experience. Based on the view that scientific knowledge is the only kind of factual knowledge, this logic was then applied across the board as though it was the paradigm to which every other kind of language must conform in order to be considered meaningful. So, when the logical positivists say that a religious statement is not "meaningful" or "cognitive," they are saying no more than that it does not have meaning or cognition in the way that scientific statements have meaning or cognition. Although logical positivism is nowadays *passé*, the hegemonic mode of thinking it has inspired, appears to die hard. For instance, in Peter Donovan's otherwise even-handed book, *Religious Language*, we find him urging that the empirical ways of verifying religious language be adopted.[77] He writes, "Putting to the test of investigation through the senses is, after all, our most usual way of distinguishing what is the case from what is not."[78] Sam Harris (b. 1967), one of the so-called "New Atheists," has recently expressed a view that is redolent of pure scientism. He says, "Religious language is, without question, unscientific in its claims for what is true. We have Christians believing in the holy ghost, the resurrection of Jesus and his possible return—these are claims about biology and physics which, from a scientific point of view in the twenty-first century, should be unsustainable."[79] The presupposition that underlies these remarks is fine as far as it goes; it is one that embraces a long-held conception of language as a system of signs, "an instrument which serves to point to things known independently of it and to utter thoughts formulated prelinguistically."[80] In his Tractarian phase, it may be recalled, Wittgenstein had espoused a similar account of language. However, through careful observation, he later came to see language in a totally different light—no longer as a single calculus, but as a tool with a diversity of functioning and possibilities. For him, language simply did not have the sort of homogeneity that he once thought it had. His analogy comparing language to the handles in a control room of a locomotive is illuminating: these handles look almost alike, even have a common feature in that they are hand-operated, but are functionally different.[81] He further exemplifies that even a simple linguistic notion like "describing"

77. Donovan, *Religious Language*, 17.

78. Donovan, *Religious Language*, 17.

79. Harris cited in Saner, "Is There Any Place for Religious Faith in Science?"

80. Kerr, "Language as Hermeneutic," 494.

81. *PI* 12.

is susceptible to being variously interpreted, for the reason that "many different kinds of thing are called 'description.'"[82] All of this must have prompted him, in words we have earlier quoted, to make "a radical break with the idea that language always functions in one way." An important corollary to his later philosophy we can draw is that religious language should not be reduced to a physical or scientific language. This in turn calls for a reassessment of the tendency to shoehorn the workings of religious language into the structure of some preconceived linguistic paradigm. It needs to be said that scientifically-minded people are not the only ones who seek such reductions. Certain currents in Evangelical Christianity with their conception of religion as a rational account of the origins of the cosmos and humanity's place in it, come close to using religious language as in science. For instance, Carl F. H. Henry (1913–2003) writes, "The Bible is not a textbook on science or on history. But attention to the Bible's statements bearing on the physical sciences and history . . . will enable its readers to avoid many misconceptions to which empirical inquiry remains ongoingly vulnerable."[83]

2. Meaning as Use

In no other area of thought is the dissonance between the early and later works of Wittgenstein more marked than that pertaining to the notion of meaning. To recollect, the early Wittgenstein had held that the meaning of a word is that to which the word refers. His assumption then was that a proposition offers a "picture of reality."[84] Meaning, which he postulated as essentially concerned with "picturing," is thought to be a correlation between a word and an object. Somewhat casually put, meaning is the "hook" between the two.[85] In his later philosophy, this view was jettisoned as inadequate for reasons we have previously discussed. Instead, a very different conclusion came to be proposed, namely, that language acquires meaning as an outcome of the uses through which it is put. Or, in Wittgenstein's words, "One cannot guess how a word functions. One has to *look at* its use and learn from that."[86] By means of such a suggestion,

82. *PI* 24.

83. Henry, *God, Revelation and Authority*, 232.

84. *TLP* 4.01.

85. Smith, *Who's Afraid of Relativism?*, 41.

86. *PI* 340.

some of the past theological disputes over words might have been avoided. Thus, for instance, had scholars attended to the various uses to which a word has been put, the argument over the concept of "revelation" might not have lingered on.[87]

There is, to be sure, no mystique about the notion of use; use is not a thing or an object of some kind. Nor is meaning simply to be equated with use. To illustrate this, Wittgenstein proposes that individual words be likened to chess pieces, each being defined in terms of its function.[88] In chess, one is not concerned with the physical movement of wooden figures or with their physical properties; the game consists in the movement of certain pieces designated as king, queen, bishop and so forth according to rules and a grammar. So the question "What is a word?" then becomes analogous to the question "What is a piece in chess?" or, if we wish to be specific, "What is a knight?" Jerry H. Gill elaborates the suggested approach for us:

> The idea here is just that as one answers the question "What is a knight?" by explaining and showing the ways in which a knight may and may not be moved, so one answers the question "What is knowledge?" by explaining and illustrating how the word "knowledge" functions. By distinguishing the ways in which the word is used, and the situations in which it is accepted or rejected, one comes to an understanding of what the term means.[89]

Naturally, Wittgenstein's remarks about "meaning as use" apply to language in its religious as well as non-religious use. It is still often the case that when one wants to establish the meaning of a word one will try to connect some object-references with the word in question. One's assumption would be similar to that held by the early Wittgenstein—that the meaning of a word is correlated to the object for which the word stands—though one may not have articulated the underlying conception in quite so explicit a manner as Wittgenstein has. One is even certain that one can understand a whole sentence by simply putting together the meanings of the individual words that comprise the sentence. Wittgenstein does not say that the approach to meaning we have

---

87. See Downing, *Has Christianity a Revelation?*; Barr, *Concept of Biblical Theology.* The said dispute is later revisited in Downing, *Formation for Knowing God.*

88. See *PI* 108.

89. Gill, "Wittgenstein and Religious Language," 62–63.

described is simply wrong, but that it is not appropriate for every case of linguistic inquiry. Accordingly, he wants us to move away from "the idea that using a sentence involves imagining something for every word."[90] Hence, words like "God," "love," "grace," "redemption," and so on, are not learned by simply looking up their dictionary definitions or linking them to observable objects to which they refer. Rather, these words are learned by deriving their meaning from the role they play in the lives and experience of believers, or, to put it another way, by drawing their meaning from the application that believers make of them. And to speak about application or use is to call attention to the context in which words are used. Thus, a fixation with certain words and statements taken out of their life-context is a sure recipe for theological confusion or quarrels. As Patrick Sherry rightly observes, "if religious language seems meaningless to people today this may be because they have lost sight of the practices and the contexts with which language is associated. The remedy would be to return to the way of life in which the linguistic practices were born, to learn to be contrite, forgiving, long-suffering, hopeful and so forth."[91]

The considerations just noted point to a feature of religious language-use that is often overlooked, namely, the employment of language is almost always directed towards some *telos* or purpose, spoken within a community of faith that unites around the same.[92] Language and meaning are thus "bound up with a context of practice that is more than the repertoire of our words, and that penumbra of practices and action is essential to constituting the meaning of our words."[93] In this connection, Wittgenstein's distinction between "surface grammar" and "depth grammar" may be recalled. Surface grammar is that which "immediately impresses itself upon us about the use of a word . . . the way it is used in the construction of the sentence, the part of its use—one might say—that can be taken in by the ear."[94] By depth grammar he, of course, meant the opposite, that is, those rules of usage that are not revealed on the superficial level. The sentences, "the candidate passes her examination" and "the peace of the Lord passes understanding" appear similar in form, but they are profoundly different. In terms of its depth grammar, the verb

90. PI 449.

91. Sherry, *Religion, Truth and Language-Games*, 3–4.

92. Smith, *Who's Afraid of Relativism?*, 45.

93. Smith, *Who's Afraid of Relativism?*, 46.

94. PI 664.

in the first instance describing an event does nothing of the sort in the second. Thus, to understand what a particular passage means requires us to look beyond its form of words (i.e., its surface grammar).

Wittgenstein's notion that "meaning is use" has a further role. It deters us from assuming that religious terms or expressions are merely acts or dispositions in one's mind. When considering words like "faith," "conversion," "grace," "sin," and so on, we should take into serious account certain behavioral criteria which they epitomize. Thus, a term like "righteousness" or "holiness" must be recognized by its "fruit," and not be treated as if it were merely a mental object. To a question as to what belief amounts to, Wittgenstein's comment that "an 'inner process' stands in need of outward criteria"[95] serves to remind us that belief must always be manifested in behavior. By the same token, one's belief in God or some other tenet of faith, if genuine, will show up at various points in one's life.

3. Language-Games

The notion of "language-games," Wittgenstein writes, "is meant to bring into prominence the fact that the *speaking* of language is part of an activity, or of a form of life."[96] His intention, we have noted, is to call attention to the indissoluble connection between language and human activity. That connection seems obvious enough, but Wittgenstein rather insists that forms of human activity are the ultimate basis of all linguistic project: "What has to be accepted, the given, is—so one could say—*forms of life*."[97] For like moves in games, words or statements are context-dependent, or else they would not make sense. That is to say, their meaning is tied to their use in the context of life: "Only in the stream of thought and life do words have meaning."[98] These remarks linking meaning to use have an obvious application to religious language, as well as language in general. It is that to a large extent, one must participate in a particular form of life, or be in some sympathy with it, if one is to properly understand the language it uses. Missionaries have found out that in order to communicate with a tribe, they must not only learn its language but listen

95. *PI* 580.
96. *PI* 23.
97. *PI* II, 192.
98. *Z*, 173.

to how the tribesmen and their folks "play" with language. Something about the tribe may be learned even from jokes that are shared within it. As Wittgenstein once remarked, "a serious and good philosophical work could be written consisting entirely of jokes."[99]

Wittgenstein's stress on the multiplicity of language-games does an added service—disabusing us of thinking that logic is both *prior* to language-use as well as that it constitutes the *a priori* order of all experience.[100] But if every game has a logic of its own, may it not be that "logic is found *within* the various language-games themselves"?[101] It thus stands to reason that one can expect different shades of sense and nonsense to apply in different cases of language-use, even learning to distinguish sense from nonsense. Consider the sheer aptness of Wittgenstein's image of language as an ancient city with its maze of little streets and squares of old and new houses.[102] Under the former assumption of an overarching logic, one is likely to end up treating all of language as functioning in one same, singular way. In a recent essay, the philosopher John Caputo (b. 1940) has appropriately picked on the notion of language-games to argue against the reductionist tendency. Given the integrity and idiosyncrasy of each language-game, Caputo contends that "it would go against the idea of language games, and therefore against the very idea of language itself, to declare that everything that is going on in all the other languages can be translated into the language of just one of them."[103] Recalling the hegemony formerly exercised by theology in pre-modern times, he warns of the reduction of human values to scientific objects: "So if someone said that human compassion (ethics) is nothing other than a certain evolutionary coping mechanism (biology), that would be unfair play, a scientific reductionism, a reduction of the irreducible."[104]

In chapter 2, we noted that the parallel between language and the diversity of games had facilitated the analysis of language into separate concrete entities that can be examined in isolation.[105] Such an analysis grants that words and sentences may function in any context of

99. Malcolm, *Ludwig Wittgenstein*, 29.

100. *TLP* 5.552.

101. Keightley, *Wittgenstein, Grammar and God*, 38.

102. *PI* 18.

103. Caputo, *Philosophy and Theology*, 52.

104. Caputo, *Philosophy and Theology*, 52.

105. Specht, *Foundations of Wittgenstein's Late Philosophy*, 53–54, attributes the compounding of language into entities to Plato and Aristotle.

conversation whether it be, say, about religion or science, and that they still get their meaning by playing their part in that context. The language of religion and the language of science, to keep to our examples, remain fully susceptible of criticism, justification, and reflection within their respective areas of experience. Where religious words are concerned, we can expect their meaning to differ from their use in ordinary contexts. Thus, if one were to say "God's eye sees everything"[106] one is hardly talking about eyebrows and the like. Similarly, the words said at the Eucharist about eating the body of Christ or drinking his blood are not to be taken as suggestive of cannibalism. A Catholic is perfectly entitled to claim she is being fed "a resurrected and transfigured 'super body' that foreshadows the new reality of a new Heaven and a new earth."[107]

This brings me to an important observation about the workings of language-games that speaks directly to what I wish to argue in this study, namely the thesis that although religious language is fact-stating, it cannot be expected to yield exact definition or complete explanation about its object. In an interesting passage, Wittgenstein tauntingly asks his imagined interlocutor who reproaches inexactness but praises exactness to think about these questions:

> If I tell someone "Stand roughly here"—may not this explanation work perfectly? And may not my other one fail too? But isn't it an inexact explanation?—Yes; why shouldn't we call it "inexact"? Only let us understand what "inexact" means. For it does not mean "unusable." And let us consider what we call an "exact" explanation in contrast with this one. Perhaps something like drawing a chalk line round an area? Here it strikes us at once that the line has breadth. So a colour-edge would be more exact. But has this exactness still got a function here: isn't the engine idling?[108]

Wittgenstein is clearly not persuaded that exactness is the holy grail to be pursued at all costs. What is important, he proceeds to argue, is the attainment of one's goal in a discourse situation: "Thus the point here is what we call 'the goal.' Am I inexact when I do not give our distance from the sun to the nearest foot, or tell a joiner the width of a table to

106. *LC*, 71.

107. Foley, "Eucharist and Cannibalism."

108. *PI* 88. To another interlocutor, Wittgenstein responds, "When I give the description: 'The ground was quite covered with plants'—do you want to say I don't know what I am talking about until I can give a definition of a plant?" (*PI* 70).

the nearest thousandth of an inch?"[109] We may be tempted to think the statement "The Scottish Fold is on the mat" is more exact than "the cat is on the mat," but is the matter of exactness so clearly settled? The first statement is merely more detailed than the second, unless it is our intention to specify what kind of breed of cat is on the mat.

It must be said that we are not saying that Wittgenstein is making short shrift of the concept of exactness or giving endorsement to vague and fuzzy use of language. For him, as we have just shown, what counts is whether one succeeds in meeting one's need in making one's meaning intelligible. He goes on, "One might say that the concept 'game' is a concept with blurred edges.—'But is a blurred concept a concept at all?'—Is an indistinct photograph a picture of a person at all? Is it even always an advantage to replace an indistinct picture by a sharp one? Isn't the indistinct one often exactly what we need?"[110] Whether or not an indistinct picture is preferable to a sharp one, I suspect the passion for exactness, or conversely, the worry over imprecision in religious language, is nourished by an underlying empirical scientism that characterizes our culture and permeates our religious thinking. To be sure, most people, including believers, generally presuppose the methodology of the hard sciences to apply to all discourse situations, including God-talk—such is the extent of empirical colonization. Congruently, most believers would regard the statements they make about their religion as objectively true. However, to free religion from the grip that the scientific methodology has on it, one need not push to dichotomize between language and reality, for that may well lead to skepticism. Far better to point out that the quest for complete objectivity in scientific language is illusionary, let alone in religious language. For, as Wittgenstein puts it, "if there were evidence, this would in fact destroy the whole business."[111] The present issue is perhaps best understood in terms of the concept of language-games. Exactness and inexactness, precision and imprecision and other conceptual binaries are themes being played out in, and as, different language-games. They should be seen as such, rather than as extralinguistic moorings. But taking them out of their language-games will only create unnecessary philosophical muddles.

109. *PI* 88.
110. *PI* 71.
111. *LC*, 56.

Concluding Remarks

In this chapter, I have revisited the main features of both the early and later phases of Wittgenstein's philosophy and picked out several of his insights or ideas that have a bearing on our understanding of religious language. Given the subtlety of his work, there are potentially more applicable insights than I have been able to detect. Doubtless there are also aspects and dimensions I have outlined which I have not succeeded in teasing out their applicability to actual situations of language use or misuse. Nevertheless, I think we have put together a simple framework for looking at how language works, not least in religion. Let me provide a summary, going back to some of the ground which has been discussed.

The first thing I have sought to do was to line up with Wittgenstein in recognizing that the problems of philosophy (and theology) arise mainly "through a misinterpretation of our forms of language."[112] Questions of proof or justification of religious belief are naturally posterior to those regarding the functioning of language, for the reason that we can only judge whether something is true or false after we have agreed "the workings of language."[113] It does help to know that the concern of my work, which proposes a nuanced way of noting the cognitive status of religious language without insisting on absolute precision or completion, is a proper one.

Wittgenstein, we have seen, overturned his earlier view that a proposition "pictures" a situation in the world. Correspondingly, he moved away from the notion that the meaning of language is that to which it refers. He, however, continues to perceive the world as a linguistic one, but no longer in the sense of an absolute correspondence between language and the world. The upshot is language comes to be seen as a cipher, pointing beyond itself to what reality is. Being such a tool, language will do nicely in making its referent intelligible, but neither completion nor containment should be expected.

I have also belabored the point espoused by Wittgenstein that a proposition is capable of being true or false. That was done to show that any statement can still have sense, even if its content does not correspond with a particular existing state of affairs. The obvious application to my work is that we can say that language about God is meaningful, regardless

112. *PI* 111.
113. *PI* 109.

of whether or not it secures reference. However, what I am not suggesting is truth should take a back seat to meaning or meaningfulness.

The early Wittgenstein was often mistaken as being against religion or metaphysics. What he wrote in *TLP* about the mystical presents a very different story. As noted, Wittgenstein's understanding of God is that God is not like any fact, item or thing in the world. In other words, we could say of Wittgenstein that he was mindful and respectful of divine transcendence, that he accepted that language could never adequately bridge the distance between God and us. Hence, his famous injunction to keep silence. For my part, I am not for silence in the face of divine alterity; instead, I am concerned to enter the case that God can be spoken of—he is not "beyond language"—but that he cannot be fully defined or contained by language. Such an approach, I maintain, both honors transcendence and caters for the need for reflection.

In a culture accustomed to associating with the findings of science, my thesis proposing such a nuanced way of speaking about God may be met with derision for being vague, indeterminate, or even empty. That is going by a certain logic, namely the logic of scientific inquiry. We have seen Wittgenstein rejecting the idea that the language of science should be paradigmatic for all language, given that language is not a single calculus. Dismissing my thesis for the reason mentioned is as wrongheaded as it is to analyze religious language by the same techniques we use for handling scientific discourse.

From Wittgenstein's insight that meaning is something we *use*, two important corollaries have been drawn, namely, (i) language is not only for "picturing" things or making references to them, but also for expressing beliefs and emotions and even "to do things"; and (ii) language is a social phenomenon given that "use" must occur in a human context and involve human agency. These inferences are much in consonance with my own line of thought. For one thing, they express a similar concern to prompt a view of religious language that is "more" meaningful for going beyond the business of making objective reference to being expressive of one's beliefs, convictions, values, and the like. If language is a social phenomenon and "acquires meaning from the various procedures through which we give it particular uses in the course of our common life,"[114] does it not follow that the entire process in which we express, interpret and understand words is, like their human users themselves, fallible? While I could then

114. Keightley, *Wittgenstein, Grammar and God*, 21.

say that any claim that one can obtain exactness, precision or completion in words is naïve, I do not rule out that religious language can be "sufficiently precise" within a community of practice that learns its use.[115]

Much has been said about the language-games analogy. The idea it represents has been enormously influential. We have generously drawn on it to reject the hegemony of scientific language over religious language (or any language, vice-versa), suggest that words can only be understood in their particular "forms of life," and explain how exactitude and precision need not be viewed as the "working" norm in the religious language-game. Transposed together, these insights and resources from Wittgenstein will make a compelling case for the nuanced position I am proposing—that religious language is cognitive but cannot yield precise definition and complete explanation about its referent. Asking how religious language actually matches or captures the divine reality, and to what extent, may hopefully lead one to reflect on whether one's way of living is being shaped by the language one uses.[116]

From Wittgenstein's perspective, no absolute statements about the divine are possible because the subject-matter of religious discourse is that of which we cannot speak, that is, the mystical. This resonates with the Christian view that God is beyond the grasp of human capacity. Wittgenstein, however, allows that the mystical "shows" itself, thus bequeathing to us a system that is not entirely closed to transcendence. In his later phase, Wittgenstein maintains a respect for and an openness to the mystical, though it is not named as that. In the following chapter, we shall explore this subject more fully, and ask how we can acknowledge the mystical without renouncing expression.

---

115. For a useful discussion that absolute precision is neither possible nor necessary for meaningful communication, see Gill, *On Knowing God*, 83–86. He notes, "The criterion for determining meaningfulness is not absolute precision, but whatever degree of precision enables us to accomplish the task at hand" (86).

116. I owe this point to Harvey, *Scepticism, Relativism, and Religious Knowledge*, 10.

Chapter 4

The Mystical:
What We Cannot Speak About

The way you use the word "God" does not show whom you mean, but rather what you mean.[1]

—Ludwig Wittgenstein

Introduction

IN THE FINAL SECTIONS of *TLP*, Wittgenstein turns to a discussion of "the mystical" (*das Mystische*). His foray into logical analysis has led him to see a necessary connection between language and the world, and to the conclusion that "the sense of the world must lie outside the world."[2] He continues, "*How* things are in the world is a matter of complete indifference for what is higher. God does not reveal himself *in* the world. . . . It is not *how* things are in the world that is mystical, but *that* it exists."[3] To be sure, the "world" that Wittgenstein is ruminating here is not the world of empirical data, sensations and science; rather it is the world of facts as portrayed in propositions.[4] His next remark, which characterizes "what is mystical," also presupposes a limit to the articulatable realm: "There are, indeed, things that cannot be put into

1. *CV*, 58.
2. *TLP* 6.41.
3. *TLP* 6.432; 6.44.
4. *TLP* 1.1

79

words. They *make themselves manifest. They are what is mystical.*"[5] The delineation he speaks of—between what can be expressed (*gesagt*) and what cannot be expressed but only shown (*gezeigt*)—is later presented as the "cardinal problem" of his early philosophy.[6] In a final direct remark on the mystical, he identifies it with a certain way of viewing or feeling the world. This is how he puts it, "To view the world sub specie aeterni [sic] is to view it as a whole—a limited whole. Feeling the world as a limited whole—it is this that is mystical."[7] As is well known, these sayings and elucidations about the mystical culminate in the oft-quoted Proposition 7 which concludes the *Tractatus,* namely, "What we cannot speak about we must pass over in silence." These words, unlike those ancillary to his other propositions, are not further elaborated; they simply invoke silence, and are generally taken to be his injunction against any metaphysical or religious speculation that is conducted on the basis of a methodology borrowed from the empirical sciences.

The obvious comment should perhaps be made at this point that the precise meaning of the various passages I have cited is still controversial. The term *das Mystische* appears altogether only three times in the whole of *TLP.*[8] Used in a broad sense, it is linked by Wittgenstein to matters that are different but related, namely, "the sense of the world,"[9] "ethics,"[10] "the will,"[11] "death,"[12] "immortality,"[13] "the problems of life,"[14] "the solution of the problem of life,"[15] and—"God."[16] On the other hand, it is also used in a narrower sense to specify one form of what cannot be said but which

5. *TLP* 6.522.

6. In a letter to Bertrand Russell, cited in Anscombe, *Introduction to Wittgenstein's Tractatus,* 161, Wittgenstein considers this saying/showing delineation to be the cardinal problem of *all* philosophy.

7. *TLP* 6.45. This notion of seeing things *sub specie aeternitatis*—that is, under the aspect of eternity—can be traced to Spinoza. See Bunge et al., *Bloomsbury Companion to Spinoza,* 319–20.

8. The term also appears a few times in *NB,* but they do not add anything new or significant to our present discussion.

9. *TLP* 6.41.

10. *TLP* 6.421.

11. *TLP* 6.423.

12. *TLP* 6.4311.

13. *TLP* 6.4312.

14. *TLP* 6.52.

15. *TLP* 6.521.

16. *TLP* 6.432.

nevertheless makes itself manifest. The term is also used interchangeably with words like "transcendental," "inexpressible," and "ineffable." The use just mentioned is, linguistically, not a problem. The same, however, cannot be said about the identification of the mystical with the fact that the world "is," that it is, or that it is a limited whole. Evidently, Wittgenstein is on to something very profound, significant and—mysterious.

Our Tasks

In this chapter, I shall be concerned to explore Wittgenstein's notion of "mysticism," or to use his preferred terminology, *das Mystische*. As I have briefly stated in the last chapter and will explain more fully below, this notion is of interest to us because the mystical is properly the subject-matter of religious language;[17] it is what concerns the whole enterprise of God-talk. Whether or not we think we can speak of the mystical will affect how we perceive or use language in religion. Sallie McFague (b. 1933) goes even further to remark that unless we have a sense of mystery, we "will most likely identify God with our words."[18] In what follows, our specific task is to consider what Wittgenstein might have in mind referring to the mystical, and why he decides to use the term. This term, as Cyril Barrett (1925–2019) points out, "appears in the *Tractatus* without preparation, as though it were a household word, as if everyone was expected to know what it meant."[19] We learn from another source that Wittgenstein was simply taking over the term from his philosophical mentor, Bertrand Russell, who had used it to refer to an entirely ordinary feeling.[20] Still, Wittgenstein does apply his own meaning to it, while somewhat retaining the traditional sense associated with it. Unsurprisingly, his notion of the mystical is often seen as a mere peculiarity which does not belong to the heart of his philosophy or it is given a wide range of variant interpretations. Other than the inquiry of meaning of the mystical, I will also be attending to the all-important question about the relevance of this notion for theology. Following Wittgenstein's advice, I shall "look and see" what insights or ideas may

17. We can also say God is the object; so Glebe-Møller, "Whereof One Cannot Speak," 165.

18. McFague, *Metaphorical Theology*, 2.

19. Barrett, *Wittgenstein on Ethics and Religious Belief*, 71.

20. See Anscombe, *Introduction to Wittgenstein's Tractatus*, 170.

be appropriated to advance my claim that religious language cannot yield precise definition or complete explanation about the mystical—that is, God.

Bifurcation or Unity?

From a certain perspective, the account of the mystical does seem to introduce a bifurcation to *TLP*, splitting it between a majority first part of the book which deals with logic and language, and those last few pages in which the notion of the mystical emerges. Some have observed that the gulf between the two discussions appears large and unbridgeable;[21] others have differed. Those who think there is a split tend to view the treatment of the mystical as no "more than just an accidental part of the *Tractatus*."[22] They are also likely to dismiss those final passages on the mystical as *obiter dicta* or just curious addenda.[23] For my part, I consider the philosophy of the mystical as a culmination, rather than an afterthought, of what was discussed and developed in the preceding parts of the treatise. I am thus with those who deny any bifurcation, implying the view that Wittgenstein sees his conclusions about the mystical as following from his treatment of facts, objects, logic and language in the earlier part of the book. I expect that any gain in an understanding of Wittgenstein's treatment of the mystical will result in a further illumination of aspects of his overall philosophy, such as how logic and language are connected to religion and ethics. Eddy Zemach (b. 1935), who has also argued that the philosophy of *TLP* is "a complete philosophy," would probably endorse what I have just said given his approach to the interpretation of the work: "Just as the later part of the *Tractatus* presupposes the earlier, the earlier finds its natural and necessary completion in the later."[24] Finally, I am also not perturbed that the writer of *TLP* has devoted a greater part of his work to presenting a view of the nature of language and how it is possible to make literal and meaningful statements, only to declare towards the end there are things that can be only *shown*[25] (as opposed to *saying* or

---

21. E.g., Lazenby, *Early Wittgenstein on Religion*, 1.

22. D'hert, *Wittgenstein's Relevance for Theology*, 31. To be sure, D'hert actually thinks the mystical concerns the whole approach and purpose of *TLP*.

23. See Keightley, *Wittgenstein, Grammar and God*, 22–23.

24. Zemach, "Wittgenstein's Philosophy of the Mystical," 38.

25. In *TLP*, the word "show" is used in a technical sense. See, e.g., *TLP* 3.262; 4.022,

speaking about them*)*. I reason that Wittgenstein is intentionally leading his readers to climb up a "ladder"[26] to reach an awareness that the "logical form"—what propositions have in common with reality in order to be able to represent it—is ineffable.[27]

Why the Mystical Is of Interest

At this point, let me, as indicated, briefly explain why the discussion of the mystical is of interest to our present study. In common parlance, the word "mystical" is understood as referring to that which is transcendental, ineffable, supernatural, and hence, awe-inspiring. Thus, we would expect any event, experience or happening that is truly mystical to be totally inexplicable or unrecognizable. Now even if we agree with G. E. M. Anscombe that "mysticism" is an odd name for what Wittgenstein is referring to in those Tractarian passages we have cited, we must still acknowledge his acuity in pointing out that the mystical is something about which we must naturally be silent.[28] Such an understanding of mystery, however, has the negative implication that it is therefore logical to question the very speakability of God. In Buddhism, for instance, the proper response to the mystical is complete or almost total abstinence from God-talk. In contrast, the argument I am advancing in this work is that it is still possible to speak about God—he is not "beyond language"—without denying divine mystery. The New Testament understanding seems to me to strike the right note here: it is an essential feature of mystery that it permits itself to be grasped, though it resists objectification.[29] This is also the main thrust of my argument—that the divine cannot be fully explained or contained by language.

The present discussion on the mystical is relevant in yet another direction. Silence before God, which Wittgenstein has urged, is generally held to be the authentic response, given that human language cannot reach him. Indeed, it is often argued that silence is more powerful than

---

4.121, 4.126, 4.461; 5.541–5.5422; 6.127, 6.22.

26. *TLP* 6.54.

27. *TLP* 2.18; 4.12. It is possible to see the mystical in purely logical terms, i.e., seeing it in terms of the ineffable relation between language and the world. See Hudson, *Wittgenstein and Religious Belief*, 68–78.

28. Anscombe, *Introduction to Wittgenstein's Tractatus*, 169.

29. See Eph 1:9; 3:5; Col 1:26, 27; 1 Tim 3:16.

speech. This raises the question as to whether we still need language at all. We recall the logical positivists' antagonism toward metaphysical talk, and their acrid criticism that religious language is meaningless or nonsense. The retort is that silence is itself ambiguous and must be mediated by language for it to be meaningful. The stance of silence is that God cannot be spoken of, but the very expression of such a statement implies that one is already saying something about God. Indeed, one cannot even be silent by claiming that one's proper response to divine mystery is silence. Although set in the context of prayer, Jeff Astley's remark, "it is words that frame and lead into silence"[30] holds true for the present discussion. He also observes: "Those who pray speak into the silence, then, and in responding to the silence they come to speak better."[31] As to whether language is needed in religion, a straightforward answer may be that it is essential in giving it a "form" by which it can function, communicate, and extend. Without language as a medium, a religion would have no "continuing points of contact with wider human experience and knowledge."[32] Such a religion would be largely a private affair, one between a believer and his or her deity. Paradoxically, in the apophatic tradition of the church with its practice of moving beyond words in the face of the divine mystery, there is a reliance on language—to articulate what God is not (apophasis), rather than what God is. Indeed, some of the writings from that tradition can be as extensive as they are illuminating.

"The Mystical" or "Mysticism"?

To be sure, Wittgenstein never uses the term "mysticism" in all his three references to the mystical. I believe he is well aware that there is a slight but significant difference between "mysticism" and *das Mystische*. The former implies a system or body of beliefs held by mystics, whereas the latter does not. In choosing not to use "mysticism" I think Wittgenstein is being consistent with his declared conviction that what properly constitutes the "business" of philosophy is the "logical clarification of thoughts," rather than theories, ideas, or dogmas. In his own words,

---

30. Astley, *Exploring God-Talk*, 33.

31. Astley, *Exploring God-Talk*, 33.

32. Donovan, *Religious Language*, 2.

> Philosophy is not a body of doctrine but an activity. A philosophical work consists essentially of elucidations. Philosophy does not result in "philosophical propositions," but rather in the clarification of propositions. Without philosophy thoughts are, as it were, cloudy and indistinct: its task is to make them clear and to give them sharp boundaries.[33]

Still, one need not be overly unsettled if occasionally the two terms are used interchangeably by commentators or even by oneself. After all, both are cognates of the same word. The root word, "mystery" has quite an evolution, having been derived from the Greek. As *mysterion* it can be traced to rites, rituals or ceremonies in ancient religions where only a closed circle of priests, adherents, new converts or associates are allowed to take part in. Should something be disclosed at one of these "mystery" meetings those present must be silent about it and keep the secrecy of everything that transpired. In the New Testament, Paul and John have both mentioned and written about "mystery" on a number of occasions. This example from Paul will suffice:

> I became its servant according to God's commission that was given to me for you, to make the word of God fully known, the mystery that has been hidden throughout the ages and generations but has now been revealed to his saints. To them God chose to make known how great among the Gentiles are the riches of the glory of this mystery, which is Christ in you, the hope of glory. (Col 1:25–27)

In time, *mysterion* came also to be the word used for the sacraments of the Christian Church.[34] Earl Stanley B. Fronda, whose critique of Wittgenstein's apophaticism will be discussed shortly, has given a generally broad definition to "the mystical." He writes, "one can suppose that any philosophy, school of thought, or discursive activity (e.g., poetry) that highlights that which is ineffable and calls for silence over it, is 'mystical.'"[35] My dissatisfaction with that is: it fails to mention an aspect of mystery that is of great significance, namely, that "what is mysterious cannot lose its mysteriousness even when it is revealed."[36] Otherwise,

33. *TLP* 4.112.
34. Brown, *God and Mystery in Words*, 22.
35. Fronda, *Wittgenstein's (Misunderstood) Religious Thought*, 18.
36. Tillich, *Systematic Theology*, I, 121.

as Paul Tillich (1886–1965) argues, what is revealed is not essentially mysterious but only *seems* to be mysterious.

Wittgenstein and the Logical Positivists

Having cleared the ground so far, let us now try to get at an understanding of what Wittgenstein may have meant by *das Mystiche*. For this, I propose to recall, as my starting point, an "object lesson," which Wittgenstein is purported to have taught a number of logical positivists at a meeting of the Vienna Circle (*Wiener Kreis*)—to impress upon them that the mystical cannot be discounted in their philosophical discourse. But first a brief background about the logical positivists and their attitude towards Wittgenstein.

The movement known as "logical positivism" developed in the 1920s around Moritz Schlick who initiated the Vienna Circle. Membership of the Circle included noted thinkers like Otto Neurath (1882–1945), Hans Hahn (1879–1934), and Rudolf Carnap (1891–1970). (A. J. Ayer through his 1936 book *Language, Truth and Logic* introduced the movement to Britain, but he was not an original member of the group.) Essentially, the doctrine of logical positivism is that with the exception of mathematical and logical propositions (also called "logical constants" or tautologies), all significant propositions are truth functions of elementary propositions.[37] Thus, a statement is meaningful only if it is capable of being empirically verified as being true or false. For this reason, logical positivists came to reject metaphysics, treating such discourse as meaningless or nonsense. As religious utterances are in principle unverifiable, they too are included in the category of meaningless or nonsensical discourse. Unlike the prevailing philosophical outlook at that time, which celebrated science's ability to explain the world, and was thus unenthusiastic towards Wittgenstein's work, logical positivism embraced *TLP*, assuming it to belong to the empiricist tradition of modern thought. Wittgenstein was therefore seen and regarded as a key ally. Specifically, he was credited for the "insight that many philosophical sentences, especially in traditional metaphysics, are pseudo-sentences, devoid of cognitive content."[38] One

37. Specht cites the first explicit formulation of this principle: "A proposition has no meaning whatever, if it is in no way possible to state when the proposition is true; for the meaning of a proposition is the method of its verification" (*Foundations of Wittgenstein's Late Philosophy*, 5).

38. Carnap, *Philosophy of Rudolf Carnap*, 25.

of the passages in his book was widely embraced and used by the logical positivists as a paradigm for illustrating how the principle of empirical verification applied. As a matter of historical interest, that passage is worth recalling:

> But in order to be able to say that a point is black or white, I must first know when a point is called black, and when white: in order to be able to say, "'p' is true (or false)," I must have determined in what circumstances I call 'p' true, and in so doing I determine the sense of the proposition.[39]

Despite being well received by the Vienna Circle, Wittgenstein however kept his distance, maintaining only occasional contacts with them. He knew he had been misread, especially with regard to his position on metaphysics. This was later confirmed by Carnap, who disclosed that he and the rest of the Vienna Circle had erroneously believed their attitude toward metaphysics was similar to Wittgenstein's; they had, he further admitted, "not paid sufficient attention to the statements in his book about the mystical."[40] An agitation that Wittgenstein had long felt and which drew him further away from the logical positivists may well have been their "false confidence" in a scientism that made "it look as if *everything* were explained."[41] Brad J. Kallenberg sketches out the differences between the two parties, as follows:

> Wittgenstein never intended to *refute* the metaphysicians. He merely intended to *discipline* their use of language. Wittgenstein thought that religious mystics (such as Tolstoy) were on to something of utmost importance. He contended that the nature of language prevented direct talk about the mystical. But he never disdained the role that religious mysticism played in the life of mystics. In contrast, Wittgenstein did repudiate logical positivism for the way their scientism discounted that which is truly important.[42]

Theology today still finds itself wedged between two not dissimilar poles, a fact to which I have alluded in my introductory chapter. Either language is naively assumed to be fully competent to render the "whole truth" and to tell us precise and literal information about God, or, given

39. *TLP* 4.063.

40. Carnap cited in Lazenby, *Early Wittgenstein on Religion*, 40.

41. *TLP* 6.372.

42. Kallenberg, *Ethics as Grammar*, 170.

the prevailing spirit of skepticism, that the language of religion can have no epistemic access to reality and is only good for expressing moral or ethical intentions. The latter is well illustrated by the writings of Don Cupitt (b. 1934).[43] Both tendencies have arisen from the dualism of the mental and the physical—the Cartesian-inspired separation of the mind and the body.[44] Whereas the first tendency assumes that God is univocally and literally designated in scripture or creed, the second assumes God to be completely out of reach by means of language. Both, if I may say, need to be "disciplined" in their respective uses of language. For the consequences of how we then proceed will range from dogmatism, idolatry and absolutism and, in the case of the tendency to deny the possibility of language to express God, relativism or even nihilism.

Against this background, we return now to the object lesson that I said we would recall for the purposes of our discussion. It is on record that at a meeting of the Vienna Circle to which he was invited to speak, Wittgenstein did something rather odd.[45] He had grown impatient as the discussion veered towards a positivist direction. To everybody's surprise, he abruptly stood up, turned his back on those present, and while still facing outwards, read aloud the poetry of the Indian mystic, Rabindranath Tagore (1861–1941). It was a grand gesture on the part of Wittgenstein, one that, I believe, delivered a powerful object lesson "that the boundary of the language of logical positivism—expressed by the tight circle in which they all sat—simultaneously traced the inexpressible *das Mystische* which lay beyond it."[46] This interpretation of Wittgenstein's action is consistent with what he is trying to say in *TLP*—but which was misunderstood by the logical positivists—that there are certain things in life about which we must be silent. The logical positivists, we recall, had mistaken Wittgenstein to be wholly with them in drawing the line between what we can speak about and what we must be silent about. They had, however and, most importantly, failed to appreciate the key point of difference between them: that while they have nothing to be silent about,

---

43. Several titles of Cupitt's books are listed in the Bibliography.

44. I discussed Wittgenstein's opposition to the Cartesian dualism in chapter 2.

45. This incident of Wittgenstein reading poetry to the Vienna Circle has been retold by several writers, e.g., Hudson, *Wittgenstein and Religious Belief*, 87; Klein, *How Things Are in the World*, 244–45.

46. Kallenberg, *Ethics as Grammar*, 65–66.

"Wittgenstein passionately believes that all that really matters in human life is precisely what, in his view, we must be silent about."[47]

"That It Exists"

For Wittgenstein, we have noted, *das Mystische* is beyond the scope of articulation—it lies all together *outside* language. Recall those locutions that assert this ineffability: "There are, indeed, things that cannot be put into words. They make themselves manifest. They are what is mystical";[48] "Propositions cannot express anything higher";[49] "What we cannot speak about we must pass over in silence."[50] The view that the mystical is outside the scope of language must imply the view that nothing can be said about it. Arguably, one may even infer that it is not possible to know the mystical is there. Such an agnosticism would be nearly atheistic, since to deny the possibility of knowing the existence of the mystical comes close to discounting the mystical itself. Little wonder that the logical positivists saw him as an ally. But they had misread him, thinking he was both renouncing the expressions of, as well as denying, the mystical. I will express my disagreement with him involving the point of silence in a little more detail shortly.

At first blush, Wittgenstein's statement that "God does not reveal himself *in* the world" appears to lead in the direction of atheism too.[51] But once the wider philosophical context is factored in, a different impression is perceived: Wittgenstein is not saying that God does not exist, only that God is not within the "world" of facts. If he were part of such a world, he would be one fact among other facts, and that is precisely what the mystical is not.

Given Wittgenstein's special way of using the term "world," it is also plausible to interpret him as saying that God does not reveal himself in ways accessible to scientific or other factual investigations. Thus, we may say that though the approach that Wittgenstein has adopted holds that it is not possible to speak logically about the mystical, he does not deny that it exists. Indeed, something like God or *das Höhere* is clearly

47. Engelmann, *Letters from Ludwig Wittgenstein*, 97.
48. *TLP* 6.522.
49. *TLP* 6.42.
50. *TLP* 7.
51. *TLP* 6.432.

assumed; otherwise, how is one to account for the mystical fact that the world exists?

It is, however, not the case that Wittgenstein is uninterested in what philosophical thinkers have always returned to time and again—the case for or against the existence of God. What may have mattered more to him is the concern that one should have an appropriate attitude towards the world, an attitude in which one views and feels the world *sub specie aeterni* and "as a whole—a limited whole."[52] In consequence, the world is seen as "a cipher of transcendence." I think Wittgenstein would be quite happy to recognize such an attitude towards the world as a truly religious one. After all, as he tells us, "it is not *how* things are in the world that is mystical, but *that* it exists."[53] If, however, the attitude he is urging upon us is one which requires us never to articulate by *saying* God exists, we shall have to express our strong disagreement. This involves the point about silence that I made a while ago. We would have reason to think if he has not gone altogether too far in drawing alongside the logical positivists. Admittedly, it is a challenge to express adequately what is totally ineffable, but it is one that requires "extreme caution," not total silence. To say that something cannot be expressed does not imply that it cannot be expressed at all. Those of us who believe in God "have *heard* about him and were taught in him" (Eph 4:21), and we have an obligation to give a report or "an account" (1 Pet 3:15). If we find ourselves caught between the poles of absolute objectivity and total silence, the proper response is to navigate between them by means of a non-objectifying form of religious language which, as I said before, honors divine transcendence and caters for our need for expression. After all, as Wittgenstein himself has been careful to point out, what is mystical "shows itself"; if that is indeed the case, I believe *some* expression of "itself" must be possible through the language of religion.[54]

We should also not imagine that Wittgenstein's reluctance to address the question of the existence of God is due to any deficiency on his part about his religious belief. Based on our findings on his religious life in chapter 2, we can almost certainly rule out such a reason. While in *TLP* we are given some hints about his faith, in Wittgenstein's *Notebooks* we are shown a more articulate believer who identifies God

52. *TLP* 6.45.

53. *TLP* 6.44.

54. Keightley makes the interesting remark that the word "itself" is as important as the word "show" (*Wittgenstein, Grammar and God*, 30).

with "the meaning of life, i.e., the meaning of the world."[55] Over the years, Wittgenstein has come to believe that questions of meaning are central to philosophy, rather than questions of truth. As to whether God exists or not, such a question must necessarily involve a decision or assessment about certain statements being true or false. We know from his analysis of language, Wittgenstein is loath to engage in any enterprise that requires the objectification of God, a task that will inevitably, on his view, stretch language to go beyond its limits.

Let us be clear that to Wittgenstein's way of thinking, the reason God does not figure is not that God does not exist, but that the vocabulary for this kind of non-factual discourse is lacking. As he has already declared, "Propositions can express nothing that is higher."[56] Thus, Wittgenstein would probably regard any attempt to say what cannot be said in factual language as the spilling of nonsense. In a conversation with Drury, Wittgenstein disparagingly remarks, "Can you imagine St. Augustine saying that the existence of God was 'highly probable'?"[57] That last remark by Wittgenstein is surely an exaggeration, for it is not only perfectly imaginable for theologians and philosophers to speak of the existence of God as highly probable, many have done so. Richard Swinburne, for instance, has argued:

> It remains to me, as to so many who have thought about the matter, a source of extreme puzzlement that there should exist anything at all. . . . But there does exist something. And if there is to exist something, it seems impossible to conceive of anything simpler (and therefore *a priori* more *probable*) than the existence of God. The intrinsic *probability* of theism may be low; but it is, I suggest, relative to other hypotheses about what exists, very high.[58]

While still on the question of God's existence, a task now befalls me to share a point of application with regard to the practice of theological reflection. We have noted Wittgenstein's reluctance to stretch language to do what it cannot do. In his later philosophy, Wittgenstein would advise that words be brought back from their metaphysical use to their use in an everyday context. He tells us why we should do so: "When philosophers

55. *NB* 11.6.16.

56. *TLP* 6.42.

57. Drury, "Conversations with Wittgenstein," 105.

58. Swinburne, *Existence of God*, 283–84 (emphasis added).

use a word—'knowledge,' 'being,' 'object,' 'I,' 'proposition,' 'name'—and try to grasp the essence of the thing, one must always ask oneself: is the word ever actually used in this way in the language-game which is its original home?"[59] Likewise, in our theological reflection, we need to be mindful of the context within which the words and phrases we use are located, or from which they are drawn. Here is Kerr's extremely clear-headed counsel to all who engage in cerebral discourse about God and religion:

> Whether I mean the same by saying "I believe in God" as other people do when they say the same thing will come out at various places in our lives: our practices, aspirations, hopes, virtues, and so on. It will show in the rest of what we do whether we have faith in God. It will not be settled by our finding that we make the same correlation between our words and some item of metaphysical reality.[60]

Wittgenstein's Experience of the Mystical

There are indications in the literature that Wittgenstein's mysticism is more than an idea or hypothesis for philosophizing. Recall his remark about viewing the world *sub specie aeterni* and feeling it as a limited whole.[61] The words "viewing" and "feeling" are clearly suggestive of experience rather than theory. In this regard, one can perhaps understand why Ogden's translation of "view" (*Anschauung*) to "contemplation" has fallen out of favor with some readers: Ogden's rendering diminishes the experiential aspect that Wittgenstein has in mind.[62] Further textual evidences are to be found in the closing sections of *TLP*. The relevant passages have been cited earlier but we shall repeat them here in order to show that each of the situations related by Wittgenstein, namely, "the sense of the world," "ethics," "the will," "death," "immortality," "God," "the problems of life," and "the solution of the problem of life" is an aspect of both the view and the experience of the world as mystical. The question,

59. *PI* 161.

60. Kerr, *Theology after Wittgenstein*,153.

61. *TLP* 6.45.

62. See Morris and Dodd, "Mysticism and Nonsense in the *Tractatus*," 275. See also Atkinson, "Sub Specie Aeterni," 106. The point being made is that the word "contemplation" suggests a passive form of looking in mind, rather than an active fixing of one's attention on the world.

as Brian F. McGuinness (b. 1927) has fastidiously argued, is not whether Wittgenstein's mysticism is rooted in experience but whether "these various aspects of the *Tractatus* are concerned with a single feeling or experience or realm of experience."[63]

In an article entitled "Lectures on Ethics," Wittgenstein confesses to having had several experiences that may be characterized as mystical.[64] He considers them to be of absolute value.[65] The first is the experience *par excellence* of wondering "*at the existence of the world.*"[66] Another is the experience of "feeling *absolutely safe* . . . whatever happens."[67] Then, there is the experience of "feeling guilty" over doing something that God disapproves of.[68] These experiences which he recalls are clearly reminiscent of what Rudolf Otto (1869–1937) has famously termed *numinous experience,* the experience of the Holy or the *mysterium tremendum et fascinans.*[69] Even Wittgenstein's invocation to silence in the concluding sections of his work strikes us as a possible parallel with the "necessity of silence" felt by Otto in his response to the *numen praesens* of Yahweh.[70] In some of Wittgenstein's earliest passages, such as those cited below, we are given glimpses of his mystical experience:

> The world is *given* me, i.e., my will enters into the world completely from the outside as into something that is already there. (As for what my will is, I don't know yet.) That is why we have the feeling of being dependent on an alien will. *However this may be,* at any rate we *are* in a certain sense dependent, and what we are dependent on we call God. In this sense God would simply be fate, or, what is the same thing: The world—which is independent of our will.[71]

> How things stand, is God. God is, how things stand.[72]

---

63. McGuinness, "Mysticism of the *Tractatus,*" 319.

64. The substance of this article was delivered as a lecture to the Heretics Society in Cambridge sometime between September 1929 and December 1930.

65. *LE,* 11.

66. *LE,* 8.

67. *LE,* 9.

68. *LE,* 10.

69. Otto, *Idea of the Holy,* 1–30.

70. Otto, *Idea of the Holy,* 71.

71. *NB* 8.7.16.

72. *NB* 1.8.16.

Admittedly, the God presented in these notes appears to some to be a God of pantheism. Several commentators have arrived at such a conclusion. McGuinness, for example, writes, "True, there are references to God in the *Notebooks* and even in the *Tractatus* but clearly to a God who is identical with nature: *Deus, sive Natura*. At best Wittgenstein allows a form of pantheism . . . he might be said to hold that if there is any God, then the world is God."[73] Wittgenstein is also said to be some sort of a nature mystic who seeks to have mystical union with the divine. Discussing the question of whether Wittgenstein was a pantheist, theist, or even deist in any detail would take us too far beyond the concerns of our present study. I should like, however, to point out that some key statements in *TLP* clearly cannot be read to fit the pantheistic mold (e.g., *TLP* 3.031; 6.41–6.43, 6.432, 6.44).[74] Moreover, the traces or hints of "nature mysticism" in Wittgenstein's writings may well have been included to serve the overall aim of conveying his grand thesis—that the mystical cannot be described or talked about, but which nevertheless, shows itself. Be that as it may, we can quite confidently say that Wittgenstein "had a certainty about having come in contact with a reality beyond his own consciousness."[75] What we might have considerable less confidence about is to make the claim—as James William McClendon (1924–2000) and Brad J. Kallenberg have done—that Wittgenstein was "an authentic Christian (albeit an undogmatic and thus perhaps an irregular one)."[76] As I discussed in chapter 2, the matter of his personal religious faith cannot be easily settled, as he did not make any profession of faith, nor was he formally linked to any church.

Wittgenstein's Apophaticism

Wittgenstein is of course not the first thinker to suggest that the mystical cannot be expressed; indeed, one may even go so far as to say his understanding of the mystical is not really novel.[77] The fact is many

73. McGuinness, "Mysticism of the *Tractatus*," 321.

74. For detailed discussions that Wittgenstein's mysticism is not pantheistic, see Lazenby, *Early Wittgenstein on Religion*, 36–59; Fronda, *Wittgenstein's (Misunderstood) Religious Thought*, 27–38.

75. Glebe-Møller, "Whereof One Cannot Speak," 157.

76. McClendon and Kallenberg, "Ludwig Wittgenstein," 131.

77. Wittgenstein admits in his Preface to *TLP* that "he makes no claim to novelty in points of detail."

philosophers and theologians have struggled with and written about the inadequacy of language in this regard—possibly, with the exception of Descartes who seems to think that one can have a "clear and distinct idea" where God is concerned. Long before Wittgenstein and within the earliest Christian centuries, the "apophatic" trail has been set ablaze by Dionysius the Areopagite (whose writing we noted are better known as Pseudo-Dionysius and whom we cited earlier). This trail, we have noted above, takes the theological approach that God is best described by negation, that is, God is spoken of only in terms of what he is not, rather than what God is. It may be noted that although Aquinas opts for the way of *analogia* to understanding religious language, he considers the *via negativa* an important first step.[78] Today, apophatic theology or mystical theology is the hallmark of the Eastern Orthodox branch of Christianity, with elements of it embraced by Roman Catholic and Protestant Christians. We may safely say that the view that God is transcendent or "wholly other" and ineffable is standard doctrine within the Christian religion. The same, however, cannot be said about the view I am urging— that God is also beyond the limits of human language to contain or fully express. It is something that religious people need to be mindful of.

In his consideration of the Wittgenstein corpus, Fronda has concluded that the theology of Wittgenstein "is much more impressive for its negative suggestions than it is for its affirmative ones."[79] This observation is borne out by the fact that in the pages of *TLP* although "God" is mentioned four times, it is only in the last of these occasions that Wittgenstein says anything about God, and even then what he says about God is a negation—that God does not reveal himself in the world. Fronda enumerates a number of so-called "negative suggestions" inferred from Wittgenstein's apophaticism. We shall consider three of them, under these headings: (1) Wittgenstein's God is beyond sense, (2) Wittgenstein's negative theology evidently predominates over his affirmative theology, and (3) Statements about God are not propositions with sense.

1. Wittgenstein's God Is Beyond Sense

Fronda has proposed that the God of Wittgenstein's apophaticism is a God who is beyond sense. Thus, with Wittgenstein one can go only so far

---

78. See Stiver, *Philosophy of Religious Language*, 18, 23.

79. Fronda, *Wittgenstein's (Misunderstood) Religious Thought*, 38.

as to identify God *with* but not *as*. The *with* versus *as* distinction is easily explained as follows, "If *x* is identified as *y*, then that is to say that *x* is *y*. If *x* is identified with *y*, then that is to say that *x* somehow shares a property or belongs to a domain common with or otherwise is somehow related to *y*; nonetheless *x* has a distinct identity from *y*."[80] If we accept that Wittgenstein refrains from saying who God is, then the oft-made claim about him being a pantheist would be defeated simply on the basis that even a pantheist has to make a claim about divinity. I would, however, not go so far as to say that skepticism must then be conceded. The fact that Wittgenstein had characterized God, albeit by negation, should lead us away from supposing that nothing can be said about the divine. More rightly to suppose is the nuanced view I am concerned to defend in this study, that the God who is beyond sense, cannot be fully described or contained by what we say about him.

2. Wittgenstein's Negative Theology Evidently Predominates over His Affirmative Theology

This is seen by Fronda as a "complete reversal" since in his *Notebooks* phase Wittgenstein had made many notable and affirmative statements about God.[81] We recall the following statements:

> What do I know about God and the purpose of life? I know that this world exists. . . . The meaning of life, i.e., the meaning of the world, we can call God. And connect with this the comparison of God to a father. (11.6.16).

> In this sense God would simply be fate, or, what is the same thing: The world—which is independent of our will . . . I can make myself independent of fate. Certainly it is correct to say: Conscience is the voice of God. (8.7.16)

> How things stand, is God. God is, how things stand. (1.8.16).

Against the view that the above entries indicate that Wittgenstein's understanding of God is pantheistic, Fronda counter-argues that "the theological themes in *NB* are but one side of a theological position yet to be fully shown—*TLP* subsequently shows the other side," or that

---

80. Fronda, *Wittgenstein's (Misunderstood) Religious Thought*, 39.
81. Fronda, *Wittgenstein's (Misunderstood) Religious Thought*, 41.

they are "merely initial sketches of Wittgenstein's attempt at presenting his position on God."[82] Even better put, I think, is Fronda's suggestion that the so-called pantheistic entries, as with the whole of *NB*, are but a "ladder" on which Wittgenstein climbs up towards *TLP*.

To my way of thinking, whether Wittgenstein's theology veers more towards pantheism or not is a question that can be left to one side. What Wittgenstein was saying during a particular phase or under a particular circumstance, was an attempt on his part to approach the mystical in his own way. He presents us with a variety of theologies, none of which can claim to have a full grasp of the object of theology. Naturally, it is disconcerting to think that we might be faced with an indefinite variety of languages and meanings. This, as we have noted repeatedly, does not mean that God cannot be intelligibly spoken of, only that he cannot be fully contained by our speech.

3. Statements about God Are Not Propositions with Sense

The reason statements about God are not viewed as "propositions with sense" is that they are not intended to picture "some possible fact within the logical space covered by language."[83] These statements would be labelled meaningless or nonsensical by the logical positivists and even by Wittgenstein himself, since they are not capable of being verified or falsified. A valid point is made that even if one were to resort to the *via negativa* methodology to speak of God, the statement(s) that one makes would still be dismissed as not making sense. The "unsayable" is unsayable either by positive or negative terms. Even so, the above remarks about propositions have some relevance to my work. They may help to ease the hardened position of seeing language as essentially pictorial or referential. Perhaps, they can also explain why some religious people are usually unfazed when presented with contrarian positions seeking to refute their beliefs, and why they can go on reciting creeds, lines of scripture and the like, of which they have little or no understanding.

82. Fronda, *Wittgenstein's (Misunderstood) Religious Thought*, 41.

83. Fronda, *Wittgenstein's (Misunderstood) Religious Thought*, 41.

Why the Mystical Is Broached

In this section, I shall attempt to explain why the notion of the mystical is broached in *TLP*. I begin with "*how* the world is," that is, the world as it is conceived by Wittgenstein.[84] The reason is that I want to show that the notion of the mystical is an upshot of Wittgenstein's complex thinking concerning "the world" in its relationship to language.

In Wittgenstein's account, the world is very much the reference point around which the mystical is presented. Recall if you will, the following propositions: (a) "It is not *how* things are in the world that is mystical, but *that* it exists";[85] and (b) "Feeling the world as a limited whole—it is this that is mystical."[86] Earlier, at the beginning of his treatise Wittgenstein has provided a rather aphoristic description of the world:

> The world is all that is the case.
> The world is the totality of facts, not of things.
> The world is determined by the facts, and by their being *all* the facts.
> For the totality of facts determines what is the case, and also whatever is not the case.
> The facts in logical space are the world.
> The world divides into facts.[87]

What is clearly communicated here is that the world is all-inclusive: "it is everything that is the case." In Wittgenstein's philosophical mind, as we have noted, the world is not the world of empirical data and sensations or science, but the world of facts as portrayed in propositions. He is, in my opinion, consistent in holding to this understanding of the word "world" throughout his philosophizing years.[88] But at this phase, he is still operating according to the theory that language pictures or mirrors the world, and that meaningful language is about "what is the case." This view of language, the so-called "picture theory" has been discussed at length in chapter 2. Without letting it detain us, let us mention the all-important fact that in the thought of Wittgenstein, "his world" is matched by a particular kind of language, one that can adequately depict it. "A proposition," he

84. *TLP* 6.432.
85. *TLP* 6.44.
86. *TLP* 6.45.
87. *TLP* 1, 1.1, 1.11, 1.12, 1.13, 1.2.
88. Klein, *How Things Are in the World*, 30.

has explained, "is a picture of reality."[89] That correspondence between world and language leads him to further posit that within his world, he can work out a system of absolute necessity, objectivity and logicality—by means of language. It will be a world marked out, as he says, by a "totality of facts," and one in which the principles of certainty apply, and factuality obtains. Admittedly, many will find such a world difficult to conceive, for it is missing what makes a "world" world, namely, people, human activity, beliefs, means of expressions, and so forth.

Throwing a spanner in the works, Wittgenstein himself famously sets out to mark out a limit to the expression of thought (in language). Recall his byword, "the limits of my language mean the limits of my world."[90] For he has come to recognize that there exists an entire realm of human life which he did not or could not account for in his world-view and language-concept. Paradoxically, the drawing of a limit has enabled him to "think of both sides of this limit."[91] The case, as he would say, "is altogether like that of the eye and the field of sight. But you do not really see the eye."[92] While Wittgenstein does not explicitly affirm the existence of an *ontological* domain comprising things that language is inadequate to express, he goes on to speak of a two-realm distinction—one "*within the world*," and the other "outside the world."[93] I refer to the following:

> The sense of the world must lie outside the world. In the world everything is as it is, and everything happens as it does happen: *in* it no value exists—and if it did exist, it would have no value. If there is any value that does have value, it must lie outside the whole sphere of what happens and is the case.[94]

As we have seen in chapter 2, this is the distinction or divide between what can be said and what cannot be said but nevertheless shows itself. From the textual evidence of *TLP*, we can infer what must lie outside the world: the mystical, i.e., values, religion, ethics, aesthetics, and the like. All this while, Wittgenstein has expressed a craving for a realm or order "in which the answers to questions are symmetrically combined—*a*

89. *TLP* 4.01.
90. *TLP* 5.6.
91. *TLP*, p3.
92. *TLP* 5.633.
93. *TLP* 6.41.
94. *TLP* 6.41.

priori—to form a self-contained system."[95] As he discloses, his urge towards the mystical arises from that craving, as well as from his own dissatisfaction with science which, he claims, can only provide answers to scientific questions but not to the problems of life.[96] Thus, the realm of the mystical is for him that realm which he could not account for in his language schema.

It might be helpful to consider two attempts at explaining how the notion of the mystical came to be shaped. The first is by Christopher Yorke who believes that the notion of the mystical has been posited as a "remedy" in Wittgenstein's overall philosophical schema, which, he thinks, lacks foundation.[97] Yorke begins by properly crediting Wittgenstein for succeeding "in driving home the point that philosophy cannot exist apart from the language that gives it intelligible form."[98] Yet, he finds somewhat incongruous Wittgenstein's claim that "language alone can tell us that language can mislead us."[99] It is, as he says, an issue for him because such a position amounts to a case of having one's cake and eating it. The grievance has a familiar ring to it: it distantly echoes the criticism voiced by Russell that "Mr Wittgenstein manages to say a good deal about what cannot be said."[100] The other issue with which Yorke is concerned is Wittgenstein's exclusive focus on the linguistic in his philosophical methodology. The resultant "deflationary antiphilosophy," as Yorke calls it, lacks foundation, or in his words, "an ultimate grounding or justification outside of references to entrenched linguistic practices."[101] The upshot of Wittgenstein's overall project is "a foundational circularity, albeit a tightly coherent one."[102] It is a situation that needs to be overcome if an infinite regress is to be avoided. Yorke gives us an outline of the steps taken by Wittgenstein and the ontological completion achieved:

> This exclusive focus on the linguistic leaves us with a picture of the world that is incomplete; a yin bereft of its accompanying yang. Wittgenstein himself acknowledges this lacuna, and

95. *TLP* 5.4541.

96. *TLP* 6.52; *NB* 25.5.15.

97. Yorke, "Mystic and the Ineffable," 13.

98. Yorke, "Mystic and the Ineffable," 13.

99. Yorke, "Mystic and the Ineffable," 13.

100. *TLP*, xxi.

101. Yorke, "Mystic and the Ineffable," 13.

102. Yorke, "Mystic and the Ineffable," 13.

attempts to remedy it in his philosophic schema, via his positing of the "mystical," that which transcends language, and which
no language can describe. This move brings completion to the
Wittgensteinian ontology. There is the world, the totality of all
articulatable facts; and there is the mystical, that which cannot
be captured by the language of facts—and these two categories
exhaust the set of what is and what can be.[103]

In the second suggestion, which is by Lazenby, the notion of the
mystical is said to be raised because Wittgenstein has determined that
"the vocabulary of factual language is the only vocabulary there is."[104]
Because facts, according to the Tractarian schema, are what can be
expressed in language, there is no longer place for any ideal of "moral
facts," "religious facts," or "philosophical facts." As is frequently heard,
philosophy and theology are left with an impaired language. This follows
from Wittgenstein's successful attempt at absolutizing the division
between fact and value, a division entailed by the separation between the
world and God. Thus, God who is not a fact, but value, lies outside the
reach of language. With the world now limited to facts, the mystic—and
Wittgenstein is certainly one—must either transcend it to have union with
the mystical or remain silent. If my reading of Lazenby is correct, I think
he is implying that the notion of the mystical is posited by Wittgenstein,
the mystic, as a way of overcoming the limitation of language. Consider
these words: "Objects can only be *named.* Signs are their representatives.
I can only speak *about* them: I cannot *put them into words.* Propositions
can only say *how* things are, not *what* they are."[105] How Wittgenstein
proceeds from this point is perceptively captured by Kallenberg:

> Rather than consign the ineffable to the metaphysical dust bin,
> as did the logical positivists, Wittgenstein concluded instead
> that the route to the beyond-the-world cannot lie within
> language. The logical positivists stood on the road toward the
> mystical (*das Mystische*) in order to block the way and turn
> travellers back toward home. However, Wittgenstein stood as
> a moral sage at the crossroads not to turn travelers back but to
> warn them which fork is a dead end. His intention all along was
> to *draw attention to the mystical* by showing that the limits of

---

103. Yorke, "Mystic and the Ineffable," 13.
104. Lazenby, *Early Wittgenstein on Religion*, 58.
105. *TLP* 3.221.

our worldly island are simultaneously the shoreline of a vast ocean.[106]

From Logic to the World

The proposal by Lazenby seems to me to have rightly recognized the central place of logic in Wittgenstein's philosophical undertaking. This should hardly come as a surprise. In his Preface to *TLP*, Wittgenstein has intimated that the problems of philosophy are due to the logic of language being misunderstood. He has also claimed that it is impossible to represent in language anything that goes against logic.[107] His thoughts on logical form and his notion of correspondence between "what pictures" (language) with "what is pictured" (reality) are the outcomes of an exercise in armchair logic. It is thus my contention that Wittgenstein's view of the mystical or God has also been partly determined by his own logical analysis. Interestingly, we read Russell aptly capturing this in his introduction to *TLP*:

> [Wittgenstein's] attitude upon this grows naturally out of his doctrine in pure logic, according to which the logical proposition is a picture (true or false) of the fact, and has in common with the fact a certain structure. . . . Everything, therefore, which is involved in the very idea of the expressiveness of language must remain incapable of being expressed in language, and is, therefore, inexpressible in a perfectly precise sense. This inexpressible contains, according to Mr. Wittgenstein, the whole of logic and philosophy.[108]

The Mystical in Later Wittgenstein

In this last section, I should like to briefly attend to a conundrum: if the mystical concerns the whole approach and intention of *TLP*, as we have claimed, why does it seem altogether absent from *PI*? One may be tempted to conclude that because Wittgenstein has jettisoned the logical schema of his earlier phase of philosophy, he has also abandoned the mystical

---

106. Kallenberg, *Ethics as Grammar*, 86.

107. *TLP* 3.03–3.032.

108. *TLP*, xx, xxi.

in his later phase. It is, of course, true that in *PI* a very different schema to language and logic obtains. Whereas he was earlier concerned with the structure of language and its logical form, he now looks at the way language properly functions in the context of the everyday. But as we have seen, more recent scholarship on Wittgenstein has rejected the view that his earlier and later philosophical positions are diametrically opposed. In the specific case of the treatment of the mystical, Wittgenstein has been consistent throughout in drawing limit(s) between what can be said and what cannot be said. To be sure, he still speaks of limits of language,[109] but no longer, as he did in *TLP*, of "the" limit. This variation finds expression in *TLP* in the quest for the structure of language, and in the later work, by bringing language back from their metaphysical to their everyday use. The reason for what amounts to fine-tuning in this case is that he has come to realize that there is no one definite limit to language, marking out what cannot be said meaningfully. If I am right that his basic view of philosophy has remained fundamentally unchanged over time, then the fact that nothing is said in his later work that hints of his abandoning a belief in the mystical must imply that his thoughts on the mystical are firmly in place.[110] If in *PI* he has been silent about that reality, it is probably because he is heeding his own injunction to remain silent in the face of what he cannot speak.

Concluding Remarks

This chapter has been concerned with the concept of the mystical which emerges towards the end of *TLP*. We have read closely what Wittgenstein has written about and outlined his position on the mystical—one which I believe is a culmination of his philosophical development. By that term, Wittgenstein clearly has in mind "God," but he is careful to include a range of other related concerns such as ethics, values, aesthetics, logic, and the like. In fact, his own working definition of "what is mystical" says it all: that which is inexpressible but nevertheless shows itself. Also, we have noted that the mystical is posited by Wittgenstein to bring completion to his ontology. The "mystical" presence, in my view, can be traced through his later work, even though the word itself is not used in

109. *PI* 119.

110. This is also the view of, among others, D'hert, Klein, and Keightley, to name just three.

PI. Lest we join his critics in accusing him of wanting to "talk only about words,"[111] I have drawn attention to his unpretentious call "to view the world sub specie aeterni [sic]," offering textual indications that he does indeed have an experience of, and not just a theory about, the mystical. It is evidently clear that the mystical or contemplative certainly manifests itself again and again in his life and thought.

I wish here to summarize and further comment on some of the ways in which Wittgenstein's notion of the mystical can apply to the claims of my thesis about religious language elaborated in my introductory chapter. Let me first touch on Wittgenstein's confession that the mystical exists, or better, that the mystical simply "is." The claim is basic, for unless God or some divine reality exists, there is simply no religion. In general, we might say that religion must involve the use of language to speak about God's existence or argue that he "is." If or when we use language in such wise, we must do so with care and restraint in order not to inadvertently foster the view that the divine is one thing or fact among other things or facts in the world. That is certainly not a conception of God we wish to evoke, out of respect for divine mystery, not to mention that we might be overstepping the bounds of language into a realm that is beyond language.

Wittgenstein, we have seen, characterizes the mystical as "inexpressible." It is so because it "lies outside the world" and is beyond the limits of language. He urges total silence on our part in the face of that reality, a position I have criticized as "going altogether too far." Nonetheless, we must agree with him that keeping silence is mostly an authentic response, especially if we do not mean "the silence which takes rescue in the ineffable, but rather the silence which is implicit in language."[112] Also, being silent is not an inappropriate posture towards that which is not entirely intelligible to us. At all events, Wittgenstein's stricture does not mean that we cannot talk about God, only that we cannot claim to have grasped him, or have him contained in words. Thus, what theology must never claim is full knowledge of, or complete explanation about God's being. For the reason that theology's proper object is the mystical, a reality of which our interpretation is to be continually revisited, it follows that the language of religion must not yield to the temptation of formulaic expressions or fixed formulations.

---

111. *PI* 370.

112. D'hert, *Wittgenstein's Relevance for Theology*, 182.

At *TLP* 6.522, Wittgenstein asserts that what is mystical makes itself manifest, that is, it shows itself. The logical positivists, we have seen, denied this. We can, and must, criticize Wittgenstein for not saying more about how the showing happens, or how one can come to know what is shown. One is left wondering if there is something of significance that, while not *said*, is perhaps *shown*? I believe there is. The idea that the mystical shows itself challenges me to "discipline" my use of language in ways that will make possible the object of my discourse to be meaningfully communicated and understood. This illustration by Wittgenstein gives me pause: "A proposition is a picture of reality. . . . I understand the proposition without having had its sense explained to me."[113] Paradoxically, religion, like philosophy, must "signify what cannot be said, by presenting clearly what can be said."[114] In other words, it is possible to show or communicate what cannot be said.

Wittgenstein, we may recall, tried to read the poetry of the Indian mystic, Tagore to the logical positivists as his way of directing them to the touch of *das Mystiche*. He was later to speak of having read another poem, that of Uhland's *Graf Eberhard's Weissdorn,* and finding it to be another instance of what he would regard as the mystical making itself manifest.[115] The poetry of those just cited as well as those by Dostoyevsky and Goethe, and books like Tolstoy's, certain detective stories and films and dramas had all been for him the vehicles through which the mystical can manifest itself. Speaking of poetry's role in all of this, some light is cast by David Jasper (b. 1951) on its relationship with religion: "Just as poetry . . . requires religion and draws inspiration from the definitions of theology, so poetry may serve as a necessary reminder to theology of mystery, hesitation and hiddenness of religious experience. Poets often understand well the nature of 'mystery.'"[116] I believe it is the depth of honest reflection about life in poetry and other forms of art, as well as their genuineness in expressing emotions, describing situations or even telling us something about ourselves that render them fit instruments whereby the mystical might show itself. Most certainly for us too, the mystical can be made manifest through these very same means. As we

113. *TLP* 4.021, 4.022.

114. *TLP* 4.115.

115. Engelmann, *Letters from Ludwig Wittgenstein*, 82–84.

116. Jasper, *Study of Literature and Religion*, 32. Jasper tells of a critic who "insisted that poets are natural theologians in whose mind originates the theology which theologians spoil by their intellectual endeavours" (6).

have been warned, we neglect the insights and beauty of poetry and the art of literature at our peril.[117] We can also expect the mystical to show itself in and through our use of first-order religious language such as prayer, worship and confession. This is amply borne out in our own experience and practice.

Finally, if art (poetry included) is a sphere in which Wittgenstein thought the mystical can show itself, surely human action is another. This is in line with the teaching of most religions that one's conduct, deed, and action testify to the God one believes in. Jesus, for instance, tells his followers, "Let your light so shine before men, that they may see your good works and give glory to your Father who is in heaven" (Matt 5:16). In Wittgenstein's case, we understand that he "made a conscious effort to live out the implications of the *Tractatus*, that is to *do* what could not be said but could be shown."[118]

The mystical, we have seen, is that which nothing whatsoever can be said except that it is mystical. Even so, we have argued that it might still be possible to talk about it, since it shows itself. To say that the mystical is inexpressible is already to put the "property" into words. However indirectly or partially, light on the mystical to be shed by means of language is, one would be concerned with the "truth" of what is or has been conveyed. It is to the question of truth that we shall now turn.

117. Jasper, *Study of Literature and Religion*, 138.
118. Hudson, *Wittgenstein and Religious Belief*, 104.

Chapter 5

The Question of Truth:
Finding "the Road from Error to Truth"

> We must begin with the mistake and transform it into what is true. That is, we must uncover the source of error; otherwise hearing what is true won't help us. . . . To convince someone of what is true, it is not enough to state it. We must find the road from error to truth.[1]
>
> —Ludwig Wittgenstein

Introduction

WE HAVE SEEN IN previous chapters (2–3) that for Wittgenstein—at least in the pre-*Tractatus* and *Tractatus* phases of his philosophizing—a certain connection always exists between his analysis of language and his conception of reality. Recall the following entry in *NB*, "The theory of logical portrayal by means of language says—quite generally: In order for it to be possible that a proposition should be true or false—agree with reality or not—for this to be possible something in the proposition must be *identical* with reality."[2] Or, consider his remarks in *TLP* that "a proposition is a picture of reality,"[3] and that "one can actually see from the proposition how everything stands logically *if* it is true."[4]

1. Wittgenstein, *Remarks on Frazer's Golden Bough*, 1e.
2. *NB* 20.10.14.
3. *TLP* 4.01.
4. *TLP* 4.023.

On Wittgenstein's view, language and reality are internally related, the nature of their relation resting on a "picturing" function. Propositions, he further remarks, are contingent, that is, they can be either true or false: their sense or meaningfulness as pictures of reality is independent of whatever facts that obtain. So, if a proposition is true, it corresponds to a fact and depicts how things are in the world; if false, it does not have these characteristics though it nevertheless remains meaningful. Given this view about propositions and the assumption that language matches the world, we are presented with a vision of the world as comprising and determined by facts.[5] This "world of facts," to borrow the description from a recent research on Wittgenstein's philosophy, "floats in a space of possibilities, and true propositions, reporting those facts, are surrounded by a space of meaningful but false propositions."[6] Curiously, how one comes to know whether a proposition "is true" or "is false" is a problem that is not addressed; it is simply assumed *a priori* that one knows what is true and what is false. For many, and especially those of us who are involved in theological reflection, Wittgenstein's postulation about language and its relation to reality naturally raises the all-important question of truth.

It is all too well known that in the later phase of his philosophical enterprise, Wittgenstein has had a change of view with regard to language. I have discussed this in chapter 2 and considered the various reasons why he had found the so-called "picture" theory inadequate. For our present purposes, we shall single out just one of the reasons for further mention. It is the issue he has had with the premise that there is a one-for-one correspondence between the simples of language and of reality. Something of his dissatisfaction with that feature is conveyed in the following passage:

> But what are the simple constituent parts of which reality is composed?—What are the simple constituent parts of a chair?— The bits of wood of which it is made? Or the molecules, or the atoms?—"Simple" means: not composite. And here the point is: in what sense "composite"? It makes no sense at all to speak absolutely of the "simple parts of a chair."[7]

5. *TLP* 1.11.

6. McCutcheon, *Religion within the Limits of Language Alone*, 10.

7. *PI* 47.

Accordingly, he introduces another manner of conceiving language which may be conveniently designated "meaning as use." This is the idea that what gives words or sentences meaning is not their correspondence with objects or states of affairs but their use in everyday activities. Wittgenstein himself offers a summary of that notion as follows, "For a *large* class of cases—though not for all—in which we employ the word "meaning" it can be defined thus: the meaning of a word is its use in the language."[8] With this shift of focus—from correspondence to use—the question of what counts as true or false arises even more strongly to the fore. Unlike the "picture theory" of language, judgement about a proposition with respect to its truth or falsity is no longer simply a reflection of an already given order, that is, in the form of objects. Determining whether words or signs of language are true or false now requires an investigation into their use within a definite language system. As Derek Bolton has pointed out, "If the use of a sign is to constitute judgement, there must be 'correct' applications of the sign, contrasted with 'incorrect.'"[9]

These initial remarks may have seemed to suggest that the question of what is true and what is false is only incidental to Wittgenstein's philosophical concerns. That would be quite mistaken. In fact, the question of truth is ever before him, constituting a key element in his work. As we shall see, his views and arguments with respect to truth in both phases of his philosophical life are no musings casually offered; rather, they are premised upon tacit, even pre-conceived, assumptions of what is required to call a statement "true." For instance, what Wittgenstein says in *TLP* about propositions being contingent seems determined by some *a priori* concepts of truth and falsity. It is thus understandable for Hans-Johann Glock (b. 1960) to make the claim in his dictionary article that "there is no theory of truth which has not been ascribed to Wittgenstein."[10] Still having Wittgenstein in mind, Glock further remarks,

> He has been "credited" with a coherence theory, a pragmatic theory, a consensus theory. The reality of the matter is straightforward. The early Wittgenstein developed a sophisticated version of the correspondence theory, while the later Wittgenstein, together with Ramsey, pioneered the redundancy theory.[11]

8. *PI* 43.
9. Bolton, *Approach to Wittgenstein's Philosophy*, 136.
10. Glock, *Wittgenstein Dictionary*, 365.
11. Glock, *Wittgenstein Dictionary*, 365.

That in Wittgenstein's major works certain underlying theories of truth have been detected and analyzed is also an indication that the "truth" theme has been much ruminated upon, never mind that scholars and commentators on Wittgenstein are not agreed as to which theory of truth should properly be ascribed to him or to which period of his philosophy. Later in the chapter, we shall have opportunity to consider some of the theories which are said to have guided Wittgenstein in his conception of what truth is.

Our Tasks

Before proceeding further, I should explain why the question of truth, besides being important, is relevant to our overall consideration of the place of language in speaking about God. My earlier discussion has underlined the priority of meaning over truth. This is correct as far as it goes; it is, however, not intended to sidestep concerns about the truth or falsity of particular religious concepts. Indeed, our understanding of a statement is facilitated by our having some knowledge of what it would have to obtain for it to be true, and possibly how it is to be verified. Moreover, in arguing—as I do in my work—that religious language is fact-stating (though not revealing or disclosing all there is to know about the divine reality), I cannot expect to duck the question of its truth or falsity. The language-user not only has to distill fact from "noise," he or she may even have to negotiate an agreement on what fact is. Thus, taking up the truth question here is required of us. On the part of Wittgenstein, meaning and truth are never collapsed into a single whole. He distinguishes between them in the following remark:

> If I were to say "I have never been on the moon—but that I may be mistaken" that would be idiotic. For even the thought that I might have been transported there, by unknown means . . . would not give me any right to speak of a possible mistake here.[12]

In the present chapter, we shall attempt to get a grip on what Wittgenstein means by "truth" or by the predicate "is true," terms he regularly uses in his writings. Our study will necessarily draw us into an engagement with some of the theories of truth attributed to Wittgenstein and whether his position is more reflective of realism or anti-realism.

12. *OC* 662; see also 630–31.

We shall, however, not be drawn into the debate between realists and anti-realists. As truth and language are vitally related (via meaning), some passing, but by no means insouciant, attention will be given to the role played by the latter in the service of the former. Attention to the metaphysical question "What is truth?" seems required of us for reasons I will state later, so a response to this enduring issue will be included. The whole purpose of our present study is to gain not only an understanding of truth as an epistemic concept, but also an understanding of the relationship between truth and language.

What Is Truth?

We begin by attending to a vexatious question in philosophical discussions about truth—"What is truth?"—a question famously put to Jesus by the Roman Procurator, Pontius Pilate (John 18:38).[13] In doing so we shall be able to set the stage for considering Wittgenstein's account of truth, and also introduce some of the standing issues that are essential for understanding truth-as-a-theological-problem. In his book, *Trinity and Truth*, Bruce D. Marshall makes a distinction which he thinks is important in talk about truth. He posits that there is a difference between asking what truth is and asking what is true.[14] The former is concerned with *defining* what truth is or comprises, whereas the latter is concerned with how one goes about *deciding* whether a particular belief is true. To be sure, both questions are closely related with one another, though often confused. The distinction, Marshall contends, serves a useful function. He writes,

> By itself, an account of what it is for the Christian community's beliefs to be true will not necessarily enable anyone, including Christians, to decide whether those beliefs are actually true. Decisions about the truth of beliefs or utterances require not simply a characterization of truth, but criteria of truth, by appeal to which we can distinguish true beliefs and utterances

13. The general opinion about him is that he was not at all keen to probe deeper into how truth should be determined; indeed, he seems uninterested even in the very subject itself, mouthing out the question only to cut short Jesus' talk about bearing witness to the truth.

14. He tells us that such a distinction has become commonplace in philosophical discussions, though in practice it is not always observed. See Marshall, *Trinity and Truth*, 6, 8.

from false ones, those to which our characterization of truth applies from those to which it does not.[15]

Be that as it may, I cite this distinction to indicate that in asking the question "What is truth?" we are concerned with getting at a characterization of truth, that is, with defining what truth is. What is being asked is: what do we mean to say of a sentence, a belief or a claim, that it is true? While the other question—"what is true?"—is not really a question about truth at all; it does not analyze "truth" or "is true" in any way, being chiefly concerned about *criteria* for deciding the truth or otherwise of a claim or statement.[16]

Importance of the Truth Question

The question that so troubled Pilate, even though he either did not want or wait for an answer, is of course not original to him.[17] It had been asked by philosophers and thinkers since the earliest times; indeed, it is still very much with us. Some reasons for its prevalence come easily to mind. Essentially, to ask about truth is to raise the question of being, or if you prefer, the question of reality. What we demand in the asking, as Martin Heidegger (1889–1976) tells us, "is an answer to the question as to where we stand today" or "what our situation is today."[18] According to Heidegger, when the early philosophers inquired into the question of truth they were not concerned with truth "in the sense of a theory of knowledge," but with it as "the science that considers beings as beings, that is, with regard to their being."[19] We further learn from him that there was already in those pre-critical days an assumption that "being actually 'goes together' with truth."[20] Thus, we may say it is our latter-day confusion of truth with knowledge that has spawned the theory that truth has "the structure of an agreement between knowing and the

15. Marshall, *Trinity and Truth*, 6, 8.

16. Compare Kirkham, *Theories of Truth*, 26–27. Kirkham distinguishes between theories of truth and theories of justification. The latter, he says, "neither state the necessary and sufficient conditions for truth nor give the meaning of 'truth.'" While he is correct to draw the line, I do not think we should be too pedantic over the matter.

17. For not staying for an answer, Pilate was complimented by Austin, who remarks, "Pilate was in advance of his time" (Austin, "Truth," 111).

18. Heidegger, "On the Essence of Truth," 296.

19. Heidegger, *Being and Time*, 197.

20. Heidegger, *Being and Time*, 197.

object in the sense of a correspondence of one being (subject) to another (object)."[21] Another reason why the truth question dies hard has to do with what truth inherently is. Given its vital connections with human concerns such as language, thought and action, truth is the key to how we think about the world and how we live in it. Many issues of life relate to truth, such that they rely on or are impinged upon by notions about what truth is. For instance, truth and belief are so deeply wound together that when one tells another about what one believes, the implication is that those beliefs are held to be true. It also appears that we cannot do without the concept of truth, for, as Donald Davidson (1917–2003) has asserted, "without the idea of truth we would not be thinking creatures, nor would we understand what it is for someone else to be a thinking creature."[22] This partially explains why whenever we express an opinion, make an assertion, or report an incident and so forth, we presuppose the notion of truth—even though the word is not actually used. Last but not least, the Christian religion which makes claims to having true beliefs about God has long been concerned about truth; indeed, in its theological reflection and praxis, truth is what it essentially seeks. Thus, it is certainly more than a truism for the Christian to say that "one cannot have the concept of belief without having the concept of truth."[23]

Characterization of Truth

"What is truth?" will continue to be asked despite the many attempts over the centuries to give it a proper answer. One of the most straightforward characterizations of truth comes from the pen of Aristotle who writes, "To say of what is that it is not, or of what is not that it is, is false, while to say of what is that it is, and of what is not that it is not, is true."[24] Though so simple, the definition has triggered an array of questions: What do we mean by "say"? What is "is"? What is its negation? How does what we say relate to what is?[25] Up to the present time, opinions are still divided as to whether Aristotle's characterization of truth is to be understood as indicating a correspondence view of truth, or to be interpreted in a

21. Heidegger, *Being and Time*, 201.

22. Davidson, *Truth, Language, and History*, 16.

23. Marshall, *Trinity and Truth*, 10.

24. Aristotle, *Metaphysics* IV, 7.

25. Long, *Speaking of God*, 1.

deflationary way. St. Augustine's classic definition of truth—"That is *true* which is"—has also been critically looked at, and found to be inadequate for "speaking about the *truth* of things" only.[26] The upshot of this sort of characterization of truth is that the predicate "is true" is taken as more or less synonymous with "is real," leading to talk about "the truth" as roughly the same as talk about "the ultimately real." The practice of using the two predicate terms of "is true" and "is real" inter-changeably is especially common among philosophers and thinkers. Plato, for instance, uses the two terms as virtual synonyms in *The Republic* and many other contexts. Then there is Philo of Alexandria (25 BCE–50 CE) who likens God—whom he believes to be the true God—to a coin that is genuine rather than counterfeit. Even Hume takes truth to consist in agreement to "either the real relations of ideas, or to real existence and matter of fact."[27] In a discussion on the "rootedness" of truth in *The Nature of Doctrine*, George Lindbeck proposes that we do not think of the correspondence of religious propositions to reality as an attribute that the propositions have but as "a function of their role in constituting a form of life, a way of being in the world, which itself corresponds to the Most Important, the Ultimately Real."[28] In the context of what he has written, the expression "the Ultimately Real" refers to God who is also Truth. Lindbeck whose treatment of truth will be further discussed later, is among many contemporary thinkers who have attempted (rightly, to me) to characterize truth by underpinning it with something simpler or clearer to comprehend. Their efforts may not prove to be entirely satisfactory; but this can only be expected given the nature of truth. It would, however, be wrongheaded if all attempts to characterize truth are given up. Thus, though G. E. Moore, Bertrand Russell, Frege, Tarski, and others have said that truth is "an indefinable concept" they have not refrained from writing about it and trying to relate them to other concepts like belief, desire, cause and action.[29] Nor should we.

26. Aquinas, *Summa Theologiae* 1.16.1.

27. Hume, *Treatise of Human Nature*, 527.

28. *ND*, 65.

29. See Davidson, *Truth, Language, and History*, 21.

Truth as a Person

We turn next to the notion of "truth as a person," a notion which must seem strange to those who are not identified or associated with the Christian religion. Both the Roman Catholic and the Protestant traditions are wholly united in maintaining just such a notion, principally derived from the Gospel according to John. To be sure, saying "truth-as-a-person" or "truth-is-a-person" does require some explication if we are to use the expression to more fully capture the Johannine logic. That truth is personal is of course a basic claim. Thus, truth is not merely an abstract idea, a concept or even a fact. Most importantly, truth is a person and this person is none other than Jesus of Nazareth who has said, "I am the way, and the truth, and the life" (John 14:6). Yet in John's Gospel, Jesus is also presented as *not* being the truth all by himself. For instance, he is said to be "full of grace and truth" (1:14) having come from the Father. And just as the law was given through the prophet Moses, "grace and truth came through Jesus Christ" (1:17). He himself speaks of another whom he would send after his departure—"the Spirit of truth who comes from the Father" (15:26). Then in a response to Pilate's famous question about truth, Jesus discloses his life's mission: "For this I was born, and for this I came into the world, to testify to the truth. Everyone who belongs to the truth listens to my voice" (18:37). From these considerations has emerged a particular Christian worldview that (a) the idea of truth cannot be separated from the person of truth, namely Jesus Christ; (b) Jesus is "the truth" only in virtue of his unique relation to God the Father;[30] and (c) truth is not a thing to be discovered, rather, it is an encounter with a person. Though unique in the details of its tenets, the so-called Christian concept probably draws inspiration from Plato for whom truth is transcendental, and is related to Being itself, the highest Being, the One, the Good, the True, and the Beautiful. Returning to the exchange between Pilate and Jesus,[31] the poignancy of the narrative should not be lost on us: Pilate's inability to see in Jesus the face of truth even as he asked to know what the truth is.

---

30. Marshall, *Trinity and Truth*, 2.

31. We may note that a recent study of the text of the Fourth Gospel has suggested a heavy debt to Stoicism and Platonism. See Engberg-Pedersen, *John and Philosophy*, 60–64.

Truth Skepticism

This brings us to the issue of skepticism directed at the concept of truth. This sort of skepticism has acquired an appellation, namely "truth skepticism." In his discussion on "Forms of Truth Skepticism," Scott Soames (b. 1946) uses the term to cover a wide range of skeptical views that question the notion of truth, including skepticism about whether there is such a thing as truth, and skepticism about whether truth is knowable, theoretically fruitful, or definable.[32] Skepticism as a philosophical school of thought or method is no new thing: it has a long and influential history going back to Socrates.[33] It is not a single position; there are different depths to it.[34] Shallow forms of skepticism mildly deny that we know a few of things we claim to know, while the deepest form denies we can know anything at all. There is also a radical form, which not only asserts that we cannot know anything at all, it includes the claim that we cannot know about knowing anything. Yet, as A. C. Grayling (b. 1949) has appropriately pointed out, "skepticism is not well described as [merely] doubt or denial, nor is it properly understood without limitation of subject matter. Rather, it is best and most sharply characterized as a motivated challenge, in a specified area of discourse, to the makers of epistemic claims in that discourse."[35] For this reason—that truth skepticism operates within a specified area of discourse, namely the discourse on truth, and has influenced our notion of truth and caused different metaphysical and epistemological views to emerge in response to its challenge—we must linger a little longer upon it.

It must seem reasonable to recognize that the assault on truth is probably what has led many thinkers towards skepticism. Given that we know truth generally has had a good press—it is almost always regarded as a good thing and of intrinsic value—we must ask the question: why has it come under attack, with its importance challenged or diminished? Davidson in an essay entitled "Truth Rehabilitated" seems to have a ready answer.[36] According to him, a "categorical mistake" on the part of

32. Soames, *Understanding Truth*, 20.

33. Socrates is noted for his skeptical claim that he knows nothing, or at least, nothing worthwhile.

34. See Lehrer, *Theory of Knowledge*, 205–6.

35. Grayling, *Scepticism and the Possibility of Knowledge*, 171.

36. "Truth Rehabilitated," first delivered in October 1997, is now published as a chapter in Davidson, *Truth, Language, and History*, 3–17.

philosophy to regard truth as an object has had the effect of emblazoning certain philosophers to "represent truth as something grander than it is, or to endow it with powers it does not have" and claim for themselves that as philosophers they "were privy to some special or foundational species of truth without which science could not hope to advance."[37] There arose naturally a negative reaction to such pretensions to superior access to truths from the other disciplines; some in philosophy were uneasy too. Davidson cites Friedrich Nietzsche (1844–1900) and John Dewey (1859–1952) as representatives of the philosophers who reacted, and who did so by undertaking a re-evaluation of the concept of truth. In the example Davidson gives—that of Dewey's—truth was redefined to be something of which we approve, or that which we think is good or useful. Dewey's declaration—"a belief or theory is true, if and only if, it promotes human affairs"[38]—became a highly influential slogan despite its reductionism. As one who is concerned about the confusion caused by those who made the categorical mistake and who is desirous of restoring the concept of truth to its key role in understanding the world, Davidson offers a corrective, "Truth isn't an object, and so it can't be true; truth is a concept, and is intelligibly attributed to things like sentences, utterances, beliefs and propositions, entities which have a propositional content."[39]

Perhaps a more formidable factor contributing to the rise of truth skepticism is the philosophical view that one can never be absolutely certain of the truth of any sentence or statement. Why is certainty elusive? In his book, *Creation Out of Nothing*, Don Cupitt, drawing inspiration from Michel de Montaigne (1533–1592), writes:

> For various reasons we can never be quite certain of the truth of any proposition, *p*. For (*a*) *p* is not self-evident. There are so many opinions held about everything in this uncertain world that we will always be able to find someone who disputes *p*. Furthermore, (*b*) such is the nature of human debate that a clever advocate can always counter the arguments for any particular point of view by developing an equally rational-sounding case for the opposite point of view. . . . And finally, (*c*) *p* can never be completely proved from its premises *q* and *r* because such a proof would require us either to accept *q* and *r* (or *their* premises) dogmatically and without proof, or to find

37. Davidson, *Truth, Language, and History*, 3–4.

38. Davidson, *Truth, Language, and History*, 3–4.

39. Davidson, *Truth, Language, and History*, 3–4.

p somehow hidden within *q* and *r*, as in the syllogism. The only other possibility is an infinite regress, from *q* and *r* back to *s, t, u,* and *v*, and so on forever. So nothing can ever be completely and transparently proved all the way back.[40]

In my view, Cupitt has made quite a strong case for the nihilistic conclusions that he then goes on to draw—nothing in the world and in life is fixed or sacrosanct. If the making of the world according to Kant is conceptual (that is, with the mind imposing concepts upon what we experience), it is linguistic to Cupitt. Thus, for the latter, it is "only within and by means of language [that] the world and humanity get constituted as formed and intelligible realities."[41] In that world with which he is now confronted, "everything is contingent, a product of history and open to reassessment, including all my own ideas about God and metaphysics. There are no guarantees and no certainties. Nothing is entrenched and everything is negotiable."[42] What then is the upshot of all this for the notion of truth? While truth is not denied, it is simply deflated as "the property of being true."[43] Cupitt casts doubt on the old belief of truth as One, objective, absolute and unchanging. Instead of us continuing to think of truth as something given from beyond, he urges us to think of truth as "personal" and as "something plural, something generated by the play of language, something that we ourselves create and continually recreate."[44] This particular perspective, he adds, comes from the *practice* of working at the various local uses of "truth." While on the subject of world making, Cupitt also mentions the option of materialism advanced by Karl Marx (1818–1883) whose standing claim has been that there has to be a substratum of formless matter out there in the first place "for human consciousness to arise from and for human labor to work upon."[45] But then, as Cupitt rightly observes the swing back in modern thought is not to materialism but to a qualified form of it, namely, "semiotic materialism," which is the materialism of the sign.[46]

40. Cupitt, *Creation out of Nothing*, 24.

41. Cupitt, *Creation out of Nothing*, 10.

42. Cupitt, *Creation out of Nothing*, 16.

43. Cupitt, *Creation out of Nothing*, 40.

44. Cupitt, *Creation out of Nothing*, 85.

45. Cupitt, *Creation out of Nothing*, 10,12.

46. Cupitt, *Creation out of Nothing*, 10, 12.

The skeptical argument against truth, it must be admitted is as robust as it is formidable. We are, as Cupitt reminds us, "spoken by language" and it is language "that alone gives us the classifications by which we order our world."[47] Being thus constituted, we are unable to step out of our own skins to have access to any extra-linguistic meanings and truths. We are urged by Richard Rorty, if I read him correctly, to drop the whole idea of truth as if it were out there awaiting to be discovered. He writes,

> To say that truth is not out there is simply to say that where there are no sentences there is no truth, that sentences are elements of human languages, and that human languages are human creations. Truth cannot be out there—cannot exist independently of the human mind—because sentences cannot so exist, or be out there. The world is out there, but descriptions of the world are not. Only descriptions of the world can be true or false.[48]

The Early Wittgenstein's View of Truth

Let us now return to Wittgenstein and consider where he stands in all this. As mentioned in my introductory remarks, the question of truth has been an inevitable one for the philosophy of Wittgenstein, early and late. To be sure, Wittgenstein's main concern has been with the "logic of language" and the proper use of language in clarifying thought.[49] It may be recalled that in his two landmark works, he has given hints of having been beset by a linguistic muddle: in *TLP*, he pinpoints it as a "misunderstanding of the logic of our language"[50] and in *PI*, it is "a misinterpretation of our forms of language."[51] Recall, too, that Wittgenstein has been widely credited for the celebrated "linguistic turn," a thought revolution which constructively moved contemporary philosophy from a concern with the question of truth to that of meaning.[52] Still, and as earlier noted, all

---

47. Cupitt, *Creation out of Nothing*, 35.

48. Rorty, *Contingency, Irony, and Solidarity*, 5.

49. This is also the view of Martin, *From Nietzsche to Wittgenstein*, 173. He observes that Wittgenstein's "tremendous drive to get clear about the logic of language is manifested in all the writings right up to the end of his life."

50. *TLP*, p3.

51. *PI* 111.

52. The question of truth is a function of the relationship between language and reality, while the question of meaning is an intra-systematic question of coherence. For

through the different phases of his philosophizing, the question of truth remains one of his ongoing concerns. In the pages of *TLP* we find him vigorously working out what conditions are necessary for determining the truth or falsehood of a proposition.[53] For good measure, in that same work he even throws in an analogy about an imagined black spot on white paper, to illustrate that to be able to say "*p*" is true or false is already to have made a presupposition about the circumstances for calling "*p*" true or false.[54] In his later works, while continuing to give a sustained treatment to the question of meaning, he returns every so often to the question of truth, seeking to render it clear for us. Not surprisingly, there is unanimity among scholars and writers that truth in Wittgenstein is neither denied nor dismissed; and that he even believes it is possible to discover truth. Where we find them dissenting is over which theory or theories of truth should properly be attributed to him to account for his notion of truth. To pursue one of our aims in this chapter, namely, the clarification of the concept of truth in Wittgenstein, I propose that we set out and consider his attitudes to truth during both his early and later periods of thought.

Scholarly opinion on Wittgenstein's conception of truth is almost unanimous in affirming that the early Wittgenstein presupposes a correspondence theory of truth. Paul Horwich (b. 1947), for example, in his essay "Wittgenstein on Truth" points out that a correspondence theory of truth seems to jump out of the pages of *TLP*.[55] Glock, whom we have cited above, ascribes to the early Wittgenstein a correspondence theory too, though in a later work he would argue that the standard interpretations on correspondence have been mistaken.[56] P. M. S. Hacker has detected (i) a "variant of metaphysical realism in the *Tractatus* ontology of simple sempiternal objects, of complexes and of facts" which is learnt from Russell and Frege, and (ii) an "assumption that the fundamental role of words is to name entities (although this role was denied to logical operators and to categorial expressions) and of sentences to describe

---

an explanation on why the latter takes precedence over the former, see my discussion on the "linguistic turn" in chapter 1.

53. E.g., *TLP* 4.024.

54. See *TLP* 4.063.

55. To be sure, Horwich has had some reservations about the applicability of that label. He prefers to call Wittgenstein's theory "a limited correspondence theory of *representation*." See Horwich, "Wittgenstein on Truth," 96–98.

56. See Glock, "Truth in the *Tractatus*," 345–68.

how things are in reality."[57] These factors, Hacker notes, unite to define Wittgenstein's thinking that "there must be a connection of meaning between words and the entities they name, that language acquires content by means of such a connection with reality."[58] The account here given by Hacker is clearly a version of the correspondence theory. More examples could be adduced but the point is that most commentators on Wittgenstein are agreed that a correspondence theory has provided the basis for his early conception of truth.

Now the correspondence theory of truth is a theory that has a long and enduring history. It is still much favored and is thought to best capture the concept of truth. It may be briefly explained as the view that truth is a relationship of correspondence between words, ideas or beliefs (known as "truth bearers") on the one hand, and reality (or "truth maker") on the other. In the relationship, there is a "match" between the two different sorts of things, between truth-bearers and the truth-maker. So, words, ideas or beliefs are true if and only if they "copy" their reality, to use an expression by William James (1842–1910).[59] Aquinas is often cited as a major figure in Christian theology who has thought about truth in terms of a relationship of correspondence. As well as declaring *veritas est adaequatio rei et intellectus*[60] (truth is the equation of thing and intellect), he also claims, "since the true is in the intellect in so far as it is conformed to the object understood, the aspect of the true must needs pass from the intellect to the object understood, so that also the thing understood is said to be true in so far as it has some relation to the intellect."[61] An alternative way of spelling out the correspondence relation is to say that a proposition or statement is true if and only if what it is is isomorphic with that which it is about. Or, as David Fergusson (b. 1956) contends, "what truth we do confess is established ultimately by the way things are."[62] Sometimes, the theory is given the following formulaic expression: "It is true that p if and only if p."[63]

---

57. Hacker, *Wittgenstein: Connections and Controversies*, 6.

58. Hacker, *Wittgenstein: Connections and Controversies*, 6.

59. See Lecture 6 in James, *Pragmatism*.

60. Aquinas, *Questiones Disputatae de Veritate* 1.1–3.

61. Aquinas, *Summa Theologiae* 1.16.1.

62. Fergusson, "Meaning, Truth and Realism," 198.

63. Rundle points out that Dummett has suggested that the correspondence theory expresses one important feature of the concept of truth that is missing from the formula, namely, "that a statement is true only if there is something in the world *in*

Historically, this understanding of truth is also known in philosophical circles as "realism."[64] The reason for this is instructive. The correspondence theory of truth relies on there being objects which are real, or states of affairs (facts) which are true. Andrew Newman (b. 1948) who professes to stand within a tradition that is realist about universals, explains, "There is an obvious connection between realism about universals and the correspondence theory of truth, since realism about universals implies that there is something in the world other than particulars in virtue of which sentences and propositions are true."[65] It is tempting to simply ascribe the correspondence theory of truth to Wittgenstein on the basis of his realist convictions at the time of writing *TLP*. Certainly, a correspondence theory of truth of any sort is dependent on some form of realism. But the relationship between the two positions is not one that is mutually necessary. Christopher Insole helps to clarify matters:

> Although the idea of reality as what is there anyway may go naturally with talk of "truth fitting the facts," there is no compulsion on the realist to flesh out this metaphorical talk with any detailed articulation of "truth as correspondence." Realism can be stated without invoking any explanatory or substantial notion of truth. As we saw . . . realism is quite compatible with minimalist and deflationary accounts of truth.[66]

All the same, the correspondence theory of truth is not without problems. As our intention here is not to evaluate the theory in detail, only a few major issues will be looked at. A common objection to the theory, one which we have briefly discussed in the section on skepticism, is that truth is epistemologically neither accessible, nor ascertainable. But even if this were granted, it would still not follow that the theory of truth in the sense of correspondence with reality is invalidated. Secondly, the correspondence theory is often challenged on the grounds that the specific relation of correspondence or agreement is vague, or even incoherent.

---

virtue of which it is true" (*Wittgenstein and Contemporary Philosophy of Language*, 153). Horwich, too, has criticized this formula as "mysterious" (Horwich, "Wittgenstein on Truth," 101).

64. The two main forms of realism are the transcendent realism of Plato, Frege, and others, and the immanent realism of Russell, Armstrong, and perhaps Aristotle. For more on these forms of realism, see Newman, *Correspondence Theory of Truth*, 20–32.

65. Newman, *Correspondence Theory of Truth*, 2.

66. Insole, *Realist Hope*, 83.

"Truth means, as a matter of course, agreement, correspondence of idea and fact," Dewey says, but he immediately goes on, "but what do agreement, correspondence mean?"[67] Here, we may usefully reference an analysis of the correspondence theory by Garth L. Hallett in which he compares two different ways of considering "correspondence." He observes, "The traditional thesis position was right in characterizing truth as correspondence, in the straightforward sense of similarity, but wrong in supposing that the similarity holds between likenesses in the minds of believers or speakers and the things they believe or speak about."[68] Hallett's differentiation is helpful but I am not sure if it can successfully overcome the objection of vagueness because there is still the challenge of explaining how beliefs and reality are similar "in the straightforward sense of similarity." Then there is the conundrum of understanding how words and statements can possibly correspond to things in the world. Indeed, how do the words "snow is white" correspond to the fact that snow is white on the ground? This brings us to a final objection. Heidegger's problem with the theory of correspondence is that correspondentism perpetrates violence upon objects. How so? "By defining truth in terms of the correspondence between one's ideas and a thing's fundamental reality, one may end up identifying that fundamental reality with one's ideas about it, thereby making oneself its ultimate measure and cutting it down to the size of one's categories. The danger, then, is that if one understands truth in terms of an isomorphism relation between one's ideas and an object's fundamental reality, such that one identifies the truth of, say, a cat with one's idea of felinity, the truth of a woman with one's idea of femininity, and so on, then one may make one's antecedent ideas the measure of these objects and thereby do violence to them."[69] One has to admit that Heidegger's objection, rendered in the clear words of Kevin W. Hector, deserves to be taken seriously by all.

We must now ask the pertinent question: does *TLP* contain the correspondence theory of truth? Our response will be briefly presented as much has been already said to indicate that the early Wittgenstein did think of truth in terms of correspondence. In his work on the correspondence theory of truth, Newman tells us that Wittgenstein makes no formal announcement as to what truth consists in, even if

67. Dewey cited in Davidson, "Structure and Content of Truth," 280.
68. Hallett, *Theology within the Bounds of Language*, 42.
69. Hector, *Theology without Metaphysics*, 207.

the notions of truth and falsity are main features in his philosophical discourse.[70] He also mentions that though Wittgenstein's work is devoted to the correspondence theory of truth, he does not use the term "correspondence theory of truth."[71] Be that as it may, I shall try to show that against the backdrop of his discussion of the proposition in *TLP*, a correspondence theory of truth seems to make sense. Though it is not my intention in this discussion to provide an exegesis, some references to the philosopher's text are inevitable.

The earlier sections of *TLP* seem to set out an ontology of sorts, maintaining, as we have noted, that language and reality are linked. Propositions of language are thus thought to have the capacity to picture reality or mirror its objects. In Wittgenstein's own words, "A proposition is a picture of reality. A proposition is a model of the reality as we imagine it."[72] Here are a few more statements which are explicit about that particular feature,

> The sign through which we express the thought I call the propositional sign. And the proposition is the propositional sign in its projective relation to the world.[73]

> In a proposition a thought can be expressed in such a way that elements of the propositional sign correspond to the objects of the thought.[74]

> The configuration of objects in a situation corresponds to the configuration of simple signs in the propositional sign.[75]

> The proposition shows its sense. The proposition shows how things stand, if it is true. And it says, that they do so stand.[76]

To show why we think a correspondence theory of truth should be ascribed to Wittgenstein rather than some other theory, we must ask how a proposition can represent a situation in the world. The answer, based on what we have learned about propositions, is that a proposition names

70. Newman, *Correspondence Theory of Truth*, 53.

71. Newman, *Correspondence Theory of Truth*, 10.

72. *TLP* 4.01.

73. *TLP* 3.12.

74. *TLP* 3.2.

75. *TLP* 3.21.

76. *TLP* 4.022.

or stands for a state of affairs, not unlike how a realistic picture, or a map, or an architect's model, represents what it does. Following many other scholars, some—and I cite a very recent example in Istvan Danka—have read *TLP* as establishing "a one-to-one correspondence between the realm of facts and propositions, claiming that the two are isomorphic."[77] This is the famous "picture theory" which we alluded to in the beginning. "Clearly," as Horwich rightly asserts, "*depiction of a possible fact* is to be treated as a form of *correspondence* to it."[78] To conclude, we may aptly say of the early Wittgenstein that his conception of truth is supplemented if not undergirded by a correspondence theory of truth.

The Later Wittgenstein's View of Truth

Wittgenstein's view on truth in his later phase is markedly different from the one he has earlier held. The shift in his thinking, we have noted, is known to have begun soon after the completion of *TLP*, or at least after his disavowal of the "picture theory" of language. Whereas the "picture theory" has been put forth initially as a fundamental guide to conceiving the nature of language, it is now viewed in *PI* as "a primitive idea of the way language functions."[79] The new thinking differs from the old in an important way, namely, that the signs of language are thought to have meaning not on account of their correspondence with objects but because of the use they are put to. A succinct exposition of Wittgenstein's revised position by James K. A. Smith in which two features of language use and the dynamics of meaning are highlighted, is relevant here:

> First, language is *used* for something. It is employed for some end, spoken within a community of practice that has some *telos*, that is trying to get something done. . . . Language use is always caught up in teleological communities of practice, which means that even reference and ostensive teaching are always already embedded in wider contexts of action and practice. Second, in some sense language and meaning are *bigger* than words. Language and meaning are bound up with a context of practice that is more than the repertoire of our words, and that

---

77. Danka, "A Case Study on the Limits of Ironic Redescription," 70.

78. Horwich, "Wittgenstein on Truth," 98.

79. *PI* 2.

penumbra of practices and action is essential to constituting the
meaning of our words.[80]

What Smith does not mention, but presumably knows, is the ramification
for the concept of truth that comes with the change in Wittgenstein's
philosophy. Given that truth is rooted in language, one's concept of
language will inevitably affect and bear on one's concept of truth. In
Wittgenstein's case, the impact on his concept of truth that results from
his changed position concerning language has been very considerable.

Wittgenstein, we have noted, is unabashed about admitting that
mistakes have been made in *TLP*. In one of his self-criticisms which
appears in *PI*, he describes his earlier notion of the proposition as "a bad
picture." He invites his reader to reason with him,

> Now it looks as if the definition—a proposition is whatever
> can be true or false—determined what a proposition was, by
> saying: what fits the concept "true," or what the concept "true"
> fits, is a proposition. So it is as if we had a concept of true and
> false, which we could use to determine what is and what is not
> a proposition. What *engages* with the concept of truth (as with a
> cogwheel), is a proposition. But this is a bad picture.[81]

On the view being criticized, the concepts "true" and "false" are held to
be prior to the concept "proposition." The implication appears to be that
we first operate with a clear concept of truth and falsity, and then on the
basis of that, we decide what is, or, is not, a proposition. Wittgenstein
now comes to realize that the concept of truth and falsity and the concept
of proposition are actually interdependent; one is not necessarily prior
to another. His argument, in words from a paraphrase by Jerry H. Gill,
is as follows, "The concept 'true' is no more prior to, nor independent of,
the concept 'proposition' than the concept 'check' is logically prior to, or
independent of, the concept 'king' in the statement, 'The king in chess is
the piece that one can check.'"[82] Thus, to say, as he has said in *TLP*, that
"a proposition is whatever can be true or false" is simply to say that "we
only predicate 'true' and 'false' of what we call a proposition"—and no
more. To persist in defining or thinking of a proposition as before, that
is, as "whatever can be true or false" is not satisfactory since "we do not
have a grasp of truth and falsity independently of having a conception of

80. Smith, *Who's Afraid of Relativism?*, 45–46.

81. *PI* 136.

82. Gill, "Wittgenstein's Concept of Truth," 72.

the nature of their possible bearers."[83] Or, more succinctly put, we simply cannot get out of our own skins.[84] All three terms used in the discussion, namely "proposition," "true," and "false," should be seen as interrelated in our language. Consequently, Wittgenstein concludes by maintaining that "what a proposition is is in one sense determined by the rules of sentence formation (in English for example), and in another sense by the use of the sign in the language-game."[85] We shall consider these two suggested ways of approaching the proposition.

It is sometimes held that in Wittgenstein the basic contrast between his earlier and later phases "is that between a realist semantics based on truth-conditions, and an anti-realist semantics which settles for assertability or justifiability-conditions."[86] It is then said that he rejects the idea that sentences have truth conditions in favor of assertability conditions. This inference that the question of truth for Wittgenstein is fixed in terms of assertability conditions is mistaken; I suspect it is more the result of a confusion arising from his rejection of the correspondence theory of truth, the now all-too-familiar theory that holds that propositions are true by virtue of their correspondence to objects or facts. The clear fact of the matter is that Wittgenstein does not reject truth conditions; what he does is revise his conception of a truth condition by insisting that truth conditions are determined by conventional rules of sentence formation which tell us the circumstances under which it is correct to predicate "is true" of our statements. It is worth noting Wittgenstein's reason for insisting on rules or grammar. In his early phase, his concern has been to look at language in terms of its possibilities of sense and nonsense, convinced that the "one essence" resident and hidden in all language could be found and "brought to light."[87] The quest "to grasp the incomparable essence of language"[88] is abandoned by the later Wittgenstein who finds that "*essence* is expressed by grammar"[89] rather than in factual propositions. In other words, if we wish to speak of or about what a thing is, that is, what its "essence" is,

83. Rundle, *Wittgenstein and Contemporary Philosophy of Language*, 150.

84. Since I have made this statement more than once in this work, I must qualify that I am not suggesting that there is no reality outside language.

85. *PI* 136.

86. Glock, *Wittgenstein Dictionary*, 382.

87. *PI* 91.

88. *PI* 97.

89. *PI* 371.

we shall not only have to talk about the thing itself, but also how the grammar in which the words we use pertaining to it functions.

The other suggestion by Wittgenstein that a proposition be understood in terms of its use in a "language-game" if adopted, will greatly impact our concept of truth like no other. "The sentence," he has said, "has no sense outside the language-game."[90] What the term "language-game" means has been discussed in chapter 2, so we need not be detained in trying to define it. In any event, like the term "form-of-life," there is really no strict definition to it. However, for our present purposes, let us simply take it to represent "a complete unit of human linguistic behavior," within which the behavior of people and the language they use are closely woven together.[91] As such, it is extremely useful as a methodological tool for illuminating the way language actually operates.

One of the most important insights engendered by the notion of language-games is that context and setting are integrally linked to meaning. Previously under the "picture theory," meaning is the correlation between a word and an object or thing. Meaning is thus a matter of straightforward reference: "A word refers to a thing and the 'hook' between the two is meaning."[92] The notion of language-games, however, conveys a different idea: the meanings of the propositions of language are bound up with a context of practice, and may not be separated from "the actions" into which they are woven. Differently put, a proposition or sentence may have no particular fixed meaning that is always attached to it; instead, its meaning can vary according to the language-game within which it is used and the part it plays in the language-game. Indeed, that same proposition or sentence can even have different meanings in different language-games, as it has no essential core of meaning. Wittgenstein draws on the analogy of the artichoke to illustrate the point he is now making. Like an artichoke which has no essence but many layers of leaves, so there is no essence to all propositions, nor by implication to language itself.[93] Understanding meaning, which makes possible truth, must now require that we look at the language-games, the sentences, the activities, the situation—indeed the larger context—with which they are intertwined. Recall again that Wittgenstein has said that outside a language-game, the

90. Wittgenstein, *Remarks on the Philosophy of Psychology*, 488.

91. Bell, "Wittgenstein and Descriptive Theology," 5.

92. Smith, *Who's Afraid of Relativism?*, 41.

93. *PI* 164.

sentence has no sense.[94] I may not agree with his remarks cited below explaining why one looks for the meaning of an expression by dwelling on the expression itself, but his point that we should always think of the practice with which the expression is used, is well taken:

> There is always the danger of wanting to find an expression's meaning by contemplating the expression itself, and the frame of mind in which one uses it, instead of always thinking of the practice. That is why one repeats the expression to oneself so often, because it is as if one must see what one is looking for in the expression and in the feeling it gives one.[95]

Wittgenstein famously states that "the term 'language-game' is meant to bring into prominence the fact that the speaking of language is part of an activity, or of a form of life."[96] Consequently, and in almost all cases, "the meaning of a word is its use in the language."[97] Against the traditional view that understands language to be independent of human action and to have an ontological groundedness, Wittgenstein's philosophy posits a different view—that language is connected and bound up with human action, and that meaning arises from the way the signs of language are used. In this connection, he writes,

> Giving grounds, however, justifying the evidence, comes to an end;—but the end is not certain propositions' striking us immediately as true, i.e., it is not a kind of seeing on our part; it is *our acting*, which lies at the bottom of the language-game.[98]

Now if meaningful propositions are defined by their use or by "our acting" then meaning should no longer be deemed to be "correlated with that which must be either true or false, and 'truth' becomes just another language-game or games (within the multiplicity of games)."[99] It would thus be simplistic to ground meaning to any sort of reference or representation, or to think of the meaning of a specific word as consisting

---

94. It seems that Frege had said something similar. Compare the remark by Davidson: "Frege said only in the context of a sentence does a word have meaning; in the same vein he might have added that only in the context of the language does a sentence (and therefore a word) have meaning" ("Truth and Meaning," 308).

95. *OC* 601.

96. *PI* 23.

97. *PI* 43.

98. *OC* 204.

99. Martin, *From Nietzsche to Wittgenstein*, 278.

only in the object signified. Glen Martin has made a strong case against Wittgenstein's formerly-held premise about the paradigmatic nature of the proposition. He argues as follows:

> The idea that a proposition pictures the world in such a way as to be true or false was itself just a picture which it seemed could only be applied in one way. Wittgenstein says that it seemed "that the picture forced a particular application upon us." (*PI* 140). But any picture can be applied in some other way: what constitutes isomorphic mapping depends on how one applies that picture. Not only is the notion of a "proposition" not restricted to that of "truth or falsity" but the idea of something being either true or false is itself of no help because *even that picture* has yet to be applied and can be applied in more than one way (that is, the meanings of the words "true" and "false" may vary depending on their application).[100]

The issue concerning the arbitrary nature of truth is one that naturally arises from Wittgenstein's notion of language-games and his idea that "the meaning of a word is its use in the language." To recap, Wittgenstein has pointed out that the meanings of the signs of language are inseparably connected with the practices with which they are interwoven in a language-game. Consequently, "what is true" and "what is false" may vary, depending on their context. His assertion that "meaning is use" shifts the focus from an ontological or referential interpretation of meaning to seeing it as defined by human action. What the assertion further implies has been clearly spelled out by Smith:

> To observe that "meaning is use" is to recognize that meaning is always game-relative—which is to say that meaning is always *conventional*. It depends; more specifically, meaning depends on the conventions of a community of practice—what Wittgenstein variously describes as a "language game" or a "form of life." . . . So the claim that "meaning is use" is, at root, a deeply *social* account of meaning.[101]

Now Wittgenstein himself has anticipated being quizzed: "So you are saying that human agreement decides what is true and what is false?"[102] His immediate response—"It is what human beings *say* that

---

100. Martin, *From Nietzsche to Wittgenstein*, 279.

101. Smith, *Who's Afraid of Relativism?*, 48.

102. *PI* 241.

is true and false; and they agree in the language they use"—reveals an awareness of his interlocutor's criticism that his view has implied a relativistic conception of truth, that is to say, the view that "true" and "false" are simply a matter of agreement in opinions. Brilliantly, he argues that the agreement in question refers to an agreement of opinion about "form of life," not an agreement of opinion about matters of fact. Jerry Gill enlightens us by clarifying that "agreement in form of life is logically prior to agreement about what is and what is not the case" and that "agreements in factual judgement also play an important part in the make-up of a form of life."[103] My own view is that Wittgenstein's critic is clearly mistaken in thinking that the view of truth he seeks to espouse is one that is arbitrary or relativistic. This is, however, not to deny that some form of relativism is rooted in Wittgenstein's philosophy.[104]

We shall turn now to the theory of truth which, by broad scholarly consensus, the later Wittgenstein is said to have explicitly held.[105] This is the so-called deflationary theory.[106] According to Horwich, the term "deflationary" is applied to accounts of truth that emphasize the following features: (i) truth has no traditional explicit definition; (ii) the nature of the concept is implicitly fixed by the way that each statement specifies its own condition for being true; (iii) it is an extremely superficial concept; and (iv) it is merely a useful expressive device.[107] Thus from a deflationary perspective, "truth" is a purely logical concept; the predicate "is true" serving only to express generalizations over sentences, propositions, claims, assertions or beliefs.

---

103. Gill, "Wittgenstein's Concept of Truth," 73. Gill's clarification is based on Wittgenstein's remarks in *PI* 242.

104. Smith, *Who's Afraid of Relativism?*, 40, offers a reasoned defense of "Christian relativism" as being more "attentive to our dependence in ways that realism and representationalism are not." He believes it can better account for aspects of our creaturehood, namely our contingency, dependency, and sociality. See Smith, *Who's Afraid of Relativism?*, 16, 30.

105. Scholars who attribute a deflationary theory to Wittgenstein include Donald Davidson, Hans-Johann Gluck, Paul Horwich, Richard Rorty, Bede Rundle, and James K. A. Smith.

106. There are competing theories of deflationism, namely, the redundancy theory, the minimalist theory, Tarski's theory, the prosentential theory or the disquotation theory. The differences between the varieties need not concern us as they are not significant, nor are they germane to our present discussion. See Horwich, *Truth, Meaning, Reality*, 19–20.

107. Horwich, "Wittgenstein on Truth," 99–100.

Here, it needs to be said that those who advocate deflationism do not necessarily deny truth, nor do they shy away from affirming that some claim or belief is true. But they do "deny that truth involves anything like the kind of *relation* that the correspondence theorist sees at its heart."[108]

Wittgenstein's remarks on "this is how things are" are often cited as providing the clearest evidence for his deflationism.[109] Against the backdrop of a discussion of the proposition, he maintains that to ascribe truth to a proposition is the same as asserting the proposition itself. He writes,

> At bottom, giving "This is how things are" as the general form of propositions is the same as giving the definition: a proposition is whatever can be true or false. For instead of "This is how things are" I could have said "This is true." (Or again "This is false.") But we have
> 'p' is true = p
> 'p' is false = not-p.[110]

On the analysis of "true" and "false" just shown, we have a situation in which the predicates "is true" and "is false" may simply be dispensed with. The reason is all too obvious: they are both redundant, since "p is true" is logically equivalent to "p," and "p is false" is logically equivalent to "not-p." F. P. Ramsey's classic statements are illustrative of what is now known as the principle of redundancy: "It is true that Caesar was murdered" means no more than that Caesar was murdered, and "It is false that Caesar was murdered" means that Caesar was not murdered.[111] Ramsey further adds that "is true" and "is false" are "phrases we sometimes use for emphasis or for stylistic reasons, or to indicate the position occupied by the statement in our argument."[112] If he is right, we would not even require the concept of truth at all. Indeed, why do we even continue to use the term "true" if there is nothing that the truth predicate sets forth which cannot be set forth without it? In any event, Wittgenstein seems to have adopted Ramsey's analysis when he presents the following formulation, "What he says is true = Things are as he says."[113] One might also say being "true"

108. Rundle, *Wittgenstein and Contemporary Philosophy of Language*, 152.

109. *PI* 136.

110. *PI* 136.

111. Ramsey cited in Sahlin, *Philosophy of F. P. Ramsey*, 57–58.

112. Sahlin, *Philosophy of F. P. Ramsey*, 57–58.

113. *PG*, 123.

and "false" are just a matter of being "as stated" or "as denied," so "What he said was no doubt true" becoming "Things were no doubt as he stated" and "What he no doubt said was false" becoming "Things were no doubt not as he stated."[114] Here it is important to clarify that to say that "true" is redundant does not amount to saying the concept of truth is also redundant.

As we might expect, there are issues with the deflationary view of truth. I can think of three, though I believe a detailed analysis of the theory—which is beyond the scope of our present study as well as my competence—may throw up more. Firstly, in spite of the caveat that deflationists are not truth-denying, their claim that the word "true" in a statement is redundant, or that to say a statement is true is merely another way of asserting it, will appear to suggest that we can simply "walk away" from metaphysical and theological questions concerning truth.[115] What this does, if true, is push these questions to the peripherals of intellectual discourse. The upshot is we are no further forward in understanding the concept of truth. Nor does the redundancy approach have anything important to offer on the relation between truth and meaning. In the second place, the elimination of the word "true" seems to serve little purpose, if it simply means the substitution of another phrase in its place. A case can be made for the reversal of the redundancy approach by arguing that the word "true" is more than just an assertion variable: "the term merits a definition applicable in all its occurrences, albeit one which may reveal it as eliminable in certain of these."[116] Thirdly, we would argue that as a theory it is not all-comprehensive for it is not always possible to eliminate the word "true" in a statement. Here is a good example: "Everything that follows from what John just said is true." In this assertion, we do need "true," for we cannot assert everything that follows from what John said.[117] In light of these issues and given what we know of Wittgenstein's aversion to philosophical theorizing, we have good reason to think that he may after all not be as fully deflationary as he is made out to be. That said, the deflationary account of truth should still be recognized for its usefulness in directing us away from thinking

---

114. See Rundle, *Wittgenstein and Contemporary Philosophy of Language*, 150.

115. Long, *Speaking of God*, 271.

116. Rundle, *Wittgenstein and Contemporary Philosophy of Language*, 151.

117. Stoutland, "Wittgenstein," 210–11.

"that truth is a mechanism by which concepts in our heads magically hook onto entities outside of our heads."[118]

Truth after Wittgenstein

In the final section of the chapter, I wish to discuss how truth, as we understand it, relates to language. In particular, I will consider a number of issues of truth with regard to my work—that we may make statements about God which tell us facts about God, but that our words can neither yield a complete explanation nor an exhaustive conception of the divine reality. In considering the issues, I will try to bear in mind the light that Wittgenstein has shed.

1. A Crisis of Truth?

In recent years, it has become something of a commonplace for some commentators within the traditional wing of the Christian religion to raise the alarm that there is a "crisis of truth." Their variable claim is that the notion of truth is being undermined or rejected, or that there is even a "total war on truth itself."[119] While still Pope, Joseph Ratzinger wrote that "our faith is decisively opposed to the attitude of resignation that considers man incapable of truth—as if this were more than he could cope with. This attitude of resignation with regard to truth . . . lies at the heart of the crisis of the West, the crisis of Europe."[120] Postmodernity or more accurately, postmodernism is usually blamed for eroding the foundations of belief by fostering the "shifty" view that there is no such thing as objective reality, truth and so forth.[121] We are accordingly urged to do battle with the postmodernists in preventing further "truth decay" and to return to an embrace of "absolute truth."[122] Actually, in the issue of the treatment of truth by postmodernism, matters are not quite so simple as these commentators have painted. According to Smith, the thrust of postmodernist theorists is not that there is no such thing as truth, but that truth is to be explained in terms of a framework very different to the one

118. Smith, *Who's Afraid of Relativism?*, 27,

119. Mohler, "Modernity's Assault on Truth."

120. Benedict XVI, "Apostolic Journey."

121. Moreland, *Kingdom Triangle*, 77.

122. E.g., Groothuis, *Truth Decay*.

deployed by the traditionalist. The postmodernist theorists, he explains, "don't deny truth, nor do they forfeit the ability to be able to say 'X is true'; they just don't think that truth is a mechanism by which concepts in our heads magically hook onto entities outside of our heads."[123] In keeping with their way of thinking about truth, postmodernists are likely to admit to subscribing to a theory of truth already familiar to us and earlier discussed, namely, the "deflationary" theory, in preference to either the correspondence or the coherence theories. They would typically make the minimalist claim that to assert a statement true is simply to assert the very statement itself.

In view of the misapprehension that postmodernism denies truth, it may be worth noting the clarification by Rorty, probably the most prominent defender of postmodernism, that he is not dismissive of truth:

> To say that we should drop the idea of truth as out there waiting to be discovered is not to say that we have discovered that, out there, there is *no* truth. It is to say that our purposes would be served best by ceasing to see truth as a deep matter, as a topic of philosophical interest, or "true" as a term which repays "analysis."[124]

To dispel any remaining doubts that the postmodernists are not claiming that there is no truth, let us appeal to the witness of another noted postmodernist, Jacques Derrida (1930–2004), who although known for challenging the concept of truth and making it tremble, did not seek "to eradicate the possibility of objective truth."[125] In a remark made within parenthesis, Derrida explicates what truth is: "(truth as an unveiling of that which is in its Being, or as an adequation between a judicative statement and the thing itself.)"[126] His essay "University without Condition" explores the concept of truth under four headings for kinds of truth, namely, adequation, revelation, object of theoretico-constative discourses and poetico-performative events.[127] Then referring to truth as "enigmatic," he remarks, "However enigmatic it may be, the reference to truth remains fundamental enough to be found."[128]

123. Smith, *Who's Afraid of Relativism?*, 27.
124. Rorty, *Contingency, Irony, and Solidarity*, 8 (emphasis added).
125. Knowles, *Beyond Evangelicalism*, 23.
126. Derrida, *Margins of Philosophy*, 322.
127. Derrida, *Without Alibi*, 202–3.
128. Derrida, *Without Alibi*, 202–3.

Admittedly, the postmodernist view of truth will not sit well with those who think of truth as some "thing" that is objectively and silently standing over us to be sought for and discovered. Our unease may have all to do with the way reality is "pictured." According to Charles Taylor, most of us are enthralled to the habit of assuming that our grasp of reality "outside" must come *through* ideas or representations we have *a priori* formed of it "inside" our minds. "We grasp the world through something, what is outside through something inner."[129] Calling this the "inside/outside" (I/O) structuring framework, Taylor outlines the process by which the mind's constructions occur: "The input is combined, computed over, or structured by the mind to construct a view of what lies outside."[130] Under this Descartes-inspired I/O framework, we relate to the world by setting up a certain distinction between inside and outside, seeing knowledge as exclusively grounded in ideas or "representations" which are then given objective status.

The relevance of all this for the purposes of our discussion is not merely that Rorty (or postmodernism) believes in truth and adopts a deflationary approach to it, or that the inside/outside "picture" of knowledge and truth is still insidiously and powerfully at work in shaping our thinking. What I see as having more relevance is, first, the claim by Rorty that "where there are no sentences there is no truth" and secondly, his idea that "most of reality is indifferent to our descriptions of it, and that the human self is created by the use of a vocabulary rather than being adequately or inadequately expressed in a vocabulary."[131] Factoring in his other remarks about truth—that truth is "made" rather than "found" and that truth is a property of sentences or propositions—we may infer that truth for him is more like a human activity which has a particular place within a language game, than a "hard scientific fact," and, that it is not something that simply stands outside our sphere of linguistic signs and concepts awaiting to be discovered. Although traversing slightly different routes of thought, both he and Wittgenstein seem to have arrived at similar conclusions respecting the notion of truth and reality. Both are adamant in their claim that truth is socially, or even better put, linguistically constructed. At the risk of oversimplifying matters, would it not help if I propose a clarification that while truth is indeed objective,

129. Taylor, "Merleau-Ponty and the Epistemological Picture," 26–28.
130. Taylor, "Merleau-Ponty and the Epistemological Picture," 26–28.
131. Rorty, *Contingency, Irony, and Solidarity*, 7.

it however cannot be known objectively? Thus, just like the way we get to know the world, we shall know or encounter truth only linguistically— through texts, representations, conceptions.

This last remark is especially significant for what I have in mind because the question of truth naturally arises when language is used for religious purposes. In the case of lectures, sermons and formulations of doctrine such as creeds, declarations, "statements of faith" or "articles of faith," the question as to the truth or falsity of their claims will surface as a matter of course, once their content or sense is understood by the believer, even if not very fully. The question of truth, however, does not arise in the case of first-order language like prayers, commandments, litanies as these are not statemental—that is, they do not express any propositions. A prayer asking God for healing or blessing, for instance, is an utterance that is neither true nor false. Nor does the question arise for utterances that "do" things—the type which Austin calls "performatives"[132]—such as "I christen this ship the *Queen Elizabeth*" or "I dedicate this building to the glory of God." None of these utterances is either true or false; but the mere act of uttering one has the effect of performing the action specified in that particular utterance. Sherry's interesting example of a non-religious work to illustrate the point that some item may be essential without containing many or even any truths may be cited: the Highway Code—essential for the rules and regulations and recommendations it prescribes for the motorist and yet it contains very few truths.[133]

Other than a few exceptions which we have noted, most instances of the religious use of language presuppose the notion of truth, even if the user herself denies that truth is real or knowable or sets out to use language to bear false witness. That is why the issue of truth in religious language is so crucial and cannot be side-stepped. In the case of doctrines and creedal statements, it may be readily conceded that they "function as informative propositions or truth claims about objective realities."[134] In other words, they purport to disclose important facts and insights concerning God, human existence, the world, the Eschaton, and so forth. Thus, doctrines and creedal statements do play a vital role in defining beliefs, shaping values, and ordering lives. They are generally held as important and true. In consequence, they have drawn different and

132. Austin, *How to Do Things with Words*, 7.

133. Sherry, *Religion, Truth and Language-Games*, 62.

134. *ND*, 16.

varied understandings and interpretations to themselves, and these have in turn generated among the believing communities accord as well as discord—regrettably more of the latter than of the former. The quarrels, acrimonies and even violence among believers over differences rooted in doctrines and teachings are only too well known. It is not surprising that an evaluation of the truth or falsity, accuracy or inaccuracy, and correctness or incorrectness of the claims made is consistently being demanded.

2. Truth-Value

I turn now to a brief consideration of the question of the truth-value of religious language. Let me clarify that we are not concerned with wanting to prove any particular religion or religious belief true. Our burden is rather to understand "truth" as it is claimed by religious statements such as doctrines and creeds to possess. As Wittgenstein puts it, "If a proposition has no sense, nothing corresponds to it, since it does not designate a thing (a truth-value) which might have properties called 'false' or 'true.'"[135]

The question about truth-value has attracted two well-known responses. The first is by R. B. Braithwaite (1900–1990) who takes the view that religious assertions are primarily used to "announce allegiance to a set of moral principles,"[136] and that this "use" (in guiding conduct) renders them meaningful: they are then deemed to have passed the verificationist test.[137] The other response is by those who think that religious reflection and discourse has its own unique criteria of truth. Their basic point is that the word "true" carries a different meaning in religion from its use in ordinary discourse. While it is a fact that language about God or religion is very different from, say, language about science or business, yet it is surely improper to confuse the concept of truth especially when we have sought to emphasize that truth is a property of linguistic entities. The term "true" as well as its opposite term "false" should always retain the same meaning no matter what is being talked about, and no matter how great the differences are between a particular object of discourse and another. My suggestion is that the basic continuity

135. *TLP* 4.063.

136. Braithwaite, "Empiricist's View," 82.

137. Braithwaite, "Empiricist's View," 77.

between "truth" in religion and "truth" in everyday life be assiduously maintained, and the attempted substitution of the empirical sense of truth by a religious or spiritual sense of truth be abandoned. We shall still have room for "truth" in the aesthetic, literary or existential sense of the word. There is great wisdom in insisting upon a continuity between the realms of the religious and the non-religious with respect to the concept of truth, for unless religious language is grounded in the wider, everyday life, it will fail to make the vital connections needed to stake its claim to truth. Sherry similarly cautions that if religion operated with its own kind of truth "we are in danger of isolating religion from other spheres of life and thereby perhaps trivialising it."[138]

This last remark may appear to contradict the position I have earlier defended—that truth in religion and truth in other spheres of life should be continuous. I should therefore explain that my stated position refers to the sense in which "truth" is defined, that it should be unequivocal in every case. However, how truth is understood by users of religious language is a different matter, and so it is with the question of what religious statements are about with respect to truth that I am concerned. I hope it is obvious that the question I am asking is different to the one of "What kind of truth do religious statements have?" I can perhaps put what I have in view in another way by borrowing a useful distinction suggested by T. F. Torrance (1913–2007), the distinction between the "truth of being" (which is truth itself) and the "truth of statement" (which is a statement about truth).[139] The former is ontologically prior to the latter and may be more or less synonymous with reality or the essence of things; whereas the latter is our conception or articulation of truth.[140] Naturally and in keeping with the purpose of our inquiry, our concern here is with the latter. The observant reader might have perceived that the distinction I made between the question of what religious statements are about with respect to truth and the question of what kind of truth religious statements have, corresponds closely but inversely to Torrance's distinction between the truth of being and the truth of statement. Be that as it may, I hope it is by now clear that the ultimate subject-matter with which religious language is concerned is God—his being, his reality and his overture to the created order. This is not to deny that there are

138. Sherry, *Religion, Truth and Language-Games*, 62.

139. Torrance, *Reality and Scientific Theology*, 143.

140. Torrance, *Reality and Scientific Theology*, 141.

several strands to religious language and that many kinds of facts, issues and even entities are also included within the scope of regular religious discourse. To have God as subject-matter is sheer grace; it is only possible because "God opens himself to us and informs us of himself in a way that no created being can."[141] While God is open to some understanding on our part, he remains the "wholly other" who is ineffable and mysterious and beyond all knowing. Torrance's reminder is as noteworthy as it is profoundly put, "We may apprehend God but we cannot comprehend him."[142] Recall that it was Wittgenstein's encounter with what he could only refer to as "the mystical" that drew his famous conclusion—"What we cannot speak about we must pass over in silence."[143] All this about the divine being is commonly known, and we are again reminded that the religious use of language for the discourse of such a reality is *sui generis*, which is not the same as saying it is not going to be problematic.

In Torrance's distinction referred to above, he rightly gives priority to the "truth of being" over the "truth of statements" and for a sound reason. He writes, "The Reality of God ever remains the Source of all our authentic concepts of him and the unchanging Ground of all our faithful formalizations of his revelation."[144] In other words, the Being of God is *a priori* to the language which seeks to express him, whereas religious statements even if they are about him are derived and "ever open to further clarification, fuller amplification, and change."[145] The aim he aspires in such a "stratification of truth" as he labels it, is "to show the subordination of all our conceptual and linguistic formulations to the inherent intelligibility of reality."[146] Yet, the lapse in identifying statements or linguistic formulations about truth with truth itself is not uncommon. I venture to suggest that it is exactly such an identification that has led to doctrines, creeds and statements of faith being objectified or absolutized. In the circumstances, doctrines, creeds and statements about truth would have nearly replaced truth. That a concerned Pope John XXIII had to advise the assembled fathers of his church at the Second Vatican Council to distinguish the substance of the faith from "the formulation

---

141. Torrance, *Reality and Scientific Theology*, 138.

142. Torrance, *Reality and Scientific Theology*, 139.

143. *TLP* 7.

144. Torrance, *Reality and Scientific Theology*, 139.

145. Torrance, *Reality and Scientific Theology*, 139.

146. Torrance, *Reality and Scientific Theology*, 146.

in which it is clothed"[147] is indicative of the prevalence of such ill-advised identification. We recall the bitter and acrimonious divisions in the church which had been and still are the result of differences rooted in doctrines and teachings. The failure to make the needed distinction has bewitched many into thinking that doctrines and religious statements are propositionally precise representations of the truth of being, with the upshot that doctrinal differences have become more difficult to reconcile, if not totally irreconcilable. Lindbeck's caricature of the propositionalist's intransigence with respect to doctrinal reconciliation is of particular relevance here: "For a propositionalist, if a doctrine is once true it is always true, and if it is false, it is always false."[148]

3. Cognitive/Non-Cognitive Distinction

As users of ordinary religious language, believers mostly take the God described thereby as their object of faith. They do also hold and regard the tenets and creeds of their religion as true—that these statements or propositions are descriptive of "what is the case." These believers will thus resist any suggestion that their religious claims are merely expressive, or, non-cognitive. The two-fold distinction that emerges may be briefly characterized as follows: the former is concerned with how matters are cognitively to be described and explained; the latter is concerned with how they are to be subjectively favored or disfavored.[149] For remarks such as the following, Wittgenstein is often thought to be an advocate of non-cognitivism in religion:

> I can well imagine a religion in which there are no doctrines, so that nothing is spoken. Clearly then, the essence of religion can have nothing to do with what is said—or rather if anything is said, then this itself is an element in religious behaviour, and not a theory. Further, no question accordingly arises whether the words are true or false or meaningless.[150]

For my part, the cognitivist/non-cognitivist distinction—let us term it such—is not a useful one, for it may reflect little more than a

147. John XXIII, "*Gaudet Mater Ecclesia.*"

148. *ND*, 16.

149. I have adapted this characterization from Stevenson, *Ethics and Language*, 4.

150. Waismann, *Wittgenstein and the Vienna Circle*, 117. I dispute the common interpretation that Wittgenstein is such an advocate.

difference in how we look at things. Statements of belief can sometimes be both expressive *and* cognitive, depending on the surrounding practice in which they are held. Moreover, admitting that they are expressive does not entail the surrender of the claim of truth. Nor should my espousal that religious language is cognitive be allowable only if I also insist on there being strict applicable definition and complete clarity.

I suspect the concern that religious claims must be as far as possible descriptive and fact-stating, is a consequence of the thinking that religion must explain things objectively. As Wittgenstein aptly observes, "Philosophers constantly see the method of science before their eyes, and are irresistibly tempted to ask and answer questions in the way science does. This tendency is the real source of metaphysics, and leads the philosopher into complete darkness."[151] These remarks could just as well apply to religious people.

While we credit science for the immense gain in our knowledge of "how things are in the world," we ought to recognize that religion makes its own contribution as well. What religion uniquely delivers has been picked up by the atheist philosopher, Tim Crane (b. 1962):

> Religion attempts to make sense of the world by seeing a kind of meaning or significance in things. This kind of significance does not need laws or generalizations, just the sense that the everyday world we experience is not all there is, and that behind it all is the mystery of God's presence, or more abstractly, the unseen order.[152]

Crane not only correctly identifies divine mystery as the concern of religion, he proposes that how that element is approached or embraced lies at the heart of the difference between the two "magisteria" of religion and science. He elaborates:

> Science too has its share of mysteries. . . . But one aim of science is to minimize such things, to reduce the number of primitive concepts or primitive explanations. The religious attitude is very different. It does not seek to minimize mystery. Mysteries are accepted as a consequence of what, for the religious, make the world meaningful.[153]

151. *BB*, 18.

152. Crane, *Meaning of Belief*, 40.

153. Crane, *Meaning of Belief*, 72.

As we have pointed out in our introductory chapter, religious people should not assume that the scientific method of explanation of things is the only one that counts. Science makes no such hegemonic claim for itself, although the same cannot be said for its ideological form known as "scientism." The important point for religious people to note is they should not assume that religion must explain its claims in the manner required by science. In the face of divine mystery, what is central to religion is a commitment to finding meaning, rather than a quest for complete explanation or certainty. This is the attitude encapsulated by Anselm's maxim, *Credo ut intelligam*—I believe so that I may understand. We might even say such an attitude of faith is an integral part of the language-game(s) in which religious people participate.

4. Relativism

Let us now take up the issue of relativism, for a possible objection might be raised that my work seems unconcerned about getting at the absolute truth. Truth, after all, is what theology seeks and what theological reflections aim to deliver by means of language. John Caputo has recently made the remark that "relativism means there is no Truth."[154] His point is, with so many competing truths around and one is as good as another, who can say what is true? To be sure, Caputo is not in support of relativism, having criticized it for not coming up with a theory of truth and thus rendering us unable to say that anything is wrong.[155] A more common difficulty with relativism finds expression in the cry of those who encounter the claim that truth is relative, the cry that "truth is *arbitrary*—anything goes."[156] As expected, relativism so-conceived is seen as a threat to truth which must then be opposed. Those religious people who think this way would "often invoke 'absolute truth' as both a casualty and antidote. What's threatened by relativism is 'absolute' truth, and yet the only thing that can deliver us from relativism is 'absolute' truth."[157] Smith whose words I have just quoted, thinks that the practice of affixing the qualifier "absolute" to truth ought to be re-evaluated. His worry is the use of the term must lead to a theological conundrum, namely,

154. Caputo, *Truth*, 7.
155. Caputo, *Truth*, 9.
156. Smith, *Who's Afraid of Relativism?*, 29.
157. Smith, *Who's Afraid of Relativism?*, 29.

the question whether we as contingent and finite beings can attain "absoluteness." If we respond in the affirmative, are we not failing to own up to our contingency and dependence as creatures? Indeed, any claim to absoluteness is sheer hubris. For my part, I simply take the position that absolute truth is an ideal which is for God to dispense; as far as we are concerned our task is to seek it. On the other hand, saying that truth is relative is not the same as denying truth or playing fast-and-lose with truth. "It is simply," as Smith rightly argues, "to recognize the conditions of our knowledge that are coincident with our status as finite, created, social beings."[158]

Wittgenstein, we have seen, on being accused of maintaining that truth is decided by human agreement, astutely replied "It is what human beings *say* that is true and false; and they agree in the *language* they use."[159] His relativism is a response to the problem of meaning which in turn is "the possession of a role and a place in a 'language' or a 'form of life.'"[160] Another way of looking at the present argument is to relate it to our ability to discover how things are in the world. That the world is knowable to us, even if only in a very limited and infinitesimal degree, is a valid case for believing that there is a great variety of truths, even relative and tentatively-held ones. For the world is a store-house of many things, and the human quest for knowledge has yielded much fruit and enabled us to discover many truths. Any attempt to dismiss the view that there are particular truths in favor of the Neo-platonic idea of one single "absolute truth" is, I think, wrongheaded.

It would be wrongheaded too to conclude that religion is unconcerned with making factual or historical claims. That "there is no God but Allah and Muhammad is his messenger" is both a factual and historical claim. To Christians, the resurrection of Jesus Christ is a historical occurrence of such significance that *if* it did not happen, many will, with St. Paul, declare faith to be "in vain" (1 Cor 15:14). Wittgenstein seems to have adopted the same position when he makes the following confession:

> What inclines even me to believe in Christ's resurrection? I play as it were with the thought.—If he did not rise from the dead, then he decomposed in the grave like every human being. *He is*

---

158. Smith, *Who's Afraid of Relativism?*, 30.

159. *PI* 241.

160. Keightley, *Wittgenstein, Grammar and God*, 110.

dead and decomposed. In that case he is a teacher, like any other and can no longer *help*; and we are once more orphaned and alone.[161]

To be sure, he has also said that "Christianity is not based on a historical truth."[162] His point may well be that if a religious claim is generally held by others to be false, the believer may still choose not to accept that opinion, since religion is not of the same language-game as that played by its critics. Catholics have exemplified such a response to contrarian positions by continuing to believe in transubstantiation even though others may not think wine has changed in any way.[163]

Concluding Remarks

In this chapter, several key issues concerning the concept of truth have been raised and addressed, if only briefly. Admittedly, the concept continues to be controversial. It certainly defies attempts to underpin it with something more fundamental or easier to grasp, despite it being rigorously discussed since the earliest times. Yet, there can be no question of side-stepping the concept because truth is, and always will be, theology's proper goal. In any event, our analysis of language and its use must lead us to a consideration of truth, for one of the basic functions of language is to convey meaning which, in turn, makes "truth" possible.

Wittgenstein's position on meaning has been the main thrust in the shaping of his concept of truth. His great insight—that the meaning of a word is not to be correlated with the object that corresponds with the word but rather with its use—provides the basis for delinking meaning from any sort of reference or representation. And if meaning is constituted through use, it becomes clear that "true" as a word must function "within the activity of using language (language game) and its meaning is determined by the part it plays in this language."[164] This suggests that the notion of truth must pertain to language; Rorty's oft-quoted line that sentences are needed for there to be truth points in the same direction.

161. *CV*, 38.
162. *CV*, 37.
163. *OC* 239.
164. Gill, "Wittgenstein's Concept of Truth," 74.

If truth is linguistic, the notion of truth must be more than an epistemic concept. In the words of Caputo, truth is "a function of the light of God that shines on things and with which God illumines our minds."[165] Indeed, "God is truth" adds Caputo, a remark reminiscent of Christ's own claim. While it may be claimed that "true" assertions can be made which deliver on factual knowledge, they are marked by "rough edges" and are certainly incapable of rendering complete explanations or precise definitions. Yet, we should not be perturbed that we can never fully reconcile the explicit and the inexpressible, or that we have constantly to strive for more completion and clarity. We accept that we are dealing with mystery which discloses itself while remaining ever hidden. To echo Crane's sense of the matter, we need not suppose ourselves to be falling short of our belief, and it is not as if "were we more intelligent or better informed, we would be able to figure God out."[166]

In earlier chapters, I have made occasional references to the ecumenist, George Lindbeck whose work has been acclaimed for applying Wittgenstein's categories to religious language. Lindbeck's main concerns are: firstly, the nature of church doctrines and how they should function in ways that could help to reconcile theological difference, and secondly, the development of a cultural-linguistic model for conceiving religion. Our interest in him arises from the way he develops Wittgenstein's ideas in depth. In our next chapter, we turn to examine his influential book, *Nature of Doctrine* in some detail.

165. Caputo, *Truth*, 29.
166. Crane, *Meaning of Belief*, 56.

Chapter 6

Linguistic Analogy in Lindbeck's Theories of Religion and Doctrine

> It has become customary . . . to emphasize neither the cognitive nor the experiential-expressive aspects of religion; rather, emphasis is placed on those respects in which religions resemble languages with their correlative forms of life and are thus similar to cultures.[1]
>
> —George A. Lindbeck

Introduction

IN OUR INTRODUCTORY CHAPTER, we alluded to the attempt by the theologian and ecumenist George Lindbeck to develop a theological approach based essentially on Wittgenstein's categories and insights. Lindbeck is noted for being one of the first theologians to appropriate Wittgenstein. His work, the *Nature of Doctrine* (*ND*), developing the philosopher's ideas in depth, has been enormously influential. These factors however are not the only ones we have considered for focusing on him here. We have a more compelling reason—that it will be instructive for us to look at how Wittgenstein's tools have been applied to theological issues by other minds. Lindbeck's exploration may also provide ideas which are useful to my present project.

By way of introduction, let me indicate that what interests me most about Lindbeck is his vision of locating the conceptualization of religion

1. *ND*, 17–18.

in the characteristics of language. I refer to his so-called "cultural-linguistic" theory on religion and doctrine, the main elements of which may be briefly recalled. A religion is to be seen as resembling a language together with its correlative form(s) of life and is thus similar to a culture. A religion is neither a system of beliefs, nor a set of symbols expressing attitudes, feelings, or sentiments. Rather, it is like an idiom that allows for the construing of reality and the living of life. And, like a language or culture, religion is essentially communal in character. Extending the analogy of language to the doctrines of a religion, Lindbeck proposes that doctrines be regarded as rules that govern discourse, reflection and practice. Or, more technically expressed, they are "second-order" statements concerning belief and action, rather than "first-order" propositions or truth claims about God or the world.[2] Although controversial, these "programmatic" proposals have been hailed as amounting to a "paradigm shift" for the conceptualization of the nature of religion and religious doctrine.[3] To demonstrate the superiority or importance of the "cultural-linguistic" approach to religion—for reasons we shall shortly see—Lindbeck contrasts his theory of religion and doctrine with two other dominant theories. The first is the "cognitive-propositional" theory which "emphasizes the cognitive aspects of religion and stresses the ways in which church doctrines function as informative propositions or truth claims about objective realities."[4] The second, which Lindbeck labels the "experiential-expressive" theory because of its tendency towards the subjective, interprets doctrines as non-cognitive symbols of inner feelings, attitudes, or existential orientations.[5] Although Lindbeck does not specifically say so, what he has presented are "ideal types"[6] of theory of religion, that is, they are constructs or models for the

2. In Lindbeck, the distinction between "first-order" and "second-order" statements is important. The former refers to ontological statements that have cognitive content, i.e., they make assertion about the being of God; whereas the latter refers to guidelines or rules that regulate the uses of "first-order" language. Doctrines, in his model, are "second-order" rules governing how one speaks about or refers to God on the "first-order" level of prayer and confession. See *ND*, 69, 80, 94.

3. See, for example, Ford, "Review of *The Nature of Doctrine*," 277; Pecknold, *Transforming Postliberal Theology*, 14; Fosset, *Upon This Rock*, 7.

4. *ND*, 16.

5. *ND*, 16.

6. "An ideal type is formed from characteristics and elements of the given phenomena, but it is not meant to correspond to all of the characteristics of any one particular case. It is not meant to refer to perfect things, moral ideals nor to statistical

purpose of conceptual study and heuristic analysis. As such, they should not be, but are often, confused with "what is the case." I believe some of Lindbeck's critics would have been less nit-picking if they knew the theories were meant to be "ideal types."[7]

Our Tasks

In what follows, I will say more about each of the three theories of religion and doctrine. However, the treatment will not be exhaustive, as our task is mainly to show how language and grammar are used as descriptive analogies within his overall conception of the roles of language in religion. In this connection, a summary of Lindbeck's position by David H. Kelsey (b. 1932) in terms of a chain of language-related metaphors may be aptly recalled: "A religion (in this case, Christianity) is (like) a culture; a culture is (like) a language; and as French grammar is to the French language, so is Christian doctrine to Christianity."[8] In the development of his own "cultural-linguistic" theory, Lindbeck has been quite forthright about his reliance on Wittgenstein's philosophy of language. Indeed, he discloses that the roots of his theory, especially on the linguistic side, go back to that philosopher.[9] His generous acknowledgement says it all: "Wittgenstein's influence . . . has served as a major stimulus to my thinking (even if in ways that those more knowledgeable in Wittgenstein might not approve.)"[10] So, where and in what manner he has applied the stimulus from the philosopher will also be explored. Naturally we will also want to assess if his appropriation of Wittgenstein has been effective or otherwise. Overall, we will concentrate on the linguistic analogy to look out for tools and insights which may have something to contribute to my own work. In the later part of the chapter we will examine Lindbeck's understanding of truth which is central to his entire project. We will also discuss both the promise and problems that Lindbeck's cultural-linguistic approach to religion and doctrine holds for the theological enterprise. The final

---

averages but rather to stress certain elements common to most cases of the given phenomena" ("Ideal Type").

7. Ford, "Review of *The Nature of Doctrine*," 277, has the good insight of seeing them as "ideal" types, as does Gill, *Moral Leadership in a Postmodern Age*, 51–54.

8. Kelsey, "Church Discourse and Public Realm," 8.

9. *ND*, 20.

10. *ND*, 24.

section of the chapter will be devoted to an assessment of some of the key assumptions that underlie that approach.

There is a whisper that however novel or useful Lindbeck's programmatic proposals on religion and doctrine may be, they are these days not much considered, or that they are *passé*. After all, more than three decades have gone by since he first presented them in *ND*. And it does seem that the high level of interest which initially and for some ensuing years greeted the slim volume has waned considerably. Our position, however, is that the "cultural-linguistic" or "postliberal" (a term used by Lindbeck himself and which appears in the subtitle of his work) approach to religion and doctrine still holds great promise, and that it has aspects which are pedagogically useful. Far from being obsolete, Lindbeck's ideas are still being explored and discussed in scholarly circles. In the recent decade or so, we have witnessed the publication of a number of studies on Lindbeck or that are related to his themes; among those who have so published we count the following (to name only a few): Adonis Vidu (2005), C. C. Pecknold (2005), Kevin J. Vanhoozer (2005), Paul Dehart (2006), D. Stephen Long (2009), Steven Knowles (2010), Robert L. Fossett (2013), John Allan Knight (2013), Ronald Michener (2013), James K. A. Smith (2014), and David Trenery (2014).[11] Lindbeck's theses have also continued to receive attention in numerous handbooks on or guides to theology; the two more popular ones are, namely, *The Modern Theologians* (2005), edited by David Ford, and *The Cambridge Companion to Postmodern Theology* (2003), edited by Kevin J. Vanhoozer. I believe we can expect more studies on postliberal theology to be produced. Pecknold's generous remarks about Lindbeck's groundbreaking book will surely find wide agreement:

> For better or for worse, what began in 1984 . . . is now one of the most pedagogically powerful representations of postliberal theology to date. . . . Both the profound pedagogical effect of Lindbeck's slim volume, and the representational status it has gained as a contemporary classic of postliberalism seem to suggest . . . it is a work of some enduring significance.[12]

---

11. See the Bibliography for full details of the works produced by these writers.

12. Pecknold, *Transforming Postliberal Theology*, 3.

Background

It is necessary to discussion of Lindbeck's theses about the nature of religion and doctrine that we know something of the background to the development of his "cultural-linguistic" theory and his claim that it is superior or preferable to the rival "cognitive-propositional" and the "experiential-expressive" theories. Why it is so will, I hope, become clear presently. For many years Lindbeck, as an active participant in ecumenical discussions, has been dissatisfied with the inadequacy of existing models of religion to deal with what he terms "doctrinal reconciliation without capitulation."[13] The question that puzzles him the most is: how can doctrines that were once held to be contradictory to each other be reconciled and yet remain unchanged?[14] Or, to use a different phraseology from a recent critique of Lindbeck's work, "how it is that certain linguistic usages can serve to mark the boundaries of communal belonging?"[15] Lindbeck recalls too that reports of agreements reached on church-dividing topics such as baptism, the Eucharist, ministry, justification, the papacy and so on, are often received with suspicion that those so engaged in ecumenical dialogues (himself included) are self-deceived victims of their own desire for reconciliation, for these very discussants would continue—by their own admission—to adhere to their original, long-held convictions. The problem, as Lindbeck sees it, is not that the claim to have achieved doctrinal reconciliation is false but that the categories for dealing with doctrinal reconciliation available to these folk are inadequate.[16] The theory that Lindbeck now puts forward and writes about in *ND* is therefore intended as a response to the aforesaid conundrum. Equally, the metaphors and the central analogy of "religion as language" that fund Lindbeck's argument are selected purely on the basis that they are effective for resolving that particular problematic. The claim then that his own theory of religion and doctrine is the superior or preferred theory is made strictly within an ecumenical context.[17] Whether his claim is justified or not, however, must at this point be left

13. *ND*, 16.

14. *ND*, 15, 78.

15. Dehart, *Trial of the Witnesses*, 156.

16. *ND*, 7, 15.

17. Frei tells us to "forget the rule or regulative approach, forget the cultural-linguistic theory," unless this ecumenical reality is taken into account ("Epilogue," 278).

an open question; but the background just presented should be kept in mind as we proceed to consider his ideas.

So how have the "cognitive-propositional" and "experiential-expressive" theories failed the ecumenical cause, whereas Lindbeck's "cultural-linguistic" theory seems to have succeeded? According to Lindbeck, the first two theories do not measure up because by their very nature the possibility of doctrinal reconciliation is simply denied: one requires us to reject doctrinal reconciliation, while the other would have us reject doctrinal constancy.[18] In the "cognitive-propositional" theory, the possibility of doctrinal reconciliation is simply ruled out unless the differing sides are prepared to capitulate or retract. For under this theory, doctrines are held as norms about beliefs and practice, and so are not open to reformulation. Lindbeck elaborates,

> For a propositionalist, if a doctrine is once true, it is always true, and if it is once false, it is always false. This implies, for example, that the historic affirmations and denials of transubstantiation can never be harmonized. Agreement can be reached only if one or both sides abandon their positions. Thus, on this view, doctrinal reconciliation without capitulation is impossible because there is no significant sense in which the meaning of a doctrine can change while remaining the same.[19]

In the second type of theory, given its focus on the "experiential-expressive" dimension of religion and a lack of serious interest in questions of diversity, doctrinal harmony has been reduced to resolving underlying feelings, attitudes, existential orientations or practices rather than doctrinal differences which presumably are left unsettled. Indeed, in this tradition "doctrines function as nondiscursive symbols, they are polyvalent in import and therefore subject to changes of meaning or even to a total loss of meaningfulness."[20] After all, for experiential-expressive symbolists, the essence of religion is an experience or mode of consciousness that relates to the transcendent, with doctrines serving only as nondiscursive symbols—they can remain the same even if their meanings have changed, or they can alter without any change

18. *ND*, 16.

19. *ND*, 16–17. Both McGrath and Vanhoozer have objected to Lindbeck's claim that doctrines are treated by propositionalists as "eternally true." They have also accused him of being simplistic in representing the propositional position as such. See McGrath, *Genesis of Doctrine*, 16–17; Vanhoozer, *Drama of Doctrine*, 88.

20. *ND*, 17.

of meaning. Indeed, as Trenery has observed, on the "experiential-expressive" approach to religion and doctrine, "any degree of variation in doctrinal formulation appears to be consistent with an underlying unity of religious experience."[21]

Caveats

Before proceeding further, several clarifications or caveats pertaining to the present discussion issued by Lindbeck himself may be briefly noted.

1. Doctrine and Religion Are Interdependent on Each Other

At the outset, Lindbeck insists that the problem of doctrine "is not confined to doctrines per se, but extends to the notion of religion itself."[22] The reason is there is an "interdependent" relationship between theories of religion and theories of doctrine, so that "deficiencies in one area are inseparable from deficiencies in the other."[23] This is certainly true. Indeed, from what is gleaned from the celebrated anthropologist Clifford Geertz (1926–2006), the dynamics are even greater, with doctrine in significant inter-relationship not only with religion (i.e., schemes of symbolization and representation) but with the wider community.[24] No sooner does one begin to explore the nature of doctrine than one is thrown into an inquiry that embraces the whole of religion. It should therefore occasion no surprise that Lindbeck is not concerned with enumerating specific doctrines (such as those relating to the Trinity, Christology, infallibility, the Eucharist, and so on). Neither is he concerned to attempt any assessment on claims as to which statements should have or should not have doctrinal status. In other words, rather than seek to "decide material questions," he is only concerned "to provide a framework for their discussion."[25] Sensing the need for a "non-controversial" description of doctrines, he offers the following:

21. Trenery, *Alasdair MacIntyre*, 147.
22. *ND*, 7.
23. *ND*, 7.
24. See McGrath, *Genesis of Doctrine*, 11.
25. *ND*, 10.

> Church doctrines are communally authoritative teachings regarding beliefs and practices that are considered essential to the identity or welfare of the group in question. They may be formally stated or informally operative, but in any case they indicate what constitutes faithful adherence to a community.[26]

The stress on doctrines as "teachings regarding beliefs and practices" is a reiteration that the role of doctrines is a second-order one. Doctrines are not first-order formulations of beliefs which shape practices; they are authoritative insofar as they function as *rules* governing discourse, attitude, and action. Recall the analogy that religion is the language and doctrines are the grammar of religion. The following remark may be instructive: "The system therefore consists of a 'first-order' (the actual performances of particular 'sentences') and a 'second-order' (the grammar by which those sentences are regulated), and Lindbeck keeps a fairly rigid boundary between the two."[27]

2. Language

It seems that Lindbeck has issued a clarification on "language" which will have a bearing on a correct understanding of his argument. I borrow the following remarks, which appear as a footnote in John Allan Knight's chapter on "George Lindbeck and Frei's Later Work":

> First, [Lindbeck] means language to include any form of symbolic action that has a conventionalized meaning. Second, he doesn't mean that an action or its meaning is necessarily *exhausted* by its linguistic constitution. Third, we might engage in activities that are not linguistically constituted. But these activities are not distinctively human. That is, what it means to be human is to exist in a culture, to take part in a form of life that is regulated by a language game. Activities that are distinctively human, then, will be linguistically constituted.[28]

In the main body of his chapter, Knight has suggested that when Lindbeck says an activity is linguistically constituted, what he means is that it is "constituted by a *particular* linguistic system."[29] Functioning like

---

26. *ND*, 74.

27. Higton, "Frei's Christology and Lindbeck's Cultural-Linguistic Theory," 84.

28. Knight, *Liberalism versus Postliberalism*, 202n15.

29. Knight, *Liberalism versus Postliberalism*, 202.

a language, religion informs our thought, structures our worldview, and orders our culture. "Therefore," Knight imputes Lindbeck as implying, "there cannot be any such thing as religion in general, and, more generally, humans have incommensurable experiences. To speak of the religious quality of all experience, from a cultural-linguistic point of view, is to use language to which no meaning can ultimately be assigned."[30]

It is also vital to discussion of the "cultural-linguistic" approach to note Lindbeck's insistence that language precedes and is *prior* to religious experience. The order is strictly as follows: language comes first, the world and experience second. Put differently, "it is necessary to have the means for expressing an experience in order to have it, and the richer our expressive or linguistic system, the more subtle, varied and differentiated can be our experience."[31] Such an understanding of language will surely challenge the commonly held assumption that experience being extra-linguistic is the bedrock of religious belief. Even so, might Lindbeck's claim of the priority of language over experience be equally extreme and so equally wrongheaded? Do language and experience not interact rather than one being wholly determinative of the other?

3. Culture

Next, Lindbeck is careful to explain the analogy he uses in saying that religion (also) resembles a culture. While he affirms Paul Tillich's formulation that "religion is the substance of culture, and culture is the form of religion"[32]—by which he understands religion as an individualistic sense of ultimate concern as well as, collectively, the vitalizing source of all significant cultural achievements—he does not collapse the distinctions between the two. Religion, unlike a culture, has a more specifiable domain, namely, whatever that is taken as most important.[33] It is by virtue of their domain concerning that which is most important that religions are such comprehensive interpretive schemes that can structure and shape all human experience and understanding of life, self, and world. Yet, culture is an instructive analogy for Lindbeck's purposes as it lays stress on the elements of "exchange and collective elaboration

---

30. Knight, *Liberalism versus Postliberalism*, 202.

31. *ND*, 37.

32. Tillich, *Theology of Culture*, 42, cited in *ND*, 34.

33. *ND*, 34.

of meaningful systems"[34] which characterize all socio-cultural processes. Inspired by Geertz, "culture" is now widely understood as a semiotic medium or symbol system—like a shared language with its "ensemble of publicly available symbols which function together to structure shared possibilities of communication, interpretation, and experience."[35] Paul Dehart (b. 1964) has pointed out that these symbolic exchanges "have their own 'logic' due to the meaningful interrelations which constitute them."[36] In a footnote, Lindbeck explains, "It is this relatively greater emphasis on the internal logic or grammar of religions which differentiates what I am calling 'cultural-linguistic' approaches to religion from more one-sidedly cultural ones."[37]

Three Models of Religion

The presentation of Lindbeck's three-fold typology of theories of religion and doctrine, we have noted, is primarily a response to a longstanding concern regarding the prospect of ecumenical unity and agreement. The paramount issue is the question of the possibility of the reconciliation of doctrines, doctrines which are church-dividing as well as those which are not so. Reading the circumstances, James K. A. Smith has correctly remarked that "Lindbeck's quarry is a theory of doctrine."[38] Still, it should be quite apparent in the accounts of the theories so far presented or in the terminology used in their descriptions that they include or are aligned with different understandings of the nature of religious language. To be sure, each of these theories incorporates a view of language. Thus, a dominant metaphor—that of language—seems to be present in all of the rival views. With this perspective in mind let us consider each of the theories in turn.

34. Geertz, *Interpretation of Cultures*, 5–10, cited in Dehart, *Trial of the Witnesses*, 67.

35. Dehart, *Trial of the Witnesses*, 67.

36. Dehart, *Trial of the Witnesses*, 68.

37. *ND*, 28n16.

38. Smith, *Who's Afraid of Relativism?*, 154.

1. The Cognitive-Propositional Theory

On this "cognitive-propositional" approach, the factual aspects of religion are emphasized, and religion itself is likened to a science or a philosophy, as these were typically understood.[39] It follows that the doctrines of religion are treated as propositions that correspond to or represent what is objectively real and of ultimate importance. Such propositions (doctrines) are informative and assessable in cognitive terms, though as truth-claims they can of course be either true or false. Lindbeck does not develop this theory in great detail, though he tells us that he sees it as a pre-liberal "approach of traditional orthodoxies (as well as of many heterodoxies)" and that "it has certain affinities to the outlook on religion adopted by much Anglo-American analytic philosophy with its preoccupation with the cognitive or informational meaningfulness of religious utterances."[40] He does, however, attempt to eschew the "cognitive-propositional" position for being out of sync with modernity, even suggesting that those who still perceive or experience religion in such fashion are people who "combine unusual insecurity with naiveté."[41] We have already noted his main criticism that the propositional perspective practically rules out the possibility of doctrinal reconciliation without capitulation.

It is quite obvious that the theory of language utilized in the "cognitive-propositional" approach to religion and doctrine is that which correlates to what is commonly known as referentialism (or representationalism). A simple definition of the referential theory is that "the meaning of a word is the object to which it refers."[42] In this theory, the assumption is that there is a relationship between three terms, namely language, reality and knowledge, knowledge being "a relation of ideas ('representations') in my mind that 'correspond' to reality 'outside' my mind."[43] Knowledge acquisition, as we have previously noted, becomes "a matter of getting something 'inside' our mind to hook onto things 'outside' our minds."[44] Language is thus merely the instrument; it is supplied by God for the primary function of describing God—his being, his relation to the world and his action—in propositional form. These immaterial

---

39. *ND*, 23. Here, Lindbeck speaks of such theories as "old-fashioned."

40. *ND*,16.

41. *ND*, 21.

42. Thiselton, *Two Horizons*, 121.

43. Smith, *Who's Afraid of Relativism?*, 24.

44. Smith, *Who's Afraid of Relativism?*, 24.

"facts" about the divine reality are the primary referents of religious propositions, whose truth is dependent on their correspondence to states of affairs. An example of an extreme form of referentialism is found in the following account on the verbal inspiration of scripture by A. A. Hodge (1823–1886) who goes as far as to claim that even the choice of words in Scripture is divinely ordered:

> [By verbal inspiration] is meant that the divine influence, of whatever kind it may have been, which accompanied the sacred writers in what they wrote, extends to their expression of their thoughts in language, as well as to the thoughts themselves. The effect being that in the original autograph copies the language expresses the thought God intended to convey with infallible accuracy, so that the words as well as the thoughts are God's revelation to us.[45]

As a matter of philosophical interest, it has been averred that if the "cognitive-propositional" model is to endure in our modern times it must be founded upon or wed to a representationalist epistemology.[46]

A major problem with the referential theory of language is that it cannot "account for the variety of functions that words serve";[47] that is, it is not an all-embracing theory as it only works when we think of certain types of words, e.g., nouns like "table," "chair," "bread," names of people, etc. Wittgenstein provides a simple demonstration that language cannot be all referential:

> Now think of the following use of language: I send someone shopping. I give him a slip marked "five red apples." He takes the slip to the shopkeeper, who opens the drawer marked "apples"; then he looks up the word "red" in a table and finds a colour sample opposite it; then he says the series of cardinal numbers—I assume that he knows them by heart—up to the word "five" and for each number he takes an apple of the same colour as the sample out of the drawer.—It is in this and similar ways that one operates with words.—"But how does he know where and how he is to look up the word 'red' and what he is to do with the word 'five'?"—Well, I assume that he *acts* as I

45. Hodge, *Outlines of Theology*, 66–67, cited in Murphy, *Beyond Liberalism and Fundamentalism*, 43.

46. Smith, *Who's Afraid of Relativism?*, 155. Cathey has observed that "there is an inherent connection between 'cognitive-propositionalism' in doctrine and the epistemology of metaphysical realism" (*God in Postliberal Perspective*, 50).

47. Hovey, *Speak Thus*, 67.

have described. Explanations come to an end somewhere.—But what is the meaning of the word "five"?—No such thing was in question here, only how the word "five" is used.[48]

In the above passage, only the word "apples" makes a reference to some reality; the word "five" has no meaning other than from the way it is used, and the word "red" is meaningful in so far as it is used with reference to "apples."

Another difficulty with the referential theory and by extension, the "cognitive-propositional" approach to religion, is its tendency to isolate words or even statements from the context of the life of the people. The fact is the meaning of religious utterances does not depend only on the correspondence of what is stated or claimed to reality, but must also take into account the "patterns of acting and feeling" which help create that correspondence.[49] We recall Lindbeck's insistence that insofar as religious utterances are concerned "their correspondence to reality in the view we are expounding is not an attribute that they have when considered in and of themselves, but is only a function of their role in constituting a form of life, a way of being in the world, which itself corresponds to the Most Important, the Ultimately Real."[50] A common mistake then is to focus on the so-called "referents" in religious language, missing their wider context. Thiselton shares the following observation:

> The unbeliever does not learn the meaning of such words as "God," "love," "salvation" by being shown observable objects to which these words refer. They draw their meaning *in the first place* from the role which these words play in the lives of Christian believers, even if this does not completely exhaust their meaning for the believer himself. As Paul van Buren puts it, "To examine the word (i.e., 'God') in isolation from its context in the life of religious people is to pursue an abstraction."[51]

Proponents of the "cognitive-propositional" position often pride themselves on being passionate for and concerned about truth. This is reflected in their insistence that language can actually refer to the divine reality as well as describe factual information about God. Such

---

48. *PI* 1.

49. See Barrett, "Theology as Grammar," 157.

50. *ND*, 65.

51. Thiselton, *Two Horizons*, 123. The quote by Buren is taken from Buren, *Edges of Language*, 71.

a cognitivist disposition is certainly respectable, and in Lindbeck's reckoning, its great strength is that it admits the possibility of truth claims.[52] Yet, the cognitive aspect of religion while often important, is not primary, nor is it the only concern. Most religions also command, exhort, instruct, comfort, challenge, admonish, give encouragement, offer hope, etc. Also, an authentic religious life is frequently marked by rounds of activities that are in the main non-cognitive in nature, or only minimally so. What Lindbeck fears is that the "cognitive-propositional" tradition may trade the rich diversity of uses of religious language for a truncated view of religion, one which espouses an exhaustive cognitivism or propositionalism.

Thus, Lindbeck's rejection of the propositional approach to religion is right—for the most part. Doctrinal propositions can only attempt to express the divine mystery; they can never represent God exhaustively or unambiguously owing to the very nature of language—its inadequacy and limitedness. The words of Wittgenstein's hyperbole (as I deem them) come to mind, "to say that this proposition agrees (or does not agree) with reality would be obvious nonsense."[53] Propositions are not isolated and unmediated; the kind of referring that can occur depends on the nature of the categorical scheme and their syntax. Yet, Lindbeck's disavowal of all referential statements is problematic if he disallows that some truth may be in them. The rebuttal from Alister E. McGrath (b. 1953) strikes the needed balance:

> Human words, and the categories which they express, are stretched to their limits as they attempt to encapsulate, to communicate, something which tantalizingly refuses to be reduced to words. . . . Experience and language point beyond themselves, testifying that something lies beyond their borderlands, yet into which we tantalizingly cannot enter.[54]

2. The Experiential-Expressive Theory

Unlike the "cognitive-propositional" model, the "experiential-expressive" is not concerned with the factual aspects of religious content. Instead, it is concerned with the expressive nature of one's inner being and understands

52. *ND*, 63–64.

53. *PI* 134.

54. McGrath, *Genesis of Doctrine*, 67.

doctrines to be "non-informative and non-discursive symbols of inner feelings, attitudes, or existential orientations"[55] that are shared by all of humankind. On this view, what lies at the core of religion is a root experience or consciousness that points to an ultimate and mysterious reality. Historically, the roots of this conceptualization may be traced back to Schleiermacher (1768–1834) whose classic dictum, "The essence of religion consists in the feeling of an absolute dependence" comes easily to mind.[56] As a theory of religion, the "experiential-expressive" interpretation has always been pervasive and popular; it seems to have a special appeal to the liberal-minded. In the present age where self-expression is fashionable, it is even in the ascendancy across the board.

Here we come very close to an account of religious language that we may say seeks access not to an ultimate reality or states of affairs but to "internal dispositions."[57] Religion and what identifies a religion with is not located in the referential function of language, but in the ability of language "to provide private objectivization or public articulation of the inner encounter."[58] In short, what religious language expresses is existential orientation.[59] From the perspective of those in this linguistic tradition, the external or outer features of religion are thus the nondiscursive symbols of interior experience. This explains why on the "experiential-expressive" model of religion, doctrinal changes are not an issue as doctrines are merely a "feeble" way of enunciating the experience of one's interior life. There is, thus, as Lindbeck famously points out, "at least the logical possibility that a Buddhist and a Christian might have basically the same faith, although expressed very differently."[60]

Lindbeck sees a major problem in this model of conceiving religion and the religious language it typifies. In particular, he questions the assumption that "the various religions are diverse symbolizations of one and the same core experience of the Ultimate."[61] The notion of a common core experience, he observes, has of course permeated

55. *ND*, 16.

56. Lindbeck partially cites this dictum in his account of how the experiential tradition has developed from Schleiermacher through Rudolf Otto to Mircea Eliade and beyond. See *ND*, 20–21.

57. Dehart, *Trial of the Witnesses*, 157.

58. Dehart, *Trial of the Witnesses*, 157.

59. Murphy, *Beyond Liberalism and Fundamentalism*, 49.

60. *ND*, 17.

61. *ND*, 23.

much of contemporary Christian theology. As an example, he cites Schleiermacher's articulation—which we have earlier quoted—that the source of all religion is in the "feeling of absolute dependence,"[62] and Tillich's depiction of this experience as that of "a being grasped by ultimate concern."[63] The problem for Lindbeck, and for us, with respect to the idea of a common core experience is that "it is difficult or impossible to specify its distinctive features, and yet unless this is done, the assertion of commonality becomes logically and empirically vacuous."[64] Even Bernard Lonergan (1904–1984), a noted advocate of the "experiential-expressive" position has wisely conceded that religious experience "varies with every difference of culture, class or individual."[65] In what has been said, it would appear that Lindbeck's case against the idea of a common core experience is well argued and supported. Still, what might need to be challenged is the appeal to Schleiermacher as if experience is all that mattered to him. This is a serious misrepresentation because for Schleiermacher, the experience that comes to us still points to an ultimate reality, even if it cannot be fully conceptualized. He is also clear that while we can share in the religious experiences of others, our experiences are not all the same.[66]

Another objection against the "experiential-expressive" theory, an objection that is akin to the one just discussed, concerns a gross phenomenological inaccuracy, namely, the claim that it is experience that gives account of and shape to the external features of religion. In other words, in the interplay between "inner" experience and "outer" religious factors, it is the former that is viewed as the leading partner. This so-called "inside-out" approach is predominant in the liberal theological tradition, with its unquestioned embrace of what is commonly termed "the turn to the subject." Lindbeck mentions that thinkers from Schleiermacher through Rudolf Otto to Mircea Eliade (1907–1986) and beyond, have all held such a position, locating "ultimately significant contact with whatever is finally important to religion in the prereflective experiential depths of the self and regard[ing] the public or outer features of religion as expressive and evocative objectifications (i.e., nondiscursive symbols)

---

62. *ND*, 21.

63. *ND*, 31.

64. *ND*, 32.

65. Lonergan, *Philosophy of God, and Theology*, 50, cited in *ND*, 32.

66. Vial, *Schleiermacher*, 70.

of internal experience."[67] Consider, for instance, the following line from Schleiermacher which reflects his "inside-out" assumption concerning "outer" religious beliefs,

> There is an inner experience to which they [i.e., religious beliefs] may all be traced; they rest upon a given, and apart from this they could not have arisen by deduction or synthesis from universally recognized prepositions.[68]

But Lindbeck is unconvinced that this "inside-out" assumption can be conclusively maintained. I think he is fair to state that it is "simplistic" to claim a unilaterality that either religions produce experiences, or that experiences produce religions, for the relationship between the two is dialectical and the causality is reciprocal.[69] As before, it is also the case that it is difficult or impossible to isolate a common core experience from either religious language or behavior. He seems more inclined to say that religious experience is conceptually derivative, and that the possibility of experience itself is shaped by the "outer" dimensions of religion.

It is also at this point that Lindbeck appeals to Wittgenstein's private language argument.[70] The term "private language" is used by Wittgenstein to refer to a language which is only comprehensible to its single originator but not to others because they do not have access to its vocabulary.[71] Sometimes, the term is wrongly interpreted to mean that one cannot speak to oneself, or that one cannot withhold the things one is thinking from public view. The fact is these sort of things can be done, so clearly the term is not to be so applied or understood. In the following passage, Wittgenstein invites his readers to imagine such a language, the words of which can only be understood by the person speaking:

> But could we also imagine a language in which a person could write down or give vocal expression to his inner experiences— his feelings, moods, and the rest—for his private use?——Well, can't we do so in our ordinary language?—But that is not what I mean. The individual words of this language are to refer to what can only be known to the person speaking; to his immediate

---

67. *ND*, 21.

68. Schleiermacher, *Christian Faith*, 67.

69. *ND*, 33.

70. *ND*, 38.

71. For Wittgenstein's discussion on private language, see *PI* 244–71.

private sensations. So another person cannot understand the language.[72]

The logic that Wittgenstein uses to reach his so-called "private language" argument seems to be anything but controverted:

> "So you are saying that human agreement decides what is true and what is false?"—It is what human beings *say* that is true and false; and they agree in the *language* they use. That is not agreement in opinions but in form of life. If language is to be a means of communication there must be agreement not only in definitions but also (queer as this may sound) in judgments.[73]

Contending that because "private languages are logically impossible"[74] Lindbeck draws the following parallel:

> If so, the same would have to be said regarding private religious experiences (such as the dynamic state of being unrestrictedly in love), which are purportedly independent of any particular language game. This is not the place to assess this argument. I shall simply note that even those experiential-expressivists— such as Lonergan (or Karl Rahner and David Tracy)—who acknowledge that experience cannot be expressed except in public and intersubjective forms, do seem to maintain a kind of privacy in the origins of experience and language that, if Wittgenstein is right, is more than doubtful.[75]

3. The Cultural-Linguistic Theory

In Lindbeck's schematic assessment noted above, the "cognitive-propositional" and "experiential-expressive" approaches to religion and doctrine have both failed to adequately account for the possibility of doctrinal reconciliation without capitulation. By their very nature, the former is unable to relent on its invariability (in that the adherents continue to hold to the truth of their doctrines), while the latter seems infused with a certain variability (in that expressions of belief once held to be irreconcilable can now be interpreted in ways that allow for

72. *PI* 243.
73. *PI* 241–42.
74. *ND*, 38.
75. *ND*, 38.

their harmonization).[76] Lindbeck briefly considers a "hybrid" approach that could better account for both the variable and invariable aspects of religious traditions.[77] Despite some virtue to it, Lindbeck however jettisons this approach for being "weak in criteria for determining when a given doctrinal development is consistent with the sources of faith" and being "unable to avoid a rather greater reliance on the magisterium."[78] It is then that a new, postliberal, way of conceiving religion and doctrine known as the "cultural-linguistic" theory comes to be proposed. From a critical perspective, one wonders if Lindbeck might have been too quick to reject his own idea of a hybrid approach: might not all three theories of religion be applied to complement one another? Religious statements, especially those on doctrine, may well be a composite of propositional truth-claims, expressions of faith experiences, and rules or idioms that describe or prescribe religious duties and conduct.

Though the main elements of the "cultural-linguistic" theory have been indicated at the beginning of the chapter, it is still necessary to look at the more technical version supplied by its originator. For Lindbeck,

> a religion can be viewed as a kind of cultural and/or linguistic framework or medium that shapes the entirety of life and thought. It functions somewhat like a Kantian *a priori*. . . . It is not primarily an array of beliefs about the true and the good (though it may involve these), or a symbolism expressive of basic attitudes, feelings, or sentiments (though these will be generated). Rather it is similar to an idiom that makes possible the description of realities, the formulation of beliefs, and the experiencing of inner attitudes, feelings, and sentiments. Like a culture or language, it is a communal phenomenon that shapes the subjectivities of individuals rather than being primarily a manifestation of those subjectivities.[79]

The first thing we can say is that the linguistic analogy is drawn by Lindbeck at several important points. Observe that he emphasizes that religion itself be "viewed as a kind of cultural and/or linguistic framework or medium . . . [indeed,] similar to an idiom." In contrast with the claims of the earlier views, religion is neither a system of beliefs expressed in terms of the cognitive, nor a "symbolism" expressive of sentiments or

76. *ND*, 17.

77. *ND*, 17.

78. *ND*, 17.

79. *ND*, 33.

feelings arising from a spiritual encounter. One becomes religious as one would acquire a language or a culture; conversion or discipleship then is a kind of acculturation, for "to become a Christian involves learning the story of Israel and of Jesus well enough to interpret and experience oneself and one's world in its terms."[80] To be sure, one needs also to think of how religions can change: the reason is one is inducted into something that is potentially open-handed, as in the extreme example of the transformation of Judaism into Christianity. Being religious is also like a kind of "knowing how"—just like joining a particular linguistic and cultural community—and such knowledge cannot be passed on by second-hand. Within a religion, one must, in order to become socialized into it, embrace its "vocabulary" and learn and practice its skills. Picking up a well-known and important element in Wittgenstein's thought, Lindbeck notes:

> Lastly, just as a language (or "language games" to use Wittgenstein's phrase) is correlated with a form of life, and just as a culture has both cognitive and behavioral dimensions, so it is also in the case of a religious tradition. Its doctrines, cosmic stories or myths, and ethical directives are integrally related to the rituals it practices, the sentiments or experiences it evokes, the actions it recommends, and the institutional forms it develops.[81]

Lindbeck's use of the concept of language-games-with-a-form-of-life to connect with religious tradition with its rituals, sentiments, experiences, actions, and institutional forms, represents a key mention of Wittgenstein in *ND*. Questions however have been raised as to whether Lindbeck is right to so appropriate this Wittgenstein's concept.[82] The main complaint appears to be that as Wittgenstein never likened language as a whole, or even a realm of discourse (such as religion, philosophy, or science) to a game, what Lindbeck did was a transgression of Wittgenstein's intentions. Though I agree, following Fergus Kerr, that on textual grounds religion or anything else on a grand scale cannot count as a form of life, I do not think Lindbeck is guilty of any misuse.[83] To be pedantic, Lindbeck's comparison is drawn between the lesser elements of a religious tradition (not the

80. *ND*, 34.

81. *ND*, 33.

82. See Nicholson, "Abusing Wittgenstein," 617–29.

83. Kerr, *Theology after Wittgenstein*, 29.

whole religion) and language games/form of life. In the circumstances, his appropriation of Wittgenstein has worked out well, shedding light on aspects of his theory.

Another instance of appropriating Wittgenstein occurs at the point of proposing that doctrines be interpreted as rules. Lindbeck has proposed that church doctrines be construed "not as expressive symbols or as truth claims, but as communally authoritative rules of discourse, attitude, and action."[84] He also insists on understanding the function of doctrines in terms of their use. Unsurprisingly, once doctrines are interpreted in their function as "usage guides"[85] the conflict between preserving the fixed form of doctrinal formulation (i.e., "constancy") and allowing flexibility in their theorization (i.e., change) will at once seem less formidable.

It may occasion surprise that although he is insistent that his "cultural-linguistic" theory is superior to the "cognitive-propositional" and "experiential-expressive" ones, Lindbeck does not seek to have them completely discarded. Rather, he urges an "absorption" of these theories into his model.[86] It is, he says, a testament to the strength of the cultural-linguistic outlook that "it can accommodate and combine the distinctive and often competing emphases of the other two approaches."[87] More pertinently, as we have noted, their chief deficiency vis-à-vis the "cultural-linguistic" approach to religion is the fact that they are "more one-sidedly."

The contrast between Lindbeck's approach and the other two may be further illustrated by comparing their respective perspectives with regard to the question of language. Whereas in the earlier theories of religion the relevant dimension of language with which each is identified has been either reference or symbolization, in this "cultural-linguistic" model, the dimension of language is semantic interconnection.[88] Put differently and more strongly, the "cognitive-propositional" and "experiential-expressive" interpretations have impoverished religion—by reducing the nature of religious belief either to propositional truth on the one hand, or to the expression of religious experience on the other. These tendencies will naturally impinge on the way scripture is to be interpreted, either as texts

84. *ND*, 18.

85. Dehart, *Trial of the Witnesses*, 158.

86. Pecknold, *Transforming Postliberal Theology*, 22.

87. *ND*, 34.

88. See Dehart, *Trial of the Witnesses*, 158.

which attempt to describe and encompass an objective reality, or as texts which facilitate the expression of one's experience of the transcendent or the living of life. This is an area of study which will require further exploration.

The "Rule" Theory of Doctrine

The so-called "rule" or "regulative" theory of doctrine (hereinafter the "rule" theory) is developed in a series of arguments that begin with Lindbeck making the basic point that doctrines are "second-order reflection on the data of religion,"[89] or to say the same thing, "they are second-order rules for first-order talk."[90] Doctrines as such do not assert anything either true or false about God at all: they only speak about or describe assertions so made. Applying the linguistic analogy once again, Lindbeck likens doctrines to languages, or more precisely, to grammatical rules. No doubt the phrase "theology as grammar" by Wittgenstein probably provided the inspiration.[91] To clarify what doctrines-as-grammar means, Lindbeck explains thus,

> Some doctrines, such as those delimiting the canon and specifying the relation of Scripture and tradition, help determine the vocabulary; while others (or sometimes the same ones) instantiate syntactical rules that guide the use of this material in construing the world, community, and self, and still others provide semantic reference.[92]

Lindbeck further argues that what is most prominent in this new conception of doctrines "is their use, not as expressive symbols or as truth claims but as communally authoritative rules of discourse, attitude, and action."[93] Given that doctrines are descriptive and have a regulative function, doctrinal conflicts will be easier to overcome as differences are reconciled while the doctrines remain unchanged. "Thus," he elaborates, "oppositions between rules [i.e., doctrines] can in some instances be resolved, not by altering one or both of them, but by specifying when or where they apply, or by stipulating which of the competing directives

89. *ND*, 10.

90. Loughlin, *Telling God's Story*, 19.

91. *PI* 373.

92. *ND*, 81.

93. *ND*, 18.

takes precedence."[94] One cannot but detect here a further appropriation of a Wittgensteinian concept—that of rules operating within a language-game, serving very different roles in the game.[95] To strengthen the case for regarding doctrines as rules, Lindbeck assures his readers that there has been historical precedent. He cites as evidence the notion of *regulae fidei* which has been practiced since the earliest Christian centuries, and the subsequent recognition by later historians and systematic theologians that the role of doctrines within the teachings of the church has been largely regulative.[96]

Lindbeck devotes a chapter in his book to discuss how the "rule" theory of doctrine can be tested for its usefulness. He selects three "hard" cases, namely the classic Christological/Trinitarian affirmations, the Marian dogma and papal infallibility for examination to see whether the theory works in them.[97] To attempt to recount the detailed discussions involved in each case would take us beyond the concerns of the present study. Let it suffice to say that the requirement of the rule theory that "a distinction be made between doctrine and formulation, between content and form" seems to succeed in at least allowing for various formulations of a particular doctrine. In Christology, for instance, the believer may not deny the divinity or humanity of Jesus but within these "rules" he or she is free to give his or her own particular expression to the doctrine. The "rule" theory thus provides for several "logical possibilities" in the way the believer chooses to talk about his or her belief.[98]

The Question of Truth

I return now to the question of truth raised in the previous chapter. In the development of the "cultural-linguistic" theory of religion and doctrine, Lindbeck recognizes that one religion may profess to be "truer" than another. So he devotes an excursus in his book to dealing with the notion of "truth," drawing a distinction between two types of truth: intrasystematic and ontological. The first refers to the truth of coherence.

---

94. *ND*, 18.
95. *PI* 31.
96. *ND*, 18.
97. *ND*, 91.
98. O'Neill, "Rule Theory," 421–22.

So, an utterance is intrasystematically true if it coheres with the overall context in which it is made. Lindbeck explains as follows,

> Thus for a Christian, "God is Three and One" or "Christ is Lord" are true only as parts of a total pattern of speaking, thinking, feeling and acting. They are false when their use in any given instance is inconsistent with what the pattern as a whole affirms of God's being and will. The crusader's battle cry *"Christus est Dominus,"* for example, is false when used to authorise cleaving the skull of the infidel (even though the same words in other contexts may be a true utterance.) When thus employed, it contradicts the Christian understanding of Lordship as embodying, for example, suffering servanthood.[99]

The second kind of truth—ontological truth—is constituted by correspondence. An utterance or statement is ontologically true if its content corresponds to reality, or false if it does not. By way of illustration, the two types of truth are contrasted with reference to Shakespeare's statement in *Hamlet*: "Denmark is the land where Hamlet lived." Within the context of Shakespeare's play, the statement is intrasystematically true; if taken as history it is ontologically false.[100]

Of the two concepts of truth, Lindbeck contends that intrasystematic truth is of greater "fundamental significance."[101] He posits, "a statement . . . cannot be ontologically true unless it is intrasystematically true, but intrasystematic truth is quite possible without ontological truth."[102] In other words, ontological truth is not essential for the interpretation of doctrine, as "intrasystematic truth is quite possible without ontological truth."[103] Even so, Lindbeck cannot be labelled as dismissive of ontological correspondence. Though he rejects propositionalism along with the experiential-expressive approach to religion in favor of his own linguistic-cultural approach, he makes a return to the propositional, conceding: "we must not simply allow for the possibility that a religion may be categorically as well symbolically or expressively true; we must also allow for its possible propositional truth."[104] One may further recall that in his preferred approach, religion does not preclude the cognitivity

99. *ND*, 64.

100. *ND*, 65.

101. *ND*, 64. That intrasystematic truth is of greater significance is merely implied.

102. *ND*, 64.

103. *ND*, 64.

104. *ND*, 63.

of religious truth claims—just that "the cognitive aspect, while often important, is not primary."[105] It is important to note that the "concession" to the propositional carries a caveat that truth is to be understood as a "lived" reality. In his memorable words,

> There is . . . a sense in which truth as correspondence can retain its significance even for a religion whose truth is primarily categorial rather than propositional. A religion thought of as comparable to a cultural system, as a set of language games correlated with a form of life, may as a whole correspond or not correspond to what a theist calls God's being and will. As actually lived, a religion may be pictured as a single gigantic proposition.[106]

Thus, truth for Lindbeck cannot adequately be expressed in terms of a proposition or experience. Truth is dependent on the extent to which "objectivities are interiorized and exercised by groups or individuals in such a way as to conform them in some measure in the various dimensions of their existence to the ultimate reality and goodness that lies at the heart of things."[107] Falsity is simply the failure to achieve that end. As David Fergusson has rightly inferred, truth for Lindbeck is only attained by a "total existential conformity" of one's self to God.[108]

It may be of interest to observe how closely Lindbeck's notions of truth coincide with those held by Wittgenstein: intrasystematic truth matching Wittgenstein's later view on truth, and ontological truth matching his earlier position. The coherence of intrasystematic truth with its stress on "the total relevant context" is but another way of making the same point by Wittgenstein regarding languages functioning with language games. In Lindbeck's description of ontological truth, it is not difficult to uncover elements from both the early and later Wittgenstein.

Returning to the two types of truth—intrasystematic and ontological—it is clear that Lindbeck does not see a dissonance between them. He is of the view that the former is a necessary though insufficient condition for the latter. Consequently, he grants and assigns intrasystematic truth a greater "fundamental significance" over ontological truth. To some, Lindbeck's position at correlating the two

---

105. *ND*, 35.

106. *ND*, 51.

107. *ND*, 51.

108. Fergusson, "Meaning, Truth, and Realism," 196.

notions of truth will not satisfy, as was his unconvincing attempt at defining the notion of intrasystematic truth as equivalent to the truth of coherence—a matter to which we shall return later. For my part, I do not think the two notions require a defense, since as Fergusson has rightly observed, the conjunction between them "is held together by a Thomistic theory of meaning."[109] If this is so, we are back to a point that the later Wittgenstein has made—that meaning is prior to the concept of truth. Also, the truth or falsity of a statement is in part dependent on what it means. Fergusson's elaboration in this regard is helpful:

> Here we see an attempt to construct a doctrine of analogy . . . which holds together ideas about truth and use. In our statements about God the signified (*significatum*) corresponds to the divine being whereas the mode of signifying (*modus significandi*) does not. The statement that "God is good" affirms that there is a notion of goodness unavailable to us which applies to God. Yet although our mode of signifying is analogous to something in itself unknown its function is the performative one of enabling us to live and act as if God were good in the way we ordinarily understand goodness. The theory of analogy thus deployed enables us to hold that a religious utterance is true if it is correctly used and its significatum corresponds to God.[110]

In the provocative example of the crusader cited above, is Lindbeck correct to judge the crusader's cry "*Christus est Dominus*" false for the reason he has stated? Fergusson thinks that if Lindbeck has properly differentiated between meaning and use, a different conclusion would have prevailed: the crusader would be considered to have made a true statement; "the obscenity resides not in the fact that the statement is false but that its *use* is grotesque."[111] For, as Fergusson contends, "if the statement is ontologically true it is not because it is being properly used; it is true because of the way things are independently of my asserting them to be so."[112] It may be instructive to note that Fergusson's argument that the crusader's statement is true is one that is based on his own seeing of truth in terms of correspondence, even if he takes cognizance of Wittgenstein's insight about the place of use.

109. Fergusson, "Meaning, Truth, and Realism," 196.
110. Fergusson, "Meaning, Truth, and Realism," 196.
111. Fergusson, "Meaning, Truth, and Realism," 197 (emphasis added).
112. Fergusson, "Meaning, Truth, and Realism," 197.

The relevance of all this for my argument is that we can still claim to be making meaningfully true statements about God even when we grant that the language we use cannot and should not be pressed to yield absolute precision or comprehension about God.

Reactions/Queries

As expected, Lindbeck's "cultural-linguistic" approach has drawn "flak" from various audiences, especially those he has broadly classified as the "propositionalists" or "cognitivists" and the "experiential-expressivists." Even those who subscribe to a combination of "propositionalist" and "experiential-expressivist" views have not remained silent. Consequently, much has been written in critique of Lindbeck's approach and ideas.[113] In this section, I will look at only some of the points raised.

To be sure, some of the critics have recognized merits in the "postliberal" scheme. For instance, McGrath credits and endorses Lindbeck for his "timely and persuasive" critique of the experiential-expressive theory of doctrine.[114] Kevin Vanhoozer (b. 1957) considers his corrective of propositionalism helpful.[115] And from the pen of Hans Frei (1922–1988), a generous compliment for Lindbeck's rightful ordering of priorities—subjecting theology to be in the service of the church first, before and above the interest of the academy.[116]

The first of several rejoinders to Lindbeck's project I would like to bring up is that from D. Z. Phillips (1934–2006) who in his book, *Faith after Foundationalism* has expressed concern that theologians and philosophers may simply use the notion of grammar *itself* to determine the direction in which they want theological doctrines to develop.[117] Phillips observes that Wittgenstein's remark "theology as grammar" then becomes the "handmaid of a particular theological development."[118] He adjudges Lindbeck to be among those who have so misappropriated the notion of grammar. Lindbeck's error is in wrongly concluding "that seeing theology as a kind of grammar entails not talking of God as an

---

113. See the Bibliography for some of the responses and reviews.

114. McGrath, "Evangelical Evaluation of Postliberalism," 27.

115. Vanhoozer, *Drama of Doctrine*, 89.

116. Frei, "Epilogue," 278.

117. Phillips, *Faith after Foundationalism*, 195.

118. Phillips, *Faith after Foundationalism*, 195–96.

independent reality and ceasing to make truth claims concerning him."[119] All that one can derive from the Wittgensteinian notion, Phillips clarifies, is that such God-talk "should be understood within the grammar of the religious discourse in which it is made."[120]

Phillips makes a further complaint that he is unable to locate the "audience" that Lindbeck's book seeks to talk about and address.[121] Behind Phillips's complaint is the underlying dissatisfaction with Lindbeck for giving a "confused" account of his rival theories of religion and doctrine. Even more serious is the charge that he may have "misrepresented religious realities."[122] Hence, his remark about Lindbeck engaging in "language idling."[123]

Whereas Phillips's criticism of Lindbeck's treatment of rival views on doctrine has largely been on philosophical grounds, the criticisms advanced by others are less so. McGrath, for instance seems offended that propositionalists have been called names like "voluntarist," "intellectualist," or "literalist," and described as people who "combine unusual insecurity with naïvete."[124] B. A. Gerrish takes exception to remarks by Lindbeck that "for a propositionalist, if a doctrine is once true, it is always true, and if it is once false, it is always false"[125] and that "there are no degrees or variations in propositional truth."[126] He thinks Lindbeck's portrayal in effect imputes an inflexibility to the propositionalist that is simply false. On the contrary, he argues, "propositionalists may very well think in terms of the *relative adequacy* of a doctrinal definition, adequacy being assessed, at least initially, by reference to its original historical context."[127] They are, he claims, not closed off to the possibility of doctrines being "reappraised, reformulated, qualified, amplified, or supplemented" at some future time.[128] While he is not altogether opposed to Lindbeck's account of the propositionalist view, Vanhoozer adjudges it "thin" and

---

119. Phillips, *Faith after Foundationalism*, 211.

120. Phillips, *Faith after Foundationalism*, 211.

121. Phillips, *Faith after Foundationalism*, 197–99.

122. Phillips, *Faith after Foundationalism*, 204.

123. Phillips, *Faith after Foundationalism*, 199.

124. McGrath, "Evangelical Evaluation of Postliberalism," 29. The same criticism was first made in his *Genesis of Doctrine*, 18.

125. *ND*, 16.

126. *ND*, 47.

127. Gerrish, "Nature of Doctrine," 88.

128. Gerrish, "Nature of Doctrine," 88.

"rather simplistic."[129] My response to these criticisms is one of only partial agreement: for there can be no doubt that among those described as propositionalists are many who are indeed absolutists.

A serious criticism against the "cultural-linguistic" theory has been its assumption that language is a "given"; or as McGrath puts it, that "language" is just there.[130] To be sure, Lindbeck's claim is more a claim that language (and culture) precedes experience—that it is "a condition for religious experience."[131] "Thus," he asserts, "language, it seems, shapes domains of human existence and action that are preexperiential."[132] I suspect the root cause of the misunderstanding lies in Lindbeck's metaphor, namely, a religion is (like) a language.[133]

Behind McGrath's criticism is a more basic concern about divine revelation. Lindbeck is asked to respond as to "whether the Christian idiom, articulated in Scripture and hence in the Christian tradition emerges from accumulated human insight or from the self-disclosure of God in the Christ event."[134] Not finding an answer throughout his analysis, McGrath unfairly indicts him for "a studied evasion of the central question of revelation."[135] One wonders might the fact that Lindbeck is more concerned about theological method than theological content be a sufficient explanation for the absence of treatment of revelation in his project?

The "rule" or "regulative" theory pertaining to church doctrine may be faulted for encouraging a certain relativism. Under the refashioned theory, doctrines have become rules, or more accurately, rule-like: they no longer bear ideational content, in stark contradiction to the traditional view in which doctrines are formulations of beliefs about objective realities. So how exactly do doctrines-as-rules function? According to Lindbeck, "doctrines regulate truth claims by excluding some and permitting others, but the logic of their communally authoritative use hinders or prevents

---

129. Vanhoozer, *Drama of Doctrine*, 88.

130. McGrath, "Evangelical Evaluation of Postliberalism," 34.

131. *ND*, 37.

132. *ND*, 37.

133. Kelsey, "Church Discourse and Public Realm," 8.

134. McGrath, "Evangelical Evaluation of Postliberalism," 34.

135. McGrath, "Evangelical Evaluation of Postliberalism," 34.

them from specifying positively what is to be affirmed."[136] Given such an understanding, Lindbeck arrives at the following inference:

> Thus oppositions between rules can in some instances be resolved, not by altering one or both of them, but by specifying when or where they apply, or by stipulating which of the competing directives take precedence.[137]

Lindbeck's rule theory seems devised chiefly to secure the harmony of conflicting doctrines, even to the extent of making light their differences. Hence the criticism of relativism.

The next issue I wish to raise under the present discussion has had a brief mention in our earlier discussion about Lindbeck's notions of truth. It concerns the criticism directed at Lindbeck for advancing the view that intrasystematic truth is equivalent to the truth of coherence. We may recall his attempt at defining the concept: "Utterances are intrasystematically true when they cohere with the total relevant context, which, in the case of a religion when viewed in cultural-linguistic terms, is not only other utterances but also the correlative forms of life."[138] D. Z. Phillips's objection is that the notion of "coherence" is entirely unmediated, since "no context has been given for it."[139] In the above definition, Lindbeck's expression "cohere with the total context" has been qualified to refer to "correlative forms of life." Whatever this, and what Lindbeck has elsewhere called the "Most Important" and the "Ultimately Real" may be, they are just concepts fitted in a logical space to create an illusion.[140] More importantly, Lindbeck's twinning of intrasystematic and ontological truth has been criticized for confusing truth and use. The confusion is evident in the many statements made by Lindbeck himself where pragmatic considerations are seen to be determinative of coherence/truth value. I cite two as examples:

> Medieval scholastics spoke of truth as an adequation of the mind to the thing . . . but in the religious domain, this mental isomorphism [coherence] of the knowing and the known can

136. *ND*, 19.
137. *ND*, 18.
138. *ND*, 64.
139. Phillips, *Faith after Foundationalism*, 206.
140. Phillips, *Faith after Foundationalism*, 206.

be pictured as part and parcel of a wider conformity of the self to God.[141]

> The same point can be made by means of J. L. Austin's notion of a "performatory" use of language: a religious utterance, one might say, acquires the propositional truth of ontological correspondence only insofar as it is a performance, an act or deed, which helps create that correspondence.[142]

Evidently, in Lindbeck's construal, religious truth is a matter of the correspondence between reality (what is the Most Important, the Ultimately Real) and a lifestyle or a pattern of desired behavior. Detecting such a confusion in Lindbeck's line of approach, Fergusson gives a well-reasoned critique:

> The proper use of a statement does indeed depend on context and the warrants for assertion provided by the religion. . . . Correct use is [however] neither equivalent to nor a necessary condition of truth.[143]

Fruits

Despite the various criticisms directed at it, the "cultural-linguistic" approach to religion has a number of "fruits" which may be harvested to help us do constructive theology in what Lindbeck has termed "a postliberal age." I will now try to look at some of these. Lindbeck's crystallization of how religion is like a language and a culture, and his drawing on Wittgenstein (and other social scientists, like Geertz and Peter G. Winch [1926–1957]) may also provide some support for my own thesis about the proper place of words and statements in discourse about God.

One of the great strengths of the cultural-linguistic theory, in particular, its rule theory on doctrines, is its usefulness in serving the ecumenical cause. Of course, all hinges on whether the basic assumption that doctrines are second-order rules governing first-order talk of divine matters is readily agreed to. Traditionalists and propositionalists will need to be convinced that the doctrines they hold about the divine and

---

141. *ND*, 65.

142. *ND*, 65.

143. Fergusson, "Meaning, Truth, and Realism," 197.

such understanding of reality as they have reached, are in part a social construct.

While the "cultural-linguistic" theory can help Christians come to terms with ecumenism, it also insists upon a proper respect towards religions as distinct groups with "family resemblances" between them. Lindbeck argues against a reduction of religions to a single, universal religion. To attempt to unite all religions in the world is as foolish and unattainable as to want to reduce the world's different ways of speaking and thinking to a single language. The proposal to conceive of religions as resembling languages, together with "forms of life" associated with them (read "culture"), if pursued, will be good for fostering community life since such a conceptualization can only be fulfilled within a community. The reason is language is social; language always exists within a community. (We are reminded that private languages are logically impossible).[144] Since to be religious is to learn a language, one would need to attend to specific communities in which that language is used. It follows that constructive theology must and can only take place communally.

There is an important advantage in Lindbeck's culture-linguistic approach which one must not miss. In conceptualizing religion in the characteristics of language, Lindbeck allows that the former can be viewed from two different perspectives. That is to say, religion as a system can be interpreted as either (a) organized around a set of explicit first-order statements; or (b) constituted "by a set of stories used in specifiable ways to interpret and live in the world."[145] The difference is a significant one for revealing the level of intellectualism between the two positions. Yet, as Lindbeck observes, it is often overlooked by most believers, especially those who suppose that religious beliefs are expressed in first-order propositions that refer to objective divine realities. Characteristically, the believers in question do tend to have a "preference for doctrine and theological texts as the locus for truth-by-correspondence."[146] Lindbeck's counter-claim however is that religious truth cannot be located only on one level, i.e., whether there is correspondence or lack of correspondence; but that it must find expression in issues related to practical living. He explains,

---

144. See *ND*, 38.

145. *ND*, 64.

146. Cathey, *God in Postliberal Perspective*, 53.

For the cognitivist, it is chiefly technical theology and doctrine which are propositional, while on the [cultural-linguistic] model, propositional truth and falsity characterize ordinary religious language when it is used to mold lives through prayer, praise, preaching, and exhortation. It is only on this level that human beings linguistically exhibit their truth or falsity, their correspondence or lack of correspondence to the Ultimate Mystery.[147]

It stands to reason that when religious truth-claims are construed wholly or chiefly on the basis of correspondence, the prospect of possible error becomes unacceptable or intolerable. The idea that a religion must be error-free is seen by most adherents as essential if that religion is not to be surpassed.[148] But precisely that is how the intellectualism we spoke about is brought on. Indeed, Lindbeck thinks that both the Protestant belief in scriptural inerrancy and the Roman Catholic tradition of papal infallibility are patterned after "vulgarized forms of a rationalism descended from Greek philosophy by way of Cartesian and post-Cartesian rationalism reinforced by Newtonian science."[149] The way I see things, the intellectualistic mentality, the temper of our time, is insidiously seeking to reduce religion to concepts or tenets that all seem to hold together. This form of intellectualism is a menace to religion for failing, in Lindbeck's words, "to do justice to the fact that a religious system is more like a natural language than a formally organized set of explicit statements, and that the right use of this language, unlike a mathematical one, cannot be detached from a particular way of behaving."[150] In a way, this is what I seek to argue in my work—that assertions and statements have their proper place in religious discourse, and that such utterances need not be inerrant or infallible even if they are fact-stating. Nor should statements attempting to speak of God be expected to be precise or exhaustive, as if they are statements of science.

Last but not the least, another strength to be gained from Lindbeck's "cultural-linguistic" paradigm comes from his insistence that meaning is located within the text. The traditionalist, on the other hand, would insist on locating religious meaning outside the text.[151] The methodology of

147. *ND*, 69.

148. *ND*, 49.

149. *ND*, 51.

150. *ND*, 64.

151. *ND*, 114.

locating meaning within the text goes under the moniker "intratextual theology." Lindbeck's definition of this particular methodology has almost become classic:

> Intratextual theology redescribes reality within the scriptural framework rather than translating Scripture into extrascriptural categories. It is the text, so to speak, which absorbs the world, rather than the world the text.[152]

One can of course find faults with the "intratextual" methodology, especially if one is concerned solely with the question of truth or facticity. Lindbeck would be mistaken if he thinks that "the truth of a statement is dependent upon its location within the semantic system, rather than upon its reference to reality beyond the system."[153] Yet, there are fruits to be harvested from it to aid one's theological reflection. I cite two:

(i) the intratextual approach enables Scripture to function as the lens through which one views the world;

(ii) the intratextual method aids a reading of Scripture that is not focussed on the literal meaning of a text in isolation from its wider historical and communal settings.

Thus, an intratextual reading of Scripture will require the reader to "derive the interpretive framework that designates the theologically controlling sense from the literary structure of the text itself"[154] and not merely from isolated verses or passages. What needs to be recognized is that such intratextuality may prove a highly complex process involving skillful application of the principles of biblical criticism. Given that some biblical texts do pull in different directions, complete reconciliation may not be attainable.

Assessing George Lindbeck's Assumptions

In this concluding section, I propose to do a brief evaluation of the main assumptions which have underpinned or are reflected in Lindbeck's approach to religion. My burden is to identify implicit features in the assumptions which are relevant or useful for resisting the tendency to

152. *ND*, 118.
153. Loughlin, *Telling God's Story*, 158.
154. *ND*, 120.

situate religious language either in a metaphysical analysis concerned about objective truth-claims and exact definitions about divine reality, or in a phenomenological description of religious experience. The former, i.e., the tendency to regard language as competent to convey objective and complete accounts of the divine, is that which my own work seeks to disavow.

I start by reaffirming a point made earlier that in each of the theories of religion and doctrine discussed by Lindbeck, a backdrop of a linguistic practice is presupposed. That is, each is premised on a particular theory of the role of language. The reader will recall the correlation between all three theories with their respective types of language, namely, the "cognitive-propositional," the "experiential-expressive," and the "cultural-linguistic." That said, I should highlight the fact that Lindbeck's own "cultural-linguistic" model is not only correlated to a theory of language, it is largely driven by language as its central analogy. This analogy has been useful for him in several ways, not least in providing "the conceptual resources that underpin interpretation."[155] That Lindbeck's ideas and proposals have essentially an analogical character is thus not to be gainsaid or missed, and it is good that this observation be held in mind. For one of the temptations the general reader of Lindbeck is likely to succumb to is the failure to attend to the "principle of analogy." In all analogies, the issue is not one of arriving at complete adequacy of description or discourse, but rather an approximation of truth. By their very nature, analogies are limited since what they are principally concerned to do is make comparison between an object or idea with some other thing that is familiar but different from it. Their force depends on how they identify and illuminate the similitudes of the objects or ideas being compared (say, religion and language), and on how effectively these are brought to bear on the argument at hand. As such, they are somewhat constricted in compass and are even prone to selectivity with respect to the presenting data. All this with regard to analogies is of course well known, even Kelsey's caution about "the danger of relying on them beyond their capacity to illumine."[156] We should thus not be surprised that Lindbeck's use of the language analogy in proposing the "cultural-linguistic" theory has evoked the criticism that his project is riddled with certain obscurities. To give just one example, there is the negative

155. Dehart, *Trial of the Witnesses*, 161.
156. Kelsey, "Church Discourse and Public Realm," 30.

comment that some "other aspects of the lives of religious communities may have been obscured by this central analogy."[157] What should really surprise us are criticisms of the sort that call into question one or another aspect of the analogies in themselves.

The use of linguistic analogy by Lindbeck in driving his interpretation of religion, as well as the emphasis on language in the development of his theological perspective, are in my view, generally apt and constructive. For starters, the linguistic outlook on the religious phenomenon is thus properly raised to the fore. This contrasts with the trend prevalent within the field of the social sciences to understand religion only or mainly as a cultural phenomenon. Referring to his own theory with its distinct roots on the cultural and linguistic sides, Lindbeck observes that "it is only rarely and recently that it has become a programmatic approach to the study of religion."[158] Among theologians, the awareness of language and its place in religious life is not altogether novel but their interest has been principally concerned with the problematic of language use in expressing God, namely, human language's adequacy or inadequacy to do that. By adding "linguistic" to the term, Lindbeck is thus making the point that we cannot overlook the dimension of meaning in social interchanges, concerned as we otherwise are with discerning the dynamics of social structures or individual psyches operating on the cultural level in religion. In short, religion is "a comprehensive interpretive medium" bestowed with its own guiding logic and grammar. An important footnote in the first chapter of ND reveals Lindbeck's design, "It is this relatively greater emphasis on the internal logic or grammar of religions which differentiates what I am calling 'cultural-linguistic' approaches to religion from more one-sidedly cultural ones."[159]

We may thus justifiably state that most of the assumptions underlying the development of Lindbeck's "cultural-linguistic" theory have arisen from his sensitivity to recent shifts in the theories of religion.[160] The assumption I am about to introduce is certainly one of them. In his foreword to ND, Lindbeck refers to a view espoused by philosophers of science that in the practice of empirical and objective disciplines such as physics and chemistry, all observation terms and all observation

---

157. Dehart, *Trial of the Witnesses*, 67.

158. *ND*, 20.

159. *ND*, 28.

160. So Davaney, *Pragmatic Historicism*, 30–41.

sentences are "theory-laden"—that is to say, the facts pertaining to these are *alterable* according to the adoption of a particular theory.[161] Somewhat analogously, within a religion or among religions, the same difficulty of accounting for differences obtains—perhaps even more forcefully—with each of the theories on religion and doctrine subscribing to a particular view of what is relevant evidence for or against the adequacy of its own perspective. "There is," he concedes, "no higher neutral standpoint from which to adjudicate their competing perceptions of what is factual and/ or anomalous. Comprehensive outlooks on religion, not to mention religions themselves, are not susceptible to decisive confirmation or disconfirmation."[162] Now for a long time, philosophers and even theologians have made much of this same notion that there is no higher, neutral or impartial ground for adjudicating differences and variances of opinion between religious systems or schools of thought. Richard Rorty who has asserted both the ubiquity and contingency of language, has argued that "there is no standpoint outside the particular historically conditioned and temporary vocabulary we are presently using from which to judge this vocabulary."[163] For the textualist Don Cupitt, language is, as it were, "able to explain itself entirely in terms of itself," and so there is "no need to go outside language."[164] Indeed, "there is no eternal and impartial standpoint" from which we can assess the various perspectives that we find ourselves exploring.[165] Many other known voices have joined in to sing the same refrain that language has no outside, that there is no escape from it. On his part, Lindbeck is probably more motivated by a conciliatory desire to demonstrate that while each religion as an interpretative medium can develop its own corpus of beliefs and dogmas, and even establish its own canons of justification, there can be no basis for asserting the truth of such beliefs and dogmas against other competing claims.[166] The sheer incommensurability between religions

---

161. See *ND*, 11.

162. *ND*, 11.

163. Rorty, *Contingency, Irony, and Solidarity*, 48. He adds, "For there will be no way to rise above the language, culture, institutions, and practices one has adopted and view all these as on a par with all the others" (50).

164. Cupitt, *Long-Legged Fly*, 18.

165. Cupitt, *Long-Legged Fly*, 29.

166. It is also correct to suggest that Lindbeck is concerned to point out that a "nontheological" theory of religion such as his does not need to *demonstrate* the superiority of one religion. See Trenery, *Alasdair MacIntyre*, 166.

simply rules out any basis for doing that. Admittedly, the way I have put matters thus far may suggest that the issue of relativism does not arise, or that it can be conveniently put to one side. The case is quite otherwise: Lindbeck has had his worries over it. For example, he concedes that his "intratextuality seems wholly relativistic: it turns religions, so one can argue, into self-enclosed and incommensurable intellectual ghettoes."[167] He further adds, "If there are no universal or foundational structures and standards of judgment by which one can decide between different religious and nonreligious options, the choice of any one of them becomes, it would seem, purely irrational, a matter of arbitrary whim or blind faith."[168] We ask, does Lindbeck's "cultural-linguistic" account offer any way to overcome relativism? The plain answer, we have seen, is there is no direct or quick way to judge the truth of religious statements. If we have understood Lindbeck correctly, his model disavows the approach to truth as the preserve of atomistic, independent and individual knowers in favor of a return to a sense of religion as a "form of life" bound up with the tangible practices of a lived community. Analogous to the methods of testing scientific theories or views, "confirmation or disconfirmation occurs through an accumulation of successes or failures in making practically and cognitively coherent sense of relevant data."[169] The process of adjudication will naturally take time; and while it will "provide warrants for taking reasonableness in religion seriously"—that is, "religious claims nevertheless can be tested and argued about in various ways"—the different perspectives will not be decided on the basis of reason alone.[170] If it seems we are being put in a bind, the solution on offer is not a return to some foundationalist strategies of uncovering universal principles or structures, but an acceptance of a "tradition-guided" method of comparative assessment of rival views suggested by Alasdair MacIntyre (b. 1929).[171] For the truth of a religion, on the "cultural-linguistic" theory, is not just an objective proposition or an abstraction to be believed but a reality bound up with the traditions, practices and conventions of a believing community identified with that religion. Ironically, such a

167. *ND*, 128.

168. *ND*, 130.

169. *ND*, 131.

170. *ND*, 131.

171. This is a complex and rigorous process of assessing rival claims in the belief that it is possible to get at truth. See MacIntyre, *Whose Justice? Which Rationality?*, esp. 354–69.

characterization certainly tells more about the truth of that religion than ostensibly abstract truth-claims ever could.

Lindbeck's creative employment of the language analogy in his approach to religion is, I suggest, predicated upon the premise that human persons are linguistic and textually constructed, as is religion itself. While we have said that we are embedded in language, this is only partially the case, for the converse is not yet considered, namely that language is in us too. On this account, language is like a Kantian *a priori*, in the sense that our whole sense of the world—of what is the case—is shaped and formed by the socially-constructed discourses in which we are engaged and located. Simply put, having a language is a prerequisite for the possibility of experience, religious or otherwise. An oft-repeated claim made by Lindbeck has been that while experience occurs within the signs and symbols of language, it is the former that is shaped, molded and constituted by the latter.[172] Recall his famous contention, "There are numberless thoughts we cannot think, sentiments we cannot have, and realities we cannot perceive unless we learn to use the appropriate symbol systems."[173] This stress on language as making possible inner thoughts, sentiments, the description of realities and even the formulation of beliefs is a welcome departure from the traditional thinking that language is merely a tool or instrument for "expression" and a derivative one at that. How then does all of this relate to the external and objective reality, assuming that it is there, and is itself not a linguistic construct? I have added the qualifier "assuming that it is there" because this external and objective reality is these days commonly not assumed or is considered hypothetical by some anti-realist thinkers. In point of fact, the existence of an external and objective reality or simply "what is the case" is not denied, except by those who subscribe to an extreme form of anti-realism. Actually, it is already a very difficult thing to convince oneself or others that nothing exists out there, let alone deny that the world—yes, even the world-in-itself—exists. For there seems to be "a certain undeniable givenness to the universe" or what is objectively out there.[174] In this connection, these words from Gerard Loughlin are

172. He also expresses the view that "human beings are so thoroughly programmed genetically for language use that apart from acquiring a language they cannot properly develop physiologically . . . but remain peculiarly immature in their sensory and physical competence" (*ND*, 37).

173. *ND*, 34.

174. Grenz and Franke, *Beyond Foundationalism*, 53.

most apposite, "But one of the things that we know *in* language is that there are things *outside* language."[175] It follows that the affirmation by the Christian or the theist of the reality of God is one that can be plausibly made. However, in light of our present discussion about our linguisticity, we would want to do so while allowing that such an affirmation can take place only within language, or better, within a story. We might even insist that what we know is known only in and through language. Two theological payoffs for such a move may be briefly noted. In the first place, we are led to a reverent appreciation that the objectivity of the divine is not that of a static, fixed and perhaps impersonal reality. It is not a sort of "Thing-in-itself" or a "fact" existing in or outside the universe. Rather, the divine reality is perceived and experienced as it comes to us through the story of the gospel, as God has so ordained. Secondly, the claim that the divine objectivity is experienced via language, that it is co-temporal with our linguistically constructed reality, entails that we preserve the distinctiveness of Christian (or religious) discourse, avoiding the pitfalls of linguistic practices which tends towards absolutism or idolatry on the one pole, and expressivism or sentimentalism on the other.

As a final note, I would like to consider the concept of "form of life," which has played a critical role in Lindbeck's methodology. One of his criticisms of churches is that they have become more concerned that church members "embark on their own individual quests for symbols of transcendence," than that they themselves become "communities that socialize their members into coherent and comprehensive religious outlooks and forms of life."[176] In his book, the "cognitive-propositional" and the "experiential-expressive" models are deemed weak for not emphasizing the importance of practices of religious communities. These models seem to have failed to appreciate religion as a "form of life." In contrast, Lindbeck himself has set great store by the concept of "form of life." In his "cultural-linguistic" model, religion is conceived as akin to "languages together with their correlative forms of life."[177] From his dense articulation in connection with our present concern two further inferences may be discerned. Firstly, he privileges the performance or practice of a community against believing or profession of faith. Given that "a religion is essentially bound up with the communal *form* of its

---

175. Loughlin, *Telling God's Story*, 23.

176. *ND*, 126.

177. *ND*, 18.

practices,"[178] one becomes religious by interiorizing a set of skills by practice and training. Secondly, he regards religious truth or falsity as dependent on the success or failure of a community internalizing its religion as a form of life. To reinforce this view, Lindbeck argues that the belief that Christ's Lordship is an objective fact must still be attested by believers actually doing something about it, namely, to commit themselves to a way of life.[179] The positions we have noted are among the stock-in-trade of philosophers of language who have insisted that the question of meaning or truth cannot be decided or settled without considering the social practices within which language and justification make sense. This is another way of saying that the meaning of a proposition or statement is not simply arrived at by looking or defining at its constituent words or by trying to relate it to some possible state or states of affairs. The great service of a concept like "form of life" is in showing the language user that the meaning of propositions is not some "object" or "thing" clothed in words, but rather it is linked to the actions or activities in which those propositions are used by people.

In sum, we may say Lindbeck is right as far as he goes, leaving us with useful lessons and tools for understanding doctrine. The expression of doctrine is of course a function of religious language.

178. Smith, *Who's Afraid of Relativism?*, 159.
179. *ND*, 66.

Chapter 7

Conclusions: Reordering
How We See Language

> The problems arising through a misinterpretation of our forms of language have the character of *depth*. They are deep disquietudes; their roots are as deep in us as the forms of our language and their significance is as great as the importance of our language.[1]
>
> —Ludwig Wittgenstein

IN THIS STUDY, I have been concerned to advance the thesis that the language we use to talk about God can be fact-stating or cognitive, but that it cannot be pressed to yield a complete and exact description of the reality of God. The fact that words in themselves are often ambiguous and never completely transparent in the way they carry their meaning is obviously central here. But the root of the problem stems from the claim that God's way of being is utterly different from human being or any other mode of being present in this world, to the extent that he is beyond human discernment. Moreover, God and language appear to be incommensurable and there seems to be no common ground or point of overlap between them.[2] To borrow an expression by Aquinas, even the

1. *PI* 111.

2. The notion of incommensurability is of course borrowed from the philosophy of science. It contends that two paradigms are said to be incommensurable if there is no "third paradigm" into which they can be translated without remainder or equivocation for the purpose of providing common standard of measurement against each other.

188

"names" we use to signify God or predicate his substance "fall short of a full representation of him."[3]

As explained in my introductory chapter, it is precisely because of such difficulties that many religious people have found themselves wedged between two poles. One tendency is to regard religious statements as having no factual content, or as only amounting to the expression of moral or ethical intentions or exhortations. The other is the tendency to assume that words are perfectly fitted to render the divine completely intelligible and to give believers precise explanations. These two tendencies are known, respectively, to engender skepticism and absolutism. What my project hopes to inspire is a *via media*—something in the order of a non-objectifying form of religious language, the use made of which honors transcendence and caters for the need for self-expression.

In the preceding chapters, our consideration of the various cluster of issues concerning language—its phenomenon and "discovery," its problematic nature, the historical approaches to its employment, and so on—as well our exploration of the leading ideas in Wittgenstein and Lindbeck have provided a fund for constructing a defense for our central claim. In what follows, I shall attempt to pull the different threads together, examining the key principles and drawing some inferences—an exercise which, it is hoped, might move us further forward in the direction of "how to avoid not speaking of God."[4] This task, I anticipate, will not be a tidy one; inevitably, it will also at times appear a little repetitive as material from earlier chapters is reviewed.

Distinguishing between "Sign" and "Thing"

In chapter 1, we offered a brief sketch of how language came to be "discovered." We observed that the early Greek thinkers regarded language as an instrument or tool in the service of communicating and distinguishing thoughts. As such, it was structured in such a way that a strict separation between "sign" (*signum*) and "thing" (*res*) was always maintained, even as the etymological relations between words and what words mean were explored.[5] I believe Socrates's widely-known attempts

---

See Tilley, "Incommensurability, Intratextuality, and Fideism," 87–111.

3. Aquinas, *Summa Theologiae* 13.2.

4. This expression is a chapter title in Smith, *Speech and Theology*, 3–15.

5. The adjective "etymological" is used to limit the scope of relations between

at defining concepts like "justice," "knowledge," and "good" stem from this interest in an analytic understanding of words and their meanings. As for Plato, language is a clear reflection of what exists in reality, with words mirroring the "furniture" of the universe, which is to say forms, concepts or ideas. We note, however, that in his linguistic schema, the possibility of any sort of "essential" relation between word and thing is always ruled out since worldly reality will always fall short of the perfect ideal reality or form. This basic approach to language adopted by these early Greek thinkers has been the dominant paradigm ever since; it has certainly had a significant influence on Christian thought regarding language. Not surprisingly, throughout the history of Christianity, long and bitter disputes had been fought over what words actually mean or represent. The celebrated Arian controversy in the fourth century over whether Jesus Christ is the same as God—or, put in theological language, whether the Son is of *one* substance (*homoousios*) with the Father or is he of a *similar* substance (*homoiousios*) with the Father—is a case in point.[6] In my view, this and other important controversies that helped shape and define Christian orthodoxy may not have arisen in such an acute form if the Christian religion in its wrestling with language had made a distinction between sign and thing. The fact is that the two notions should always be distinguished because they *do* differ from one another, not least, in how they function. A sign, like an indicator, points beyond itself to what is signified, whereas a thing is a kind of stopping point, an end-in-itself. An example may help to make the distinction clear: the word "t-r-e-e" is a *sign* that one uses to point or refer to the *thing* that grows tall and green out there.[7] Any collapse of sign and thing into one indistinguishable whole, were that to happen, would probably result

---

verbal expression and meaning-content to aspects which relate to the origin and historical development of words and their meanings. Thus, to envisage a connection etymologically is to putatively trace words back to their roots to establish if there is any semblance or analogy between them and the thing named. See Milbank, *Word Made Strange*, 89.

6. Macquarrie has argued that the controversy was not so much over metaphysical essences represented by the distinction between "*homoousios*" and "*homoiousios*" as over the issue of whether Christ can be given the allegiance of faith unless he really is God (*God-Talk*, 15–16). Still, language had been a key underlying factor in the debate.

7. Smith remarks, "Signs are always instrumental. . . . You go *through* a sign to get to a thing" (*Who's Afraid of Relativism?*, 66). Certain things may themselves become signs, pointing to some further reality. Augustine teaches that certain "things" in scripture serve as signs by pointing us to Christ.

in indifference or even obliviousness on the part of the church fathers
with regard to the precise distinctions between the varieties of language
structure, function and meaning. Weighing in on this aspect of language,
Pannenberg writes, "It is thus essential to the function of the sign that
we should distinguish them. We must not equate the thing with the sign
in its weakness. Only by this distinction can the thing signified be, in a
certain sense, present by way of the sign."[8] In light of our awareness of
how words and meaning are intricately connected, I submit that in our
approach to the problem of religious language we continue to distinguish
between sign and thing.[9] To state the obvious, the notion of God's radical
otherness requires the disavowal of any conflation of the two entities.
Words we use to talk about God are distinct from the reality of God
himself. Moreover, and in the context of our present discussion, we
believe the only way we can have access to the eternal and ultimate thing
(*res*) is through the proper mediation of sign or signs (*signa*). *Res per
signa discuntur*: "things are learnt about through signs," as St. Augustine
famously insists.[10] Even so, that must not be taken to imply that signs
can signify or represent fully. Nor should they be expected to render
complete and exact descriptions. Here I recall Wittgenstein's observation
that the concepts of understanding, meaning and thinking are concepts
with "blurred edges."[11] The foregoing remarks have an obvious link to
the claims of my work: they are an invitation to theology to undertake a
careful analysis and form an accurate estimate of its own language.

Eclecticism

In the same chapter (1), the three traditional responses to the problem
of religious language were also touched upon, namely the *via negativa*
or the "apophatic way," the doctrine of analogy of Aquinas, and the
univocal way of Duns Scotus. Though these approaches are creative
and ingenious, none has won universal acceptance by the religious or
philosophical communities in either the past or the present. The reason

8. Pannenberg, *Systematic Theology*, 3:32.

9. We note the validity of Rowan Williams's reminder that "language is always
'triangulated' between the sign, the signmaker, and the signified" (*Edge of Words*, 33).
We are not suggesting that the three terms be reduced to two; it is just that in our
present discussion the role of the "signmaker" is simply assumed.

10. St. Augustine, *Teaching Christianity*, 39.

11. *PI* 71–76.

is not hard to ascertain: there are insurmountable difficulties—indeed, "fatal flaws," according to Stiver[12]—in each one of them. Yet, we may still defend them as being necessary for God-talk since the reality of God is beyond all conceptual determination. Gallantly, each of them seeks to give expression to the principle that though the transcendent God resists and is beyond language, some way must be found to express him in words, however inadequately. Not to attempt to find a way to do that is to be content with either silence—which, as I have argued, must entail the end of theology and proclamation of the faith—or the embrace of agnosticism. My suggestion is that instead of sticking to any single-track way of speaking of God, we apply an eclectic approach by drawing from and mixing the various traditional ways, even stretching language beyond its normal usage while being fully aware of the obscurities and difficulties involved. It is unwise to limit our attention to one or two of the traditional ways; even more so to generalize and insist that only one of them is the correct pattern. As we have noted, the *via negativa*, the doctrine of analogy, and the univocal way, and even methods not previously discussed in our study (for example, Origen's allegorical interpretation of Scripture or Bultmann's demythologizing approach) have failed in one way or another to offer a wholly adequate solution to the problem of religious language. My proposal to pick and apply elements which best suit the *genre* and intention of the applicable text or context may well provide a way forward. What label we use to describe our methods or approaches is not important. What we must do, having learned from Wittgenstein, is not to think that language always functions in one, standard way.[13]

Another point we can learn from Wittgenstein is the indispensability of language. "It is *in language* that it's all done."[14] Yet, the repertoire of words available to us—for the most part at least—are drawn from the everyday and carry the same range of meanings. As such, they do not have any special status. In any encounter with a religious text, one is bound to become quickly aware that the majority of the words used in it are not exclusive to religion, being, in fact, shared with and among other types of discourse. Even with terms which are decidedly religious, they are not

---

12. Stiver, *Philosophy of Religious Language*, 29.

13. *PI* 304.

14. *PG*, 143.

viewed to have come pre-packaged with *a priori* meaning.[15] Yet, we are not claiming that terms used in religion and ordinary life have exactly the same meanings at all times. Not infrequently, words applied for the purpose of speaking of God are used in ways which differ from their use in an ordinary context. Take the example of "The Lord hears the prayer of the righteous." Surely, we are not meant to think of God as having ears like ours, spreading out to catch every word the righteous utters. But in most cases, where a word is used in both religious and secular contexts, its primary meaning is that which was first established in ordinary usage, though it retains a peculiar meaning and outlook when used in religion. In this light, I make the claim that although words are good enough to disclose aspects of the divine reality, they are not so specifiable as to render precise definitions and complete explanations.

The "Linguistic Turn"

The so-called "linguistic turn" of the last century ushered in a significant revolution in our thinking about language. With its dawn, every problem of philosophy is "turned" into a problem about language, or to be more precise, into a problem dependent upon issues that have to do with language. "Most questions and propositions of the philosophers result from the fact that we do not understand the logic of our language,"[16] the early Wittgenstein tells us. The Kantian emphasis on the knowing subject with its maxim that one must first understand knowing before one can be confident about what one knows is not so much abandoned as it is by-passed by a more legitimate consideration, namely, that to understand knowing one must first deal with the language in which it is expressed. In other words, we can no longer be concerned with only questions about *what* reality is or *how* reality can be known, but with a more basic question, namely, what do we *mean* by what we say in the assumptions, claims and even conclusions we make or draw.

In religious discourse and deliberations, the philosophical shift from a concern about questions of validity or truth to a concern with meaning will have the welcome effect of encouraging more clarification than argument. Misunderstandings, disagreements, or confusions over meaning should prompt open discussions rather than fights. Regardless

15. Brümmer, *Speaking of a Personal God*, 34.

16. *TLP* 4.003.

of whether the "linguistic turn" is thought to have run its course or not,[17] it would still be an essential move to start any reflective thought not with the question of truth but by going much further back—with language and meaning.

"Meaning as Use"

Meaning, as we have noted in chapter 2, is a question around which most of Wittgenstein's works revolved. Departing from common practice, Wittgenstein goes beyond the ostensive definition of the word "meaning" to the question of its implications for connecting thought, language and the world. What concerns him, we will recall, is not the foundational or logical form of meaning—certainly not what one can easily learn from the dictionary or from one's parents or school teacher—but what language can be and do when one uses it. Wittgenstein's opposition to the illicit use of the word "meaning" to signify that which "corresponds" to a word, his catchphrase that "the meaning of a word is its use in the language," and his advice not to confuse "to mean it" with "to think of it," have attained their status as the defining marks of his renewed position on meaning.[18]

As was pointed out in chapter 3, the notion of "meaning as use" must not be interpreted as an identification of "meaning" with "use." In the appeal to "use," we are directed to "look to see" not just language *per se* but, to borrow a phrase, what "goes in language at work."[19] The view that obtains is one of language being used for something, and that such use is always within a given context of human behavior. Such "uses" are multifarious: giving or obeying orders or instructions, reporting an event, pronouncing blessings upon friends, praying, and so forth.[20] Meaning (or sense, if you like) is not some sort of an entity or thing to be sought after with a view to logical analysis or empirical investigation; rather, meaning is in the application made of the words and sentences by human persons. To see meaning in the manner proposed is bound to alter how we look

17. For an exploration of how the idea of the "linguistic turn" took shape within a specific Euro-American historiographical context, see Surkis, "When Was the Linguistic Turn?," 700–722.

18. *PI* 40; 43; 693.

19. High, *Language, Persons and Belief*, 60.

20. *PI* 23.

at language. For one, we shall be relieved of our mental "cramps" in any attempt to locate a "single picture or theory of language" or to make claims as to what the essence of language is. It is not that the classic correlation between "word" and "thing" no longer holds, but that it is inadequate as an explanation for meaning. The lone, atomic word isolated from its larger context is often taken to be the primary bearer of meaning—but in most cases, it is not. Thus, to determine what a statement or proposition means, one must go beyond the neat order in language as well as the parts that constitute it. The exhortation to look at use may well open up a new vista of understanding for the language user—that the meaning of a word may change according to how it is used. This is especially relevant in the case of religious use of language because, as we have reiterated, many of the terms associated with religion have a variety of meanings attached to them.

Another (and perhaps more significant) feature about language arising from the principle of use may be noted. Language is used for something and its employment is towards some end. It is spoken within a community of practice concerned with some *telos,* from trying to do any of the things mentioned by Wittgenstein, to engaging in theoretical reflection like God-talk. In a sense then, we can speak of language and meaning being larger than words. Once again, we shall be led to alter how we look at language: if formerly our intelligence has been under a spell of "bewitchment . . . by means of our language"[21] and our assumption has been that language is only an abstract and *a priori* thing separated from human persons, we may begin to think differently.

These remarks about meaning have a direct bearing on my work. In the first place, when I contend that religious language cannot give a complete description or explanation of the divine reality, I am directing us "away from the idea that using a sentence involves imagining something for every word."[22] I am convinced that meaning is more than reference: words do more than refer or point to things or objects. Hence, to properly understand the language of religion, we must consider its use—that is, attend to its context and to how it relates to its intended purpose. To repeat a point made earlier, one must cease to think of religious words or terms as if they are some kinds of mental activity, or as if there is only one proper meaning applicable to each of them.

21. *PI* 109.

22. *PI* 449.

"Language-Games"

Wittgenstein's elaboration of the notions of "language-games" (*Sprachspiel*) and "form of life" (*Lebensform*) has given us a good general guide as to what he means by them, though there is still some ambiguity in the way they are presented. The numerous, simple "language-games" he cites reveal the workings of language and why it functions the way it does. A language-game, we are led to infer, is the practical context in which words and linguistic exchange make sense. As a reminder that language is indeterminate and not fixed, Wittgenstein tells us that there is a multiplicity of language-games. The term "form of life" similarly evokes the idea of language and forms of human discourse being embedded in life, within its cultural, social and historical settings.

The application to religious discourse is as follows. We are to see language as something immensely down-to-earth, that it is not merely concerned with making assertions, or stating of propositional truth claims. Nor, as we have seen, is language concerned merely to point or refer to things. If "language-games" are bound up with the activities and exigencies of human existence, then "the locus of meaning is not the line that connects the dots of a word to a thing; rather, the locus of meaning is an entire web of communal practice and conventions."[23] To speak of meaning in terms of community practice and conventions is to highlight two controversial but related aspects about language. First, meaning is *contingent* rather than necessary: it is not already decreed or determined by God. Secondly and in consequence, meaning is the result of agreement reached or arrived at by the community of language users. "Meaning," to borrow Gerard Loughlin's useful presentation,

> is not something other than signs, to which signs are somehow stuck, so that I know what the sign "cat" means because it has been stuck onto cats, or what "idea" means because it has been stuck onto ideas. I know what "cat" means because it is different from "hat" and "mat" and from other words of the lexicon, . . . These strings of signs have meaning because I know how to use them to do things within my language community. I can tell someone to get the cat off the mat.[24]

Now this idea that the meaningfulness and intelligibility of sentences and statements is related to and even determined by convention is no new

23. Smith, *Who's Afraid of Relativism?*, 48.
24. Loughlin, *Telling God's Story*, 12.

thing: it was affirmed by Aristotle who recognized the effects of linguistic structure(s) and rules of usage on language.[25] From such a point of view, language is understood as a deeply social phenomenon; it "cannot be understood purely as something oral," to use Steven Knowles's expression. In this connection, Knowles also makes an interesting point: "Things unsaid must be taken into consideration, and that which is unsaid is understood within its context."[26] He further observes, "When one learns a language it is through the interaction and participation within that particular community, which is immersed in a particular culture that one understands and learns about."[27] We are to see language as something we use in a great variety of ways and for all sorts of ends. It is also to be likened to an ancient city with its maze of little streets and squares, of old and new houses, and so forth.[28] This important metaphor is suggestive of the complicated relations between the different language-games as they interface with each other. Any attempt to reduce their relations to a *simple* formula will go awry.[29] A case in point is the disastrous attempt by the logical positivists to relate and draw tight parallels between their idea of science and their idea of religious faith.

Language and Reference

We have also seen how Wittgenstein came to modify his earlier views on the relation between language and reality. In *PI*, he offered a radical critique of "referentialism" (or "representationalism"), a view of language which he had once espoused. Whereas language has had a uniform structure and thus relates in a single way to the world,[30] according to his mature philosophical phase, it no longer has; and whereas meaning has been traditionally understood as determinate and precisely demarcated,[31] Wittgenstein's new position on meaning denies and rejects such an understanding. Some philosophers of religion have read him here as

25. See Aristotle, *On Interpretation*, 17a, cited in Clarke, *Language and Natural Theology*, 19.

26. Knowles, *Beyond Evangelicalism*, 43.

27. Knowles, *Beyond Evangelicalism*, 43.

28. *PI* 18.

29. *PI* II, 154.

30. See *TLP* 4.26; 6.124.

31. *TLP* 3.23; 3.251; 4.12.

denying objective reality—that there is nothing outside language—and, as also the ruling out of "the possibility of language about God being representational or referential in a realist sense."[32] This is, in my view, a misunderstanding of Wittgenstein, arising from a failure to appreciate that his concern is with the meaning of language rather than with its reference. Consider the following remarks in which he distinguishes between existence of something in reality and the existence of the same, as part of the language in use: "'I couldn't think that something is red if red didn't exist.' What that proposition really means is the image of something red, or the existence of a red sample *as part of our language*."[33]

Another of his remarks, one that was made in his pre-Tractarian phase, reveals the clarity of his mind concerning the distinction between a proposition and its reference: "There must be something in the proposition that is identical with its reference, but the proposition cannot be identical with its reference, and so there must be something in it that is *not* identical with its reference."[34]

I have belabored the matter in question because Wittgenstein's subsequent rejection of the "picture" or "referential" theory of language is sometimes taken to the extreme—the refusal to recognize that understanding in any kind of human discourse or exchange is "at root referentialist."[35] Significantly, the scenario of the builders narrated by Wittgenstein in *PI* to demonstrate the inadequacy of the referentialist theory also serves to indicate that reference or correlation between words and objects actually makes some degree of understanding between the characters in the story possible, resulting in the subordinate worker acting in the desired way. "While understanding might sometimes involve more than reference, it seems to always involve *at least* reference as its basis."[36] Though by itself not a sufficient warrant for justifying that language about God is representational or referential, the fact is that when adherents of a religion use language to speak about God they are taking God to be the object of their discourse. In remarking that "God is real to me" or something similar, the adherents are referring to an external reality, even if we judge their claim to be merely subjective. The habit of using language

---

32. Trigg, "Wittgenstein and Social Science," 127, cited in McCutcheon, *Religion within the Limits of Language Alone*, 21.

33. *PG*, 143.

34. *NB* 22.10.14.

35. Smith, *Who's Afraid of Relativism?*, 44.

36. Smith, *Who's Afraid of Relativism?*, 44.

to *refer* to God or things in the world is one that is deeply ingrained in our being. It therefore behooves us to give due consideration to the referentialist element present in religious propositions or expressions, if we are to avoid doing violence to the integrity of religious language itself. Perhaps, we can now understand why Wittgenstein's criticism of referential language is limited to only pointing out its inadequacy as a linguistic system for every situation in which language functions.

What is more worrying to me is a certain obsession to look at language strictly and only through a representational colored lens. For one thing, a resolute focus on words or statements being representations of other things or states of affairs is likely to throw one off course perhaps into missing the whole story about the content of language. For understanding a discourse is not just a matter of associating words or statements with objects; one need to pay attention to how language operates in everyday life. To really understand and grasp the whole story one need to be a "player" within a language-game because meaning, as we have learned, is conventional. The representationalist position, however, seems to ride roughshod over the vital role which convention plays in our speaking, listening, reading, writing, and expression generally; it does so perhaps in the misplaced belief that we the language users are given language in order that we may merely comment on the world as spectators. Whereas Wittgenstein has held that language presupposes the human community and "the *speaking* of language is part of an activity, or of a form of life," those who espouse representationalism see *no* such connections. For them, language is a detached tool, closed off from the world and even from the very speakers and hearers themselves. If religious terms like repentance, forgiveness and salvation seem to be meaningless to people today, the reason may be because the Christian religion is no longer perceived to be the balm for the consciousness of moral guilt. A further worry is that under the representational or referential model of language, the relationship between language and reality is typically reduced to something like "a piecemeal correspondence between one thing (a word) and another thing (an object in the world)."[37] When this happens, meaning itself is pushed to a point where it is treated almost by default as some kind of detached object or thing dressed in words that could be captured or caged for independent investigation and classification. Think, for example, of the difficulty in explaining the

37. High, *Language, Persons and Belief*, 35.

Trinity as comprising three "persons." In a parallel development, words like "God," "soul," "mind," and the like, are similarly assumed as if they were things or substances, not unlike a myriad of other impersonal and concrete items in the world. This eventuality has been anticipated by Wittgenstein in a lecture in which he remarks, "One great trouble our language gets us into is that we take a substantive to stand for a thing or substance."[38] To be sure, the words in question are substantives but this does not mean that we are to take them as necessarily referring to things. Religious language is not exempt from the risk of being treated as a conceptual abstraction isolated from community or persons. The present discussion will have an important bearing on the questions of sense posed in our study with respect to language about God. We do right to go *beyond* explaining religious terms like "God" and so forth in the manner of ostensive definition: to engage in that sort of activity would be as wrongheaded as trying to explain numerals or colors by simply pointing. We can of course expect, following Wittgenstein, that some quarters will still want to argue that the word "god" means something like a human being and that he might have two or four arms; while someone may think that we cannot talk of God having arms—that all this God-talk is essentially about grammar.[39]

Despite the shortcomings ascribed to representation, we have defended its place in the practice of religious discourse. It is pertinent that we have a clear conception of what we mean by the term, "to represent." In his recent Gifford Lectures, Rowan Williams tells us that his use of the term "representation" is meant "to draw attention to the interesting fact that we can claim to be speaking truthfully about many aspects of our environment without actually trying on every occasion to *reproduce* or *imitate* it."[40] His disavowal of representation as a strict sort of reproduction or imitation makes a good starting point because it sets the language user "free to recognize that language may be truthful even when it is not descriptive in the strict sense."[41] Representation, Williams elaborates, is "not simply the copying, imitating, or just registering of features, it presupposes, it seems, some notion of a characteristic *form*

---

38. Wittgenstein, *Lectures, Cambridge 1930–1933*, 318.

39. Wittgenstein, *Lectures, Cambridge 1930–1933*, 321

40. Williams, *Edge of Words*, x, xi.

41. Williams, *Edge of Words*, x, xi.

of action that can be activated in different media."[42] This notion of "form of action" resonates with Wittgenstein's overall proposal in which the use of language is seen as "part of an activity, or of a form of life."[43] The relevance of such a concept to our inquiry about religious language is tremendous, in that it can help move the discussion from abstraction to practical action concerning what one must do in response to religious truth claims.

The Mystical

In chapter 4, we saw that the notion of the mystical is an issue which distanced Wittgenstein from the logical positivists. The latter had adopted a view of language that effectively ruled out metaphysics. Not so for Wittgenstein who recognized a mystical realm "in which the answers to questions are symmetrically combined—a priori—to form a self-contained system."[44] The questions he speaks of here are the important ones concerning life and death, values, ethics, religion and God. These are areas of knowledge which "must lie outside the world,"[45] in the sense that assertions about them cannot be expressed as propositions of fact. But they can make themselves manifest.

It may be appropriate here to recall the startling instruction by Wittgenstein that the propositions he had expounded and developed in his philosophy should be recognized as "nonsensical," or more precisely "as steps" of a ladder which one can use and later dispose of. I take that instruction as suggestive of the provisional nature of his whole philosophy. He is not saying that philosophizing is pointless but that it is only a preamble to "see[-ing] the world aright."[46] What is being underscored in no uncertain terms is that the whole point of his philosophy lies in pointing his readers to the sphere of the mystical. By his positing of the mystical—as that which escapes description by the use of language— Wittgenstein brings his ontology to completion.

In the face of the mystical, Wittgenstein had famously urged that we keep silence. It is important that we read his plea correctly. It is not

42. Williams, *Edge of Words*, 21.
43. *PI* 123.
44. *TLP* 5.4541.
45. *TLP* 6.41.
46. *TLP* 6.54.

a silence consequent, to borrow a phrase, upon a "positivistic disdain of the non-empirical."[47] Rather, the silence enjoined by Wittgenstein is inspired by his belief that to talk about the mystical which transcends human cognition is to trivialize it. For admittedly, "propositions can express nothing higher."[48] Nor is he, as far as we read him right, urging or implying a renunciation of language or religious discourse. For surely Wittgenstein cannot be unaware that language is indispensable and is all that we have. Again, what he is concerned to do is remind us of the "higher" function of language to direct our gaze towards the mystical in hopes that we will be ushered into and awed by its mysterious and sustaining presence.

Several implications for the user of religious language at once emerge. The first is that one must recognize that with the mystical as the object of religious language, one can never presume to be able to achieve completion or precise definition in words. Indeed, strictly speaking, the mystical or "the transcendental," to employ Wittgenstein's terminology, resists even being put into words; it lies beyond and "outside" language. There is, as most believers are agreed, a qualitative difference between the mystical (God) and humankind so that the divine reality is beyond understanding, dwelling in inaccessible light. Moreover, there are epistemological-semantic limits to what we can say about God. Donald Hudson explains the applicable logic for us: "The transcendental is the structure of language, and the reason why it cannot be put into words is the impossibility of putting into language that which must be in it already for it to be language."[49] Less technically put, and as a general rule, anything which is necessary for language to be language cannot itself be put into the words of language. To illustrate this, think of an artist who can paint a picture of anything at all *except* a picture of his own particular *way* of painting.[50] So, any move on the part of religion towards a complete hold upon the content and meaning of transcendental reality is bound to founder.

The second implication concerns Wittgenstein's point that the mystical shows itself. It is one thing to say that the mystical cannot be expressed; it is altogether another to claim that it shows itself. How does

47. Klein, *How Things Are in the World*, 244.

48. *TLP* 6.42.

49. Hudson, *Wittgenstein and Religious Belief*, 104.

50. This illustration is from Hudson, not Wittgenstein. See Hudson, *Wittgenstein and Religious Belief*, 70.

the showing work? Drawing a parallel to the language of poetry with its capacity for letting the unutterable be uttered, Keightley proposes that in a similar manner the mystical shows itself through the medium of language of religion.[51] This is certainly an attractive thought. Religious language can stand on its own and will not require to be supplemented by any other type of discourse. If so, talk about God need not be reduced to anything other than itself, though one should be mindful that the meaning of what one says in words will be more effectively disclosed if backed by appropriate behavior and action on one's part.

This leads us to the third implication for religious language that stems from Wittgenstein's insight: the whole issue of silence. As noted above, keeping silent is the appropriate way to respond to the mystical. For centuries, mystics have withdrawn themselves to spend extended periods in silent contemplation, and the practice of apophatic theology continues to be popular. Wittgenstein, in virtue of his plea to remain silent and his living up to the implications of his own teaching to *do* what could not be said but could be shown is thus justly deserving of another honor—being the champion of what has been favorably termed a "wordless faith."[52] But for the reflective user of religious language, the question as to the proper relationship between silence and articulate language remains yet unanswered. At first glance, they seem to be total opposites. Can silence even be "expressed" in language? Indeed, without the means of language silence would not exist at all because no one will know what it is. To keep silence when faced with the mystical, however, will require "a continuous effort of looking carefully at 'ordinary' reality" if one is to enter into an experience of that reality.[53] The mystical does not suddenly dawn on one, as in a flash. Paradoxically, it is only by means of language that silence is created, and by our inventing new language-games that we can hope to grasp or better, be grasped by the mystical.

The Question of Truth

Even though the present study is concerned with the understanding and use of language in talking about God, I concede that the question of truth cannot be ducked or sidestepped. Truth, as was noted in chapter 5, is what

---

51. Keightley, *Wittgenstein, Grammar and God*, 29.

52. Hudson, *Wittgenstein and Religious Belief*, 104.

53. D'hert, *Wittgenstein's Relevance for Theology*, 140.

theology seeks and what theological reflections aim to deliver. Given the essential involvement of theology with and in language—theology needs and uses language to express "what is the case"—any conscious look at the latter will have to attend to considerations of what truth itself consists in, and how it is reached. It might be added that its intersections with theology as well as with other spheres of human endeavor underscore "the characteristic human instinct to regard truth as significant."[54]

The importance of understanding the notion and function of truth is uncontroversial, as is the view that truth and language are closely related. Not to stir up any controversy, I have indicated that the essential connection between the two lies in meaning. From a Wittgensteinian perspective (that meaning is constituted through use), the word "true" is seen as a function within the activity of using language. Wittgenstein's oft-quoted words spring to mind, "It is what human beings *say* that is true and false; and they agree in the *language* they use."[55] If he is right, it would be simplistic to deal with questions about truth in religion by simply attempting to check for sufficient evidence to verify a doctrinal statement or claim. To illustrate, how does one know what is admissible evidence for verifying a proposition such as "The devil tempted me to criticize the preacher"? The appropriate thing one can and must do is consider such factors as the overarching concepts of a particular religion and both the context and way in which the meaningfulness of such a claim is expressed and grasped by the language one uses. Peter Donovan is surely on the right lines when he insists,

> The finding of observations more or less fitting the words used, the discovery of patterns in the data suggesting something like what the ideas and images of the language convey, should be seen as the *supporting of interpretations* rather than the verifying of assertions and the proving true of claims. A well-supported interpretation is still open to amendment; unlike a true proposition it does not claim to have the whole truth or say the final word. In the highly disputed field of supernatural realities, which religions take themselves to deal with, even the best-supported interpretations may still not count as a true description.[56]

54. McGrath, *Genesis of Doctrine*, 73.

55. *PI* 241.

56. Donovan, *Religious Language*, 105.

I must, however, clarify that I am not trying to confuse truth with its verification. That we verify religious assertions as well as, say, scientific ones in different ways and according to different canons is not in dispute. The word "true" when predicated of propositions of religion or science or some other discipline remains unambiguous in every case. My intention in the foregoing discussion has been to make the point that the word "true" has to do with language, not that it is to be variously interpreted. Wittgenstein makes a similar point when he remarks, "What looks as if it *had* to exist, is part of the language."[57]

In chapter 5, the reader will recall my repeated emphases that Wittgenstein and other philosophers like Rorty and Davidson, have not denied the existence of objective truth, or have they fought shy of affirming something as true. Instead, they have offered us a deflationary view of truth, a view which maintains that to ascribe truth to a proposition is the same as asserting the proposition itself.[58] Admittedly, for most of us, we have become accustomed to applying the words we use in a statement (such as "the tomb is empty") as being "true" or "false" to the objects expressed by such a statement. It seems we are stuck with a "correspondentist" frame of mind, ever seeking as much as lieth in us to know the truth. This mindset is definitely not a misplaced one for it is almost required of us to want to know "what is really the case." But given that divinity is transcendent, believers should stand ready to accept that objective truths about God will always come to them as incomplete, imprecise, and provisional, and only by means of language. Yet, as I have previously defended, we are not giving relativism or skepticism a free run.

Lindbeck's Legacy

In my evaluation of the cultural-linguistic approach to religion by Lindbeck and his appropriation of Wittgenstein's insights (chapter 6), I paid tribute to his ingenuity in applying the analogue of language to religion. I shall not repeat the discussion here, except to mention one key point that is directly relevant to my work. This is the "relatively greater emphasis on the internal logic or grammar of religion"[59] that

57. *PI* 50.
58. *PI* 136.
59. *ND*, 28.

Lindbeck has urged upon us. The idea goes back to Wittgenstein's famous statement: "Grammar tells what kind of object anything is. (Theology as grammar.)"[60] The analogue of grammar and its derivative rules proposed by Lindbeck has the merit of re-directing our whole approach toward religion—reversing how a religion is popularly construed as making ontological truth claims to it being construed in terms of how its language is structured and ordered. The thesis I am concerned to advance in this project urges the adoption of the same theological outlook, of locating the significant aspect of religion in the grammar that informs the way we reflect and do theology, rather than in the exactitude or precision of text.

Some Concluding Remarks

It remains for me to suggest a few potential directions of research which might be pursued in light of what I have presented. The first concerns theological methodology. Having now a better understanding of the nature and functioning of language and having seen how many basic issues of theology are in its language, I would urge that more attention be devoted to an analysis of language. This is not to say that we are lacking in scholars of and research pertaining to language, but rather to express the view that there must be no let-up. There is also the need to engage with more current lines of thought on language-related issues. My own present research, I admit, would have benefited more if I had also engaged with the work of the structuralists and the post-structuralists. Had I more room, the study would also have benefited from further discussion of the challenge of relativism, as well as the debate on verification and falsification. Finally, I have only made passing reference to the realism/ anti-realism divide. It would be useful to examine it as it pertains to the religious use of language.

We have learned that religion "is not primarily an array of beliefs about the true and the good (though it may involve these)"[61] but that it is also a "form of life" in which believers must locate the religious concepts they hold. The whole matter of spiritual transformation and living a good or God-centered life is therefore an important one. For as I have said, we might come to have a better understanding of what we express about the divine reality if we are in tune with the transcendent by means of

60. *PI* 373.
61. *ND*, 33.

prayer and walking with him. Detailed investigation into how the issues surrounding language can be further explored to aid or augment the spirituality of believers would be very worthwhile.

Let me now bring this whole study to a close by indicating once again that the approach to language advanced here does not rule out that words about God can be cognitive or fact-stating, only that they cannot be identified with a complete and precise description of the divine reality. Despite having "rough edges"—in that their meanings are not always transparent or strictly defined—religious words have a reliable function and are generally understandable. In that sense, God is not beyond words. All that has been said to caution against the improper use of words is not to dissuade people from speaking about God. One specific outcome to be sought after, in addition to those we spoke of at the outset of our project, is that believers may have a greater sensitivity to the role of religious language. In this regard, St. Paul (c. 4–62 CE), the one who penned the most words in the New Testament, in terms of the number of letters attributed to him, has blazed the way for us when he reveals:

> For now we see through a glass, darkly; but then face to face: now I know in part; but then shall I know even as also I am known. (1 Cor 13:12 KJV)

Bibliography

Addis, Mark. *Wittgenstein: A Guide for the Perplexed*. London: Bloomsbury, 2006.

Aldrich, Virgil C. "The Informal Logic of the Employment of Expressions." *The Philosophical Review* 63.3 (1954) 384–85.

Alston, William P. *Divine Nature and Human Language: Essays in Philosophical Theology*. Ithaca, NY: Cornell University Press, 1989.

———. "Philosophical Analysis and Structural Linguistics." *Journal of Philosophy* 59.23 (1962) 709–20.

———. *Philosophy of Language*. Englewood Cliffs, NJ: Prentice-Hall, 1964.

———. "Religious Language." In *The Oxford Handbook of Philosophy of Religion*, edited by William J. Wainwright, 220–44. Oxford: Oxford University Press, 2005.

Anscombe, G. E. M. *An Introduction to Wittgenstein's Tractatus*. London: Hutchinson, 1967.

Anselm. *De Veritate*. Translated by Jasper Hopkins and Herbert Richardson. Minneapolis, MN: Arthur J. Banning, 2000.

Aquinas, Thomas. *Summa Theologiae*. Translated by Fathers of the English Dominican Province. 1911. Reprint, New York: Benziger Bros., 1948.

———. *Questiones Disputatae de Veritate*. Translated by Robert W. Mulligan. Chicago: Henry Regnery, 1952.

Aristotle. *Metaphysics*. Translated by C. D. C. Reeve. Indiana, IN: Hackett, 2016.

———. *On Interpretation*. Translated by Harold P. Cooke. Cambridge, MA: Loeb Classical Library, 1983.

Armstrong, Karen. *The Case for God*. New York: Anchor, 2010.

Arrington, Robert L., and Mark Addis, eds. *Wittgenstein and Philosophy of Religion*. London: Routledge, 2001.

Ashford, Bruce R. "Wittgenstein's Theologians? A Survey of Ludwig Wittgenstein's Impact on Theology." *Journal of the Evangelical Theological Society* 50.2 (2007) 357–75.

Astley, Jeff. *Exploring God-Talk: Using Language in Religion*. London: Darton Longman Todd, 2004.

Astley, Jeff, and Leslie J. Francis. *Exploring Ordinary Theology: Everyday Christian Believing and the Church*. Farnham: Ashgate, 2013.

Atkinson, James. "Sub Specie Aeterni: The Mystical in the Early Writings of Ludwig Wittgenstein." PhD diss. Ottawa: University of Ottawa, 2005.

Augustine. *Teaching Christianity (De Doctrina Christiana)*. Edited by John E. Rotelle. Translated by Edmund Hill. New York: New City, 2014.

———. *The Trinity*. Translated by Edmund Hill. 2nd ed. New York: New City, 1991.

Austin, John L. *How to Do Things with Words*. Oxford: Clarendon, 1962.

———. "Truth." *Proceedings of the Aristotelian Society* 24 (1950) 111–28.

Ayer, Alfred J. *Language, Truth and Logic*. 2nd ed. New York: Dover, 1946.

———. *Ludwig Wittgenstein*. London: Penguin, 1985.

Ayer, Alfred J., et al. *The Revolution in Philosophy*. London: Macmillan, 1956.

Baker, G. P., and P. M. S. Hacker. *Wittgenstein: Understanding and Meaning. Part I: Essays*. Vol. 1 of *An Analytical Commentary on the Philosophical Investigations*. 2nd ed. Oxford: Blackwell, 2005.

Balthasar, Hans Urs von. *Truth of God*. Vol. 2 of *Theo-Logic: Theological Logical Theory*. Translated by Adrian J. Walker. San Francisco, CA: Ignatius, 2004.

Bambrough, J. Renford. *Reason, Truth and God*. London: Methuen, 1969.

Barr, James. *The Bible in the Modern World*. London: SCM, 1973.

———. *The Concept of Biblical Theology: An Old Testament Perspective*. London: SCM, 1999.

———. "The Literal, the Allegorical, and Modern Biblical Scholarship." *Journal for the Study of the Old Testament* 44 (1989) 3–17.

Barrett, Cyril. *Wittgenstein on Ethics and Religious Belief*. Oxford: Blackwell, 1991.

Barrett, Lee C. "Theology as Grammar: Regulative Principles or Paradigms and Practices." *Modern Theology* 4.2 (1988) 155–72.

Barth, Karl. *God Here and Now*. Translated by Paul M. van Buren. London: Routledge, 1964.

———. *The Word of God and Theology*. Translated by Amy Marga. London: T&T Clark, 2011.

Bassols, Alejandro Tomasini. "Wittgenstein on Language and Religion." *Revista Portuguesa de Filosofia* 64.2/4 (2008) 1291–99.

Beaney, Michael, ed. *The Oxford Handbook of the History of Analytic Philosophy*. Oxford: Oxford University Press, 2013.

———. "Wittgenstein on Language: From Simples to Samples." In *The Oxford Handbook of Philosophy of Language,* edited by Ernest Lepore and Barry C. Smith, 40–59. Oxford: Clarendon, 2006.

Bearsley, Patrick. "Augustine and Wittgenstein on Language." *Philosophy* 58.224 (1983) 229–36.

Bell, Richard H. "Theology as Grammar: Is God an Object of Understanding?" *Religious Studies* 11.3 (1975) 307–17.

———. "Wittgenstein and Descriptive Theology." *Religious Studies* 5.1 (1969) 1–18.

Benedict XVI. "Apostolic Journey of His Holiness Benedict XVI to Austria on the Occasion of the 850th Anniversary of the Foundation of the Shrine of Mariazell." Homily delivered September 8, 2007. Online. https://w2.vatican.va/content/benedict-xvi/en/homilies/2007/documents/hf_ben-xvi_hom_20070908_mariazell.html.

Bingemer, Maria Clara. *The Mystery and the World: Passion for God in Times of Unbelief*. Translated by Jovelino Ramos and Joan Ramos. Cambridge: Lutterworth, 2016.

Binkley, Timothy. *Wittgenstein's Language*. The Hague: Martinus Nijhoff, 1973.

Black, Max. *Models and Metaphor: Studies in Language and Philosophy*. Ithaca, NY: Cornell University Press, 1962.

Blackburn, Simon. "Happy 300th Birthday, David Hume!" *Oxford University Press's Academic Insights for the Thinking World* (blog), April 26, 2011. Online. https://blog.oup.com/2011/04/hume.

———. *Truth: A Guide.* Oxford: Oxford University Press, 2005.

Bloor, David. *Wittgenstein: A Social Theory of Knowledge.* New York: Columbia University Press, 1983.

Bolton, Derek. *An Approach to Wittgenstein's Philosophy.* London: Macmillan,1979.

Boone, Kathleen C. *The Bible Tells Them So: The Discourse of Protestant Fundamentalism.* London: SCM, 1990.

Borg, Marcus J. *Reading the Bible Again for the First Time: Taking the Bible Seriously but not Literally.* New York: HarperCollins, 2001.

———. *Speaking Christian: Recovering the Lost Meaning of Christian Words.* London: SPCK, 2011.

Boroditsky, Lera. "Lost in Translation." *Wall Street Journal,* July 23, 2010. Online. http://www.wsj.com/articles/SB10001424052748703467304575383131592767868.

Braaten, Carl E., ed. *Our Naming of God: Problems and Prospects of God-Talk Today.* Minneapolis, MN: Fortress, 1989.

Braithwaite, Richard B. "An Empiricist's View of the Nature of Religious Belief." In *Philosophy of Religion,* edited by Basil Mitchell, 72–91. Oxford: Oxford University Press, 1971.

Brenner, William H. "Theology as Grammar." *The Southern Journal of Philosophy* 34.4 (1996) 439–45.

Broackes, J. "Fork, Hume's." In *The Oxford Companion to Philosophy,* edited by Ted Honderich, 285. Oxford: Oxford University Press, 1995.

Brown, David. *Continental Philosophy and Modern Theology: An Engagement.* Oxford: Blackwell, 1987.

———. *Divine Generosity and Human Creativity: Theology through Symbol, Painting and Architecture.* Edited by Christopher R. Brewer and Robert MacSwain. Oxford: Routledge, 2017.

———. *God and Mystery in Words: Experience through Metaphor and Drama.* Oxford: Oxford University Press, 2008.

Brown, Stuart C. *Do Religious Claims Make Sense?* London: SCM, 1969.

Brümmer, Vincent. *Brümmer on Meaning and the Christian Faith.* Aldershot: Ashgate, 2006.

———. *Speaking of a Personal God. An Essay in Philosophical Theology.* Cambridge: Cambridge University Press, 1992.

Bunge, Wiep van, et al., eds. *The Bloomsbury Companion to Spinoza.* London: Bloomsbury, 2014.

Buren, Paul Matthew van. *The Edges of Language: An Essay in the Logic of a Religion.* London: SCM, 1972.

———. *The Secular Meaning of the Gospel.* London: SCM, 1963.

———. *Theological Explorations.* London: SCM, 1968.

Burrell, David. "Review of *The Nature of Doctrine: Religion and Theology in a Postliberal Age* by George A. Lindbeck." *Union Seminary Quarterly Review* 39.4 (1984) 322–24.

Caird, G. B. *The Language and Imagery of the Bible.* Philadelphia: Westminster, 1980.

Caputo, John D. *Philosophy and Theology.* Nashville: Abingdon, 2006.

———. *Truth. Philosophy in Transit.* London: Penguin, 2013.

Carman, Taylor, and Mark B. N. Hansen, eds. *The Cambridge Companion to Merleau-Ponty.* Cambridge: Cambridge University Press, 2005.

Carnap, Rudolf. *The Philosophy of Rudolf Carnap.* Edited by Paul Arthur Schlipp. La Salle, IL: Open Court, 1963.

Carolis, Massimo de. "Saying and Showing." *Wittgenstein-Studien* 4.1 (2013) 129–42.

Carroll, Thomas D. *Wittgenstein within the Philosophy of Religion.* Basingstoke: Palgrave Macmillan, 2014.

Cathey, Robert Andrew. *God in Postliberal Perspective: Between Realism and Non-Realism.* Farnham: Ashgate, 2009.

Cell, Edward. *Language, Existence & God: Interpretation of Moore, Russell, Ayer, Wittgenstein, Oxford Philosophy and Tillich.* New York: Abingdon, 1971.

Christian, William A., Sr. *Meaning and Truth in Religion.* Princeton, NJ: Princeton University Press, 1964.

Clack, Brian R. *An Introduction to Wittgenstein's Philosophy of Religion.* Edinburgh: Edinburgh University Press, 1999.

Clark, Gordon H. *Religion, Reason, and Revelation.* Hobbs, NM: Trinity Foundation, 1961.

———. "Special Divine Revelation as Rational." In *Revelation and the Bible,* edited by Carl F. H. Henry, 25–41. London: Tyndale, 1959.

Clarke, Bowman L. *Language and Natural Theology.* The Hague: Mouton, 1966.

Clayton, Philip. *The Problem of God in Modern Thought.* Grand Rapids, MI: Eerdmans, 2000.

Cleobury, F. H. "Wittgenstein and the Philosophy of Religion." *The Modern Churchman* 13.2 (1970) 174–81.

Comstock, Gary L. "Two Types of Narrative Theology." *Journal of the American Academy of Religion* 55.4 (1987) 687–717.

Cook, John W. "Wittgenstein and Religious Belief." *Philosophy* 63.246 (1988) 427–52.

Corner, Mark. "Review of *The Nature of Doctrine* by George A. Lindbeck." *Modern Theology* 3.1 (1986) 110–13.

Cottingham, John. "Transcending Science: Humane Models of Religious Understanding." In *New Models of Religious Understanding,* edited by Fiona Ellis, 23–41. Oxford: Oxford University Press, 2018.

Crane, Tim. *The Meaning of Belief: Religion from An Atheist's Point of View.* Cambridge, MA: Harvard University Press, 2017.

Creegan, Charles. "*Theology after Wittgenstein* by Fergus Kerr (Book Review)." *International Journal for Philosophy of Religion* 25.2 (1989) 120–22.

Crombie, I. M. "The Possibility of Theological Statements." In *Faith and Logic,* edited by Basil Mitchell, 31–83. London: George Allen & Unwin, 1957.

Cross, Richard. "Idolatry and Religious Language." *Faith and Philosophy* 25.2 (2008) 190–96.

Cupitt, Don. *After God: The Future of Religion.* New York: Basic, 1997.

———. *Creation out of Nothing.* London: SCM, 1990.

———. *The Long-Legged Fly: A Theology of Language and Desire.* London: SCM, 1987.

———. *Taking Leave of God.* London: SCM, 1980.

———. *The Time Being.* London: SCM, 1992.

Danka, Istvan. "A Case Study on the Limits of Ironic Redescription: Rorty on Wittgenstein." *Pragmatism Today* 2.1 (2011) 68–77.

Davaney, Sheila Greeve. *Pragmatic Historicism: A Theology for the Twenty-First Century*. Albany: State University of New York Press, 2000.

Davidson, Donald. "The Structure and Content of Truth." *Journal of Philosophy* 87.6 (1990) 279–328.

———. "Truth and Meaning." *Synthese* 17.3 (1967) 304–23.

———. *Truth, Language, and History*. Oxford: Clarendon ,2005.

DeHart, Paul J. *The Trial of the Witnesses: The Rise and Decline of Postliberal Theology*. Oxford: Blackwell, 2006.

Dennett, Daniel. "Ludwig Wittgenstein." *Time* 153.2 (1999) 88–90.

Depoortere, Frederiek, and Magdalen Lambkin, eds. *The Question of Theological Truth: Philosophical and Interreligious Perspectives*. Amsterdam: Brill Academic, 2012.

Derrida, Jacques. *Margins of Philosophy*. Translated Alan Bass. Chicago: University of Chicago Press, 1982.

———. *Of Grammatology*. Translated by Gayatri Chakravorty Spivak. Baltimore, MD: John Hopkins University Press, 1974.

———. *Without Alibi*. Translated by Peggy Kamuf. Stanford, CA: Stanford University Press, 2002.

Descartes, René. *Meditations on First Philosophy: With Selections from the Objections and Replies*. Edited by John Cottingham. Cambridge: Cambridge University Press, 2013.

D'hert, Ignace. *Wittgenstein's Relevance for Theology*. Bern: Herbert Lang, 1974.

Donovan, Peter. *Religious Language*. London: Sheldon ,1976.

Dorrien, Gary. "The Future of Postliberal Theology." *Christian Century* 118.21 (2001) 22–29.

———. "The Origins of Postliberalism." *Christian Century* 118.20 (2001) 16–21.

Downing, F. Gerald. *Formation for Knowing God. Imagining God: At-One-ing, Transforming, for Self-Revealing*. Cambridge: James Clarke, 2015.

———. *Has Christianity a Revelation?* London: SCM,1964.

———. "Meanings." In *What about the New Testament? Essays in Honour of Christopher Evans*, edited by Morna Hooker and Colin Hickling, 127–42. London: SCM, 1975.

Drury, Maurice O'Connor. "Conversations with Wittgenstein." In *Recollections of Wittgenstein*, edited by Rush Rhees, 79–97. Oxford: Oxford University Press, 1984.

———. *The Danger of Words*. Bristol: Thoemmes, 1996.

Ebeling, Gerhard. *Introduction to a Theological Theory of Language*. Translated by R. A. Wilson. London: Collins, 1973.

———. *The Nature of Faith*. Translated by Ronald Gregor Smith. London: Collins, 1961.

———. *Word and Faith*. Translated by James W. Leitch. London: SCM, 1963.

Eberle, Gary. *Dangerous Words: Talking about God in an Age of Fundamentalism*. Boston: Trumpeter, 2007.

Ellenbogen, Sara. *Wittgenstein's Account of Truth*. Albany: State University of New York Press, 2003.

Engberg-Pedersen, Troels. *John and Philosophy: A New Reading of the Fourth Gospel*. Oxford: Oxford University Press, 2017.

Engelmann, Paul. *Letters from Ludwig Wittgenstein: With a Memoir*. Oxford: Blackwell, 1967.

Ernst, Cornelius. *Multiple Echo: Exploration in Theology*. Edited by Fergus Kerr and Timothy Radcliffe. London: Darton Longman Todd, 1979.

Fann, K. T. *Wittgenstein's Conception of Philosophy*. Oxford: Blackwell, 1969.

Fasolt, Constantin. "Respect for the Word: What Calvin and Wittgenstein Had against Images." In *John Calvin, Myth and Reality*, edited by Amy Nelson Burnett, 165–90. Eugene, OR: Wipf & Stock, 2011.

Farrer, Austin. *Reflective Faith: Essays in Philosophical Theology*. London: SCM, 1972.

Fergusson, David. *Community, Liberalism and Christian Ethics*. Cambridge: Cambridge University Press, 1998.

———. *Faith and Its Critics: A Conversation*. Oxford: Oxford University Press, 2009.

———. "Meaning, Truth and Realism in Bultmann and Lindbeck." *Religious Studies* 26.2 (1990) 183–98.

Ferré, Frederick. *Basic Modern Philosophy of Religion*. London: George Allen & Unwin, 1968.

———. *Language, Logic and God*. London: Collins, 1961.

Feynman, Richard. *The Character of Physical Law*. Cambridge, MA: MIT Press, 1965.

Fisch, Menachem. "Taking the Linguistic Turn Seriously." *European Legacy* 13.5 (2008) 605–22.

Fodor, James. "Postliberal Theology." In *The Modern Theologians: An Introduction to Christian Theology since 1918*, edited by David F. Ford with Rachel Muers, 229–48. Malden, MA: Blackwell, 2005.

Fogelin, Robert J. *Taking Wittgenstein at His Word. A Textual Study*. Princeton: Princeton University Press, 2009.

———. *Wittgenstein*. London: Routledge & Kegan Paul, 1976.

Foley, Michael. "The Eucharist and Cannibalism." *Catholic Thing* (blog), August 6, 2011. Online. https://www.thecatholicthing.org/2011/08/06/the-eucharist-a-cannibalism.

Ford, David F. "Review of *The Nature of Doctrine: Religion and Theology in a Postliberal Age* by George A. Lindbeck." *Journal of Theological Studies* 37.1 (1986) 277–82.

Fossett, Robert L. *Upon This Rock: The Nature of Doctrine from Antifoundationalist Perspective*. Eugene, OR: Pickwick, 2013.

Fout, Jason A. "Review of *The Nature of Doctrine: Religion and Theology in a Postliberal Age* (25th Anniversary Edition)." *Reviews in Religion & Theology* 17.4 (2010) 627–30.

Fox, Craig. "Wittgenstein on Meaning and Meaning-Blindness." In *Wittgenstein: Key Concepts*, edited by Kelly Dean Jolley, 27–40. Durham: Acumen, 2010.

Frascolla, Pasquale. "The Role of the Disquotational Schema in Wittgenstein's Reflections on Truth." *Philosophical Investigations* 40.3 (2017) 205–22. doi:10.1111/phin.12161.

———. *Understanding Wittgenstein's Tractatus*. Oxford: Routledge, 2007.

Frege, Gottlob. "Sense and Reference." *The Philosophical Review* 57.3 (1948) 209–30.

———. *Translations from the Philosophical Writings of Gottlob Frege*. Edited by Peter Geach and Max Black. Oxford: Blackwell, 1970.

Frei, Hans W. *The Eclipse of Biblical Narrative: A Study in Eighteenth and Nineteenth-Century Hermeneutics*. New Haven: Yale University Press, 1974.

———. "Epilogue: George Lindbeck and the Nature of Doctrine." In *Theology and Dialogue: Essays in Conversation with George Lindbeck*, edited by Bruce D. Marshall, 275–82. Notre Dame, IN: University of Notre Dame Press, 1990.

Fronda, Earl Stanley B. *Wittgenstein's (Misunderstood) Religious Thought*. Leiden: Brill, 2010.

Garver, Newton. "Wittgenstein's Pantheism: A New Light on the Ontology of the *Tractatus*." In *Essays on Wittgenstein*, edited by E. D. Klemke, 123–37. Urbana: Illinois University Press, 1971.

Geertz, Clifford. *The Interpretation of Cultures*. New York: Basic, 1973.

Geisler, Norman L. "Wittgenstein, Ludwig." In *The Baker Encyclopedia of Christian Apologetics*, edited by Norman L. Geisler, 781–83. Grand Rapids, MI: Baker, 1998.

Geisler, Norman L., and Paul D. Feinberg. *Introduction to Philosophy: A Christian Perspective*. Grand Rapids, MI: Baker, 1980.

Gerrish, Brian A. "Review of *The Nature of Doctrine: Religion and Theology in a Postliberal Age by George A. Lindbeck*." *Journal of Religion* 68.1 (1988) 87–92.

Gilkey, Langdon. *Naming the Whirlwind: The Renewal of God-Language*. Indianapolis, IN: Bobbs-Merril, 1969.

Gill, Jerry H. *On Knowing God: New Directions for the Future of Theology*. Philadelphia: Westminster, 1981.

———. "Wittgenstein and Religious Language." *Theology Today* 21.1 (1964) 59–72.

———. "Wittgenstein's Concept of Truth." *International Philosophical Quarterly* 6.1 (1966) 71–80.

Gill, Robin. *Moral Leadership in a Postmodern Age*. Edinburgh: T&T Clark, 1997.

Glebe-Møller, Jens. "Whereof One Cannot Speak, Thereof One Must Be Silent." *Studia Theologica: Nordic Journal of Theology* 51.2 (1997) 156–67.

Glock, Hans-Johann. "Truth in the *Tractatus*." *Synthese* 148.2 (2006) 345–68.

———, ed. *A Wittgenstein Dictionary*. Oxford: Blackwell, 1996.

Graham, Gordon. *Wittgenstein and Natural Religion*. Oxford: Oxford University Press, 2014.

Grayling, A. C. *Scepticism and the Possibility of Knowledge*. London: Continuum, 2008.

Grenz, Stanley James, and John R. Franke. *Beyond Foundationalism: Shaping Theology in a Postmodern Context*. Louisville, KY: Westminster John Knox, 2001.

Grice, H. P. "Meaning." *The Philosophical Review* 66.3 (1957) 377–88.

Groothuis, Douglas. *Truth Decay: Defending Christianity against the Challenges of Postmodernism*. Downers Grove, IL: InterVarsity, 2000.

———. "Why Truth Matters Most: An Apologetic for Truth-Seeking in Postmodern Times." *Journal of Evangelical Theological Society* 47.3 (2004) 441–54.

Grünfeld, Joseph. *Science and Values*. Amsterdam: B. R. Gruner, 1973.

Hacker, P. M. S. "The Linguistic Turn in Analytic Philosophy." In *The Oxford Handbook of the History of Analytic Philosophy*, edited by Michael Beaney, 926–47. Oxford: Oxford University Press, 2013.

———. "Was He Trying to Whistle It?" In *The New Wittgenstein*, edited by A. Crary and R. Read, 353–88. London: Routledge, 2000.

———. "When the Whistling Had to Stop." In *Wittgensteinian Themes: Essays in Honour of David Pears*, edited by D. O. M. Charles and T. W. Child, 13–48. Oxford: Clarendon, 2001.

———. *Wittgenstein: Connections and Controversies*. Oxford: Oxford University Press, 2001.

———. "Wittgenstein, Ludwig Josef Johann." In *The Oxford Companion to Philosophy*, edited by Ted Honderich, 912–16. Oxford: Oxford University Press, 1995.

———. *Wittgenstein's Place in Twentieth-Century Analytic Philosophy*. Oxford: Blackwell, 1996.

Hacking, Ian. *Why Does Language Matter to Philosophy?* Cambridge: Cambridge University Press, 1975.

Hallett, Garth L. *A Companion to Wittgenstein's "Philosophical Investigations."* Ithaca, NY: Cornell University Press, 1977.

———. *Language and Truth.* New Haven: Yale University Press, 1988.

———. *Theology within the Bounds of Language: A Methodological Tour.* Albany: State University of New York, 2011.

Hanna, Robert. "From Referentialism to Human Action: The Augustinian Theory of Language." In *Wittgenstein's Philosophical Investigations: A Critical Guide*, edited by Arif Ahmed, 11–29. Cambridge: Cambridge University Press, 2010.

Hare, R. M. *The Language of Morals.* Oxford: Oxford University Press, 1964.

Harris, Harriet A. *Fundamentalism and Evangelicals.* Oxford: Oxford University Press, 1998.

Harrison, Bernard. *An Introduction to the Philosophy of Language.* London: Macmillan, 1979.

Hartnack, Justus. *Wittgenstein and Modern Philosophy.* Translated by Maurice Cranston. London: Methuen, 1965.

Harvey, Michael G. *Scepticism, Relativism, and Religious Knowledge: A Kierkegaardian Perspective Informed by Wittgenstein's Philosophy.* Cambridge: James Clarke, 2014.

———. "Wittgenstein's Notion of 'Theology as Grammar.'" *Religious Studies* 25.1 (1989) 89–103.

Haslam, Molly. "Language as Expression: A Wittgensteinian Critique of the Cultural-Linguistic Approach to Religion." *American Journal of Theology & Philosophy* 28.2 (2007) 237–50.

Hazelton, Roger. "Truth in Theology." *The Christian Century* 88.25 (1971) 772–75.

Hebblethwaite, Brian L. "God and Truth." *Kerygma und Dogma* 40.1 (1994) 2–19.

———. *The Ocean of Truth: A Defence of Objective Theism.* Cambridge: Cambridge University Press, 1988.

Hector, Kevin W. *Theology without Metaphysics: God, Language, and the Spirit of Recognition.* Cambridge: Cambridge University Press, 2011.

Heidegger, Martin. *Being and Time.* Translated by John Stambaugh. Albany: State University of New York, 1996.

———. "On the Essence of Truth." In *The Nature of Truth: Classic and Contemporary Perspectives*, edited by Michael P. Lynch, 295–316. Cambridge, MA: MIT Press, 2001.

Hengstmengel, Joost W. "'Philosophy to the Glory of God': Wittgenstein on God, Religion and Theology." *Joost Hengstmengel* (blog), February 22, 2010. Online. https://hengstmengel.wordpress.com/2010/02/22/philosophy-to-the-glory-of-god-wittgenstein-on-god-religion-and-theology.

Henry, Carl F. H. *God, Revelation and Authority. Vol. 1 God Who Speaks and Shows.* Waco, TX: Word, 1976.

———, ed. *Revelation and the Bible.* London: Tyndale, 1959.

Herder, Johann Gottfried von. "Treatise on the Origin of Language (1772)." In *Herder: Philosophical Writings*, edited by Michael N. Forster, 65–164. Cambridge: Cambridge University Press, 2002.

Herrmann, Eberhard. *Religion, Reality, and a Good Life: A Philosophical Approach to Religion.* Tübingen: Mohr Siebeck, 2004.

Hesse, Mary. "Talk of God: Royal Institute of Philosophy Lectures, Vol. 2, 1967–1968." *Philosophy* 44.170 (1969) 343–49.

Hick, John H. *Philosophy of Religion*. 4th ed. Englewood Cliffs, NJ: Prentice-Hall, 1990.

High, Dallas M. *Language, Persons, and Belief*. New York: Oxford University Press, 1967.

———, ed. *New Essays on Religious Language*. New York: Oxford University Press, 1969.

Higton, Mike. "Frei's Christology and Lindbeck's Cultural-Linguistic Theory." *Scottish Journal of Theology* 50.1 (1997) 83–96.

———. "Reconstructing the Nature of Doctrine." *Modern Theology* 30.1 (2014) 1–31.

Hodge, A. A. *Outlines of Theology*. Grand Rapids, MI: Eerdmans, 1949.

Holmer, Paul L. *The Grammar of Faith*. San Francisco: Harper & Row, 1978.

Holmes, Urban T., III. *To Speak of God*. New York: Seabury, 1974.

Horwich, Paul. *Truth*. Oxford: Oxford University Press, 1990.

———. *Truth, Meaning, Reality*. Oxford: Clarendon ,2010.

———. "Wittgenstein on Truth." *Argumenta* 3 (2016) 95–105.

Hovey, Craig R. *Speak Thus: Christian Language in Church and World*. Cambridge: James Clarke, 2008.

———. "Truth in Wittgenstein, Truth in Lindbeck." *Asbury Theological Journal* 57.1 (2002) 137–42.

Huber, Carlo. "We Can Still Speak about God." *Gregorianum* 49.4 (1968) 667–93.

Hudson, W. Donald. *Ludwig Wittgenstein: The Bearing of his Philosophy upon Religious Belief*. London: Lutterworth, 1968.

———. *Wittgenstein and Religious Belief*. London: Macmillan, 1975.

Hume, David. *Dialogues Concerning Natural Religion*. Edited by Norman Kemp Smith. 2nd ed. New York: Social Sciences, 1948.

———. *An Enquiry Concerning Human Understanding*. Edited by L. A. Selby-Bigge. 2nd ed. Oxford: Oxford University Press, 1902.

———. *The Natural History of Religion*. London: A&H Bradlaugh Bonner, 1889.

———. *A Treatise of Human Nature*. Mineola, NY: Dover, 2003.

Hunnings, Gordon. *The World and Language in Wittgenstein's Philosophy*. Albany: State University of New York Press, 1988.

Hunsinger, George. "Postliberal Theology." In *The Cambridge Companion to Postmodern Theology*, edited by Kevin J. Vanhoozer, 42–57. Cambridge: Cambridge University Press, 2003.

Hunter, J. F. M. *Understanding Wittgenstein: Studies of Philosophical Investigations*. Edinburgh: Edinburgh University Press, 1985.

Hütter, Reinhard. *Suffering Divine Things: Theology as Church Practice*. Translated by Doug Stott. Grand Rapids, MI: Eerdmans, 2000.

Hyers, Conrad. "Biblical Literalism: Constricting the Cosmic Dance." *Christian Century* 99.25 (1982) 823–27.

Hyman, John. "The Gospel According to Wittgenstein." In *Wittgenstein and Philosophy of Religion*, edited by Robert L. Arrington and Mark Addis, 1–11. London: Routledge, 2001.

"Ideal Type." *Wikipedia*. Revised January 17, 2021. Online. https://en.wikipedia.org/wiki/Ideal_type.

Incandela, Joseph M. "The Appropriation of Wittgenstein's Work by Philosophers of Religion: Towards a Re-Evaluation and an End." *Religious Studies* 21.4 (1985) 457–74.

Insole, Christopher J. *The Realist Hope: A Critique of Anti-Realist Approaches in Contemporary Philosophical Theology.* Aldershot: Ashgate, 2006.

Jackson, Timothy P. "Against Grammar." *Religious Studies Review* 11.3 (1985) 240–45.

James, William. *Pragmatism: A New Name for Some Old Ways of Thinking.* Cambridge: Cambridge University Press, 2014.

Janik, Allan, and Stephen Toulmin. *Wittgenstein's Vienna.* London: Weidenfeld & Nicolson, 1973.

Jasper, David. *Literature and Theology as Grammar of Assent.* Farnham: Ashgate, 2016.

———. *The Study of Literature and Religion: An Introduction.* London: Macmillan, 1989.

Jeffner, Anders. *The Study of Religious Language.* London: SCM, 1972.

Jennings, Theodore W., Jr. *Beyond Theism: A Grammar of God-Language.* Oxford: Oxford University Press, 1985.

John XXIII. *"Gaudet Mater Ecclesia."* Speech delivered October 11, 1962. Online. https://jakomonchak.files.wordpress.com/2012/10/john-xxiii-opening-speech. pdf.

Johnston, Paul. *Wittgenstein: Rethinking the Inner.* London: Routledge, 1993.

Jolley, Kelly Dean, ed. *Wittgenstein: Key Concepts.* Durham: Acumen, 2010

Jüngel, Eberhard. *God as the Mystery of the World: on the Foundation of the Theology of the Crucified One in the Dispute between Theism and Atheism.* Translated by Darrell L. Guder. Grand Rapids, MI: Eerdmans, 1983.

———. *Theological Essays.* Translated by J. B. Webster. Edinburgh: T&T Clark, 1989.

Kallenberg, Brad J. *Ethics as Grammar: Changing the Postmodern Subject.* Notre Dame, IN: University of Notre Dame Press, 2001.

———. "Unstuck from Yale: Theological Method after Lindbeck." *Scottish Journal of Theology* 50.2 (1997) 91–218.

Kaufman, Gordon D. "Reading Wittgenstein: Notes for Constructive Theologians." *Journal of Religion* 79.3 (1999) 404–21.

Keifert, Patrick R. "Review of *The Nature of Doctrine: Religion and Theology in a Postliberal Age* by George A. Lindbeck." *Word & World* 5.3 (1985) 342–44.

Keightley, Alan. *Wittgenstein, Grammar and God.* London: Epworth, 1976.

Kelsey, David H. "Church Discourse and Public Realm." In *Theology and Dialogue: Essays in Conversation with George Lindbeck,* edited by Bruce D. Marshall, 7–33. Notre Dame, IN: University of Notre Dame Press, 1990.

Kennick, William E. "The Language of Religion." *Philosophical Review* 65.1 (1956) 56–71.

Kenny, Anthony. *Frege.* London: Penguin, 1995.

———. *Wittgenstein.* Rev. ed. Oxford: Blackwell, 2006.

Kerr, Fergus. "Language as Hermeneutic in the Later Wittgenstein." *Tijdschrift voor Filosofie* 27.3 (1965) 491–520.

———. *Theology after Wittgenstein.* 2nd ed. London: SPCK, 1997.

———. "Wittgenstein and Theological Studies." *New Blackfriars* 63.750 (1982) 500–508.

Kimble, Kevin. "Revisiting Wittgenstein on the Nature of Religious Language." *Asian Social Science* 6.6 (2010) 73–81.

Kirkham, Richard L. *Theories of Truth: A Critical Introduction*. Cambridge, MA: MIT Press, 1992.

Klein, Terrance W. *How Things Are in the World: Metaphysics and Theology in Wittgenstein and Rahner*. Milwaukee: Marquette University Press, 2003.

Knight, John Allan. *Liberalism versus Postliberalism: The Great Divide in Twentieth-Century Theology*. Oxford: Oxford University Press, 2013.

Knowles, Steven. *Beyond Evangelicalism: The Theological Methodology of Stanley J Grenz*. Farnham: Ashgate, 2010.

Labron, Tim. *Wittgenstein and Theology*. London: T&T Clark, 2009.

Lash, Nicholas. "Review of *The Nature of Doctrine: Religion and Theology in a Postliberal Age* by George A. Lindbeck." *New Blackfriars* 66.785 (1985) 509–10.

Lazenby, J. Mark. *The Early Wittgenstein on Religion*. London: Continuum, 2006.

Lehrer, Keith. *Theory of Knowledge*. 2nd ed. New York: Westview, 2008.

Lindbeck, George A. *The Church in a Postliberal Age*. Grand Rapids, MI: Eerdmans, 2003.

———. *The Nature of Doctrine: Religion and Theology in a Postliberal Age*. London: SPCK, 1984.

———. "Response to Bruce Marshall." *The Thomist* 53.3 (1989) 403–6.

Linsky, Leonard. "Wittgenstein on Language and Some Problems of Philosophy." *Journal of Philosophy* 54.10 (1957) 285–93.

Locke, John. *An Essay Concerning Human Understanding*. Edited by P. Nidditch. Oxford: Clarendon, 1975.

Lonergan, Bernard. *Philosophy of God, and Theology*. London: Darton Longman Todd, 1973.

Long, D. Stephen. *Speaking of God: Theology, Language, and Truth*. Grand Rapids, MI: Eerdmans, 2009.

Loughlin, Gerard. *Telling God's Story: Bible, Church and Narrative Theology*. Cambridge: Cambridge University Press, 1996.

Lugton, Robert C. "Ludwig Wittgenstein: The Logic of Language." *ETC: A Review of General Semantics* 22.2 (1965)165–92.

Lynch, Michael P., ed. *The Nature of Truth: Classic and Contemporary Perspectives*. Cambridge, MA: MIT Press, 2001.

MacIntyre, Alasdair. *After Virtue: A Study in Moral Theology*. 2nd ed. Notre Dame, IN: University of Notre Dame Press, 1984.

———. *Three Rival Versions of Moral Enquiry: Encyclopaedia, Genealogy and Tradition*. Notre Dame, IN: University of Notre Dame Press, 1988.

———. *Whose Justice? Which Rationality?* London: Duckworth, 1988.

MacKinnon, Donald. "The Problem of the 'System of Projection' Appropriate to Christian Theological Statements." In vol. 5 of *Explorations in Theology*, by Donald MacKinnon, 70–89. London: SCM, 1979.

Macquarrie, John. *God-Talk: An Examination of the Language and Logic of Theology*. London: SCM, 1967.

———. *Principles of Christian Theology*. New York: Scribner's Sons, 1966.

———. *Thinking About God*. London: SCM, 1975.

Maimonides, Moses. *The Guide for the Perplexed*. 2nd ed. Translated by M. Friedlander. London: Routledge & Kegan Paul, 1904.

Malcolm, Norman. *Ludwig Wittgenstein: A Memoir*. With a Biographical Sketch by G. H. von Wright. 2nd ed. Oxford: Oxford University Press, 1984.

————. *Thought and Knowledge*. New York: Cornell University Press, 1977.

————. *Wittgenstein: A Religious Point of View?* Oxford: Routledge, 1993.

Marietta, Don E. "Is Talk of God Talk of Anything?" *International Journal for the Philosophy of Religion* 4.3 (1973) 187–95.

Marshall, Bruce D. "Introduction: The Nature of Doctrine after Twenty-Five Years." In *The Nature of Doctrine: Religion and Theology in a Postliberal Age*, by George A. Lindbeck, vii–xxvii. Twenty-Fifth Anniversary ed. Louisville, KY: Westminster John Knox, 2009.

————, ed. *Theology and Dialogue: Essays in Conversation with George Lindbeck*. Notre Dame, IN: Notre Dame University Press, 1990.

————. *Trinity and Truth*. Cambridge Studies in Christian Doctrine 3. Cambridge: Cambridge University Press, 1999.

————. "We Shall Bear the Image of the Man of Heaven: Theology and Concept of Truth." *Modern Theology* 11.1 (1995) 93–117.

Martin, Glen T. *From Nietzsche to Wittgenstein: The Problem of Truth and Nihilism in the Modern World*. New York: Peter Lang, 1989.

Martin, James Alfred. *The New Dialogue Between Philosophy and Theology*. London: Adam & Charles Black, 1966.

McClendon, James William, and Brad J. Kallenberg. "Ludwig Wittgenstein: A Christian in Philosophy." *Scottish Journal of Theology* 51.02 (1998) 131–61.

McCutcheon, Felicity. *Religion within the Limits of Language Alone: Wittgenstein on Philosophy and Religion*. Aldershot: Ashgate, 2001.

McFague, Sallie. *Metaphorical Theology: Models of God in Religious Language*. Philadelphia: Fortress, 1982.

McGinn, Colin. *Wittgenstein on Meaning*. Oxford: Blackwell, 1984.

McGinn, Marie. *Wittgenstein and the Philosophical Investigations*. Oxford: Routledge, 1997.

McGovern, Ken, and Bela Szabados. "Was Wittgenstein a Fideist? Two Views." *Sophia* 41.2 (2002) 41–54.

McGrath, Alister E. "An Evangelical Evaluation of Postliberalism." In *The Nature of Confession: Evangelicals & Postliberals in Conversation*, edited by Timothy R. Phillips and Dennis L. Okholm, 23–44. Downers Grove, IL: InterVarsity, 1996.

————. *The Genesis of Doctrine: A Study in the Foundations of Doctrinal Criticism*. Oxford: Blackwell, 1990.

————. *Reality*. Vol. 2 of *A Scientific Theology*. London: T&T Clark, 2002.

McGuinness, Brian F. "The Mysticism of the *Tractatus*." *The Philosophical Review* 75.3 (1966) 305–28.

McMullin, Ernan. "The Two Faces of Science." *Review of Metaphysics* 27.4 (1974) 655–76.

McPherson, Thomas. *Philosophy and Religious Belief*. London: Hutchinson University Library, 1974.

Medina, José. *Language: Key Concepts in Philosophy*. London: Continuum, 2005.

Merleau-Ponty, Maurice. *The Visible and the Invisible: Followed by Working Notes*. Edited by Claude Lefort. Translated by Alphonso Lingis. Evanston, IL: Northwestern University Press, 1968.

Michalson, G. E. "A Response to Lindbeck." *Modern Theology* 4.2 (1988) 107–20.

Michener, Ronald T. *Postliberal Theology: A Guide for the Perplexed*. London: Bloomsbury T&T Clark, 2013.

Milbank, John. *The Word Made Strange: Theology, Language and Culture.* Oxford: Blackwell, 1997.

Miles, Jack. "Faith and Belief: *The Evolution of God* by Robert Wright and *The Case for God* by Karen Armstrong." *Los Angeles Times*, October 11, 2009. Online. http://www.latimes.com/entertainment/arts/la-ca-karen-armstrong11-2009oct11-story.html.

Mitchell, Basil, ed. *Faith and Logic.* London: George Allen & Unwin, 1957.

———. *Philosophy of Religion.* Oxford: Oxford University Press, 1971.

Modrak, Deborah K. W. *Aristotle's Theory of Language and Meaning.* Cambridge: Cambridge University Press, 2001.

Mohler, Albert. "Modernity's Assault on Truth." *Albert Mohler* (blog), March 16, 2005. Online. https://albertmohler.com/2005/03/16/modernitys-assault-on-truth.

Monk, Ray. *Ludwig Wittgenstein: The Duty of Genius.* London: Penguin, 1991.

Moore, Andrew. *Realism and Christian Faith: God, Grammar, and Meaning.* Cambridge: Cambridge University Press, 2003.

Moore, G. E. "Wittgenstein's Lectures in 1930–33." *Mind* 63.249 (1954) 1–15.

Moreland, J. P. *Kingdom Triangle: Recover the Christian Mind, Renovate the Soul, Restore the Spirit's Power.* Grand Rapids, MI: Zondervan, 2007.

Morris, Michael, and Julian Dodd. "Mysticism and Nonsense in the *Tractatus.*" *European Journal of Philosophy* 17.2 (2009) 247–76.

Muis, Jan. "Can Christian Talk about God be Literal?" *Modern Theology* 27.4 (2011) 582–607.

Murdoch, Iris. *Metaphysics as a Guide to Morals.* London: Chatto & Windus, 1992.

———. *Sartre: Romantic Rationalist.* New Haven: Yale University Press, 1953.

———. *The Sovereignty of Good.* London: Routledge & Kegan Paul, 1970.

Murphy, Francesca Aran. *God is Not a Story: Realism Revisited.* Oxford: Oxford University Press, 2007.

Murphy, Nancey C. *Beyond Liberalism and Fundamentalism: How Modern and Postmodern Philosophy Set the Theological Agenda.* Harrisburg, PA: Trinity, 1996.

Newman, Andrew. *The Correspondence Theory of Truth: An Essay on the Metaphysics of Predication.* Cambridge: Cambridge University Press, 2002.

Nicholson, Hugh. "The Political Nature of Doctrine: A Critique of Lindbeck in Light of Recent Scholarship." *Heythrop Journal* 48.6 (2007) 858–77.

Nicholson, Michael W. "Abusing Wittgenstein: The Misuse of the Concept of Language Games in Contemporary Theology." *Journal of the Evangelical Theological Society* 39.4 (1996) 617–29.

Nieli, Russell. *Wittgenstein: From Mysticism to Ordinary Language: A Study of Viennese Positivism and the Thought of Ludwig Wittgenstein.* Albany: State University of New York Press, 1987.

Nielsen, Kai. "Wittgensteinian Fideism." *Philosophy* 42.161 (1967) 191–209.

O'Neill, Colman E. "The Rule Theory of Doctrine and Propositional Truth." *The Thomist: A Speculative Quarterly Review* 49.3 (1985) 417–42.

Otto, Rudolf. *The Idea of the Holy: An Inquiry into the Non-Rational Factor in the Idea of the Divine and Its Relation to the Rational.* New York: Oxford University Press, 1958.

Pannenberg, Wolfhart. *Basic Questions in Theology.* Vol. 2. Minneapolis, MN: Fortress, 2007.

————. *Systematic Theology.* Vol. 3. Translated by Geoffrey W. Bromiley. London: T&T Clark, 2004.

Patterson, Sue. *Word, Words and World: How a Wittgensteinian Perspective on Metaphor-Making Reveals the Theo-Logic of Reality.* Oxford: Peter Lang A. G., 2013.

Pattison, George. *The End of Theology—And the Task of Thinking about God.* London: SCM, 1998.

Pears, David. *Wittgenstein.* London: Fontana, 1971.

————. "Wittgenstein." In *The Blackwell Companion to Philosophy,* edited by N. Bunnin and E. P. Tsui-James, 811–26. 2nd ed. Oxford: Blackwell, 2002.

Pecknold, C. C. *Transforming Postliberal Theology: George Lindbeck, Pragmatism and Scripture.* London: T&T Clark, 2005.

Penner, Myron B., ed. *Christianity and the Postmodern Turn: Six Views.* Grand Rapids, MI: Brazo, 2005.

Phillips, D. Z. *The Concept of Prayer.* London: Routledge & Kegan Paul, 1965.

————. *Faith after Foundationalism.* London: Routledge, 1988.

Phillips, Timothy R., and Dennis L. Okholm, eds. *The Nature of Confession: Evangelicals & Postliberals in Conversation.* Downers Grove, IL: InterVarsity, 1996.

Pichler, Alois, and Simo Säätelä, eds. *Wittgenstein: The Philosopher and His Works.* Warschau/Berlin: De Gruyter Open, 2006.

Pitcher, George, ed. *Wittgenstein: The Philosophical Investigations.* New York: Doubleday, 1966.

Placher, William C. "Postliberal Theology." In *The Modern Theologians: An Introduction to Christian Theology in the Twentieth Century,* edited by David F. Ford, 343–56. 2nd ed. Malden, MA: Blackwell, 1997.

————. "Revisionist and Postliberal Theologies and the Public Character of Theology." *The Thomist* 49.3 (1985) 392–416.

————. *Unapologetic Theology: A Christian Voice in a Pluralistic Conversation.* Louisville, KY: Westminster/John Knox, 1989. .

Plato. *Cratylus.* Translated by Benjamin Jowett. *Project Gutenberg.* Online. http://www.gutenberg.org/ebooks/1616.

————. *The Dialogues of Plato.* 4 vols. 4th ed. Translated by B. Jowett. Oxford: Clarendon, 1871.

————. *Republic.* Edited and translated by Chris Emlyn-Jones and William Preddy. Cambridge, MA: Harvard University Press, 2013.

Pole, David. *The Later Philosophy of Wittgenstein.* London: Athlone, 1958.

Prickett, Stephen. *Words and the Word: Language, Poetics and Biblical Interpretation.* Cambridge: Cambridge University Press, 1986.

Pseudo-Dionysius the Areopagite. *On the Divine Names and the Mystical Theology.* Translated by C. E. Rolt. London: SPCK, 1920.

Putnam, Hilary. "Language and Philosophy." In *Mind, Language and Reality,* edited by Hilary Putnam, 1–32. Vol. 2 of *Philosophical Papers.* Cambridge: Cambridge University Press, 1975.

Putnam, Rhyne R. *In Defense of Doctrine: Evangelicalism, Theology, and Scripture.* Minneapolis, MN: Fortress, 2015.

Rahner, Karl. *Theological Investigations.* Vol. 9. London: Darton Longman Todd, 1972.

Ramsey, Ian T. *Religious Language: An Empirical Placing of Theological Phrases.* London: SCM, 1957.

————. "Talking about God: Models, Ancient and Modern." In *Myth and Symbol*, edited by F. W. Dillistone, 76–97. London: SPCK, 1966.

Raschke, Carl A. *The Alchemy of the Word: Language and the End of Theology*. Missoula, MT: Scholars, 1979.

Read, Rupert. *Applying Wittgenstein*. Edited by Laura Cook. London: Continuum, 2007.

Rhees, Rush. *Discussions of Wittgenstein*. London: Routledge & Kegan Paul, 1970.

————, ed. *Recollections of Wittgenstein*. Oxford: Oxford University Press, 1984.

Richards, Jay Wesley. "Truth and Meaning in George Lindbeck's *The Nature of Doctrine*." *Religious Studies* 33.1 (1997) 33–53.

Richter, Duncan J. "Ludwig Wittgenstein (1889–1951)." *Internet Encyclopedia of Philosophy*. Online. https://www.iep.utm.edu/wittgens.

Ricoeur, Paul. *Figuring the Sacred: Religion, Narrative, and Imagination*. Minneapolis, MN: Fortress, 1995.

————. *Interpretation Theory: Discourse and the Surplus of Meaning*. Fort Worth: Texas Christian University, 1976.

Rigby, Paul, et al. "The Nature of Doctrine and Scientific Progress." *Theological Studies* 52.4 (1991) 669–88.

Roach, William C. *Hermeneutics as Epistemology: A Critical Assessment of Carl F. H. Henry's Epistemological Approach to Hermeneutics*. Eugene, OR: Wipf & Stock, 2015.

Robins, R. H. *A Short History of Linguistics*. London: Routledge, 2013.

Rorty, Richard. *Contingency, Irony, and Solidarity*. Cambridge: Cambridge University Press, 1989.

————, ed. *The Linguistic Turn: Essays in Philosophical Method*. Chicago: University of Chicago Press, 1967.

————. *Philosophy and the Mirror of Nature*. Princeton: Princeton University Press, 1981.

Ross, James. "Religious Language." In *Philosophy of Religion: A Guide to the Subject*, edited by Brian Davis, 106–35. London: Cassell, 1998.

Rundle, Bede. *Wittgenstein and Contemporary Philosophy of Language*. Oxford: Basel Blackwell, 1990.

Russell, Bertrand. *Classics of Analytic Philosophy*. Edited by Robert R. Ammerman. Indianapolis, IN: Hackett, 1990.

————. *An Outline of Philosophy*. London: Allen & Unwin, 1927.

Sahlin, Nils-Eric. *The Philosophy of F. P. Ramsey*. Cambridge: Cambridge University Press, 1990.

Saner, Emine. "Is There Any Place for Religious Faith in Science?" *Guardian*, April 16, 2011. Online. https://www.theguardian.com/commentisfree/belief/2011/apr/16/conversation-science-religious-faith.

Saussure, Ferdinand de. *Course in General Linguistics*. Edited by Charles Bally and Albert Sechehaye. Translated by Wade Baskin. New York: Philosophical Library, 1959.

Schleiermacher, Friedrich. *The Christian Faith*. Edited by H. R. Mackintosh and James S. Stewart. Edinburgh: T&T Clark, 1928.

Schneiders, Sandra M. *The Revelatory Text: Interpreting the New Testament as Sacred Scripture*. 2nd ed. Collegeville, MN: Liturgical, 1999.

Schönbaumsfeld, Genia. "Worlds or Words Apart? Wittgenstein on Understanding Religious Language." *Ratio: An International Journal of Analytic Philosophy* 20.4 (2007) 422–41.

Scott, Michael. *Religious Language.* Basingstoke: Palgrave Macmillan, 2013.

Shakespeare, Steven. *Radical Orthodoxy: A Critical Introduction.* London: SPCK, 2007.

Sherry, Patrick. *Religion, Truth and Language-Games.* London: Macmillan, 1977.

Shields, Philip R. *Logic and Sin in the Writings of Ludwig Wittgenstein.* Chicago: University of Chicago Press, 1993.

Sluga, Hans, and David G. Stern, eds. *The Cambridge Companion to Wittgenstein.* Cambridge: Cambridge University Press, 1966.

Smith, Christian. *The Bible Made Impossible: Why Biblicism is Not a Truly Evangelical Reading of Scripture.* Grand Rapids, MI: Brazos, 2011.

Smith, James K. A. *Speech and Theology: Language and the Logic of Incarnation.* London: Routledge, 2002.

———. *Who's Afraid of Relativism? Community, Contingency, and Creaturehood.* Grand Rapids, MI: Baker Academic, 2014.

Smith, John E. *Experience and God.* New York: Oxford University Press, 1968.

Soames, Scott. *Understanding Truth.* New York: Oxford University Press, 1998.

Sommerville, C. John: "Is Religion a Language Game? A Real World Critique of the Cultural-Linguistic Theory." *Theology Today* 51.4 (1995) 594–99.

Sontag, Frederick. *Wittgenstein and the Mystical: Philosophy as an Ascetic Practice.* Atlanta, GA: Scholars, 1995.

Soskice, Janet M. *Metaphorical and Religious Language.* Oxford: Clarendon, 1985.

———. "Religious Language." In *A Companion to Philosophy of Religion,* edited by Charles Taliaferro et al., 348–56. 2nd ed. Oxford: Wiley-Blackwell, 2010.

Specht, Ernst Konrad. *The Foundations of Wittgenstein's Late Philosophy.* Translated by D. E. Walford. Manchester: Manchester University Press, 1963.

Steiner, George. *Real Presences.* London: Faber & Faber, 1989.

Stern, David G. "How Many Wittgensteins?" In *Wittgenstein: The Philosopher and his Works,* edited by Alois Pichler and S. Säätelä, 205–29. Warschau/Berlin: De Gruyter Open, 2006.

———. *Wittgenstein's Philosophical Investigations: An Introduction.* Cambridge: Cambridge University Press, 2004.

Stevenson, Charles L. *Ethics and Language.* New Haven: Yale University Press, 1944.

Stiver, Dan R. *The Philosophy of Religious Language: Sign, Symbol & Story.* Oxford: Blackwell, 1996.

Stoutland, Frederick. "Wittgenstein: On Certainty and Truth." *Philosophical Investigations* 21.3 (1998) 203–21.

Strawson, P. F. *Logico-Linguistic Papers.* London: Methuen, 1971.

———. "Review of Wittgenstein's Philosophical Investigations." In *Wittgenstein: The Philosophical Investigations,* edited by George Pitcher, 22–64. New York: Doubleday, 1966.

Surin, Kenneth. "'Many Religions and the One True Faith': An Examination of Lindbeck's Chapter Three." *Modern Theology* 4.2 (1988) 187–209.

Surkis, Judith. "When Was the Linguistic Turn? A Genealogy." *American Historical Review* 117.3 (2012) 700–722.

Sutherland, Stewart R. "On the Idea of a Form of Life." *Religious Studies* 11.3 (1975) 293–306.

Sweet, William. "Is the 'Intelligibility of Religious Language' Debate Dead?" *Toronto Journal of Theology* 28.2 (2012) 291–308.

Swinburne, Richard. *The Existence of God*. Rev. ed. Oxford: Oxford University Press, 2004.

Tacey, David. *Religion as Metaphor: Beyond Literal Belief*. Somerset, NJ: Transaction, 2015.

Tallis, Raymond. *Reflections of a Metaphysical Flâneur and Other Essays*. Durham, NH: Acumen, 2013.

Tanner, Kathryn. *Theories of Culture: A New Agenda for Theology*. Minneapolis, MN: Fortress, 1997.

Taylor, Charles. *Human Agency and Language*. Vol. 1 of *Philosophical Papers*. Cambridge: Cambridge University Press, 1985.

———. *The Language Animal: The Full Shape of the Human Linguistic Capacity*. Cambridge, MA: Belknap Press of Harvard University Press, 2016.

———. "Merleau-Ponty and the Epistemological Picture." In *The Cambridge Companion to Merleau-Ponty*, edited by Taylor Carman and Mark B. N. Hansen, 26–49. Cambridge: Cambridge University Press, 2005.

Thiemann, Ronald F. "Response to George Lindbeck." *Theology Today* 43.3 (1986) 377–82.

Thiselton, Anthony C. *The Two Horizons: New Testament Hermeneutics and Philosophical Description with Special Reference to Heidegger, Bultmann, Gadamer, and Wittgenstein*. Exeter: Paternoster, 1980.

Thuesen, Peter J. "George Lindbeck on Truth." *Lutheran Quarterly* 10.1 (1996) 47–58.

Tilley, Terrence W. "Incommensurability, Intratextuality, and Fideism." *Modern Theology* 5.2 (1989) 87–111.

———. *Talking of God: An Introduction to Philosophical Analysis of Religious Language*. New York: Paulist, 1978.

Tilley, Terrence W., et al. *Postmodern Theologies: The Challenge of Religious Diversity*. Eugene, OR: Wipf & Stock, 2005.

Tillich, Paul. *Dynamics of Faith*. London: George Allen & Unwin, 1957.

———. *Systematic Theology*. Vol. 1. London: SCM, 1951.

———. *Theology of Culture*. Edited by Robert C. Kimball. New York: Oxford University Press, 1959.

Torrance, Thomas F. *Reality and Scientific Theology*. Edinburgh: Scottish Academic, 1985.

Tracy, David. "Lindbeck's New Program for Theology: A Reflection." *The Thomist* 49.3 (1985) 460–72.

Travis, Charles. *The Uses of Sense: Wittgenstein's Philosophy of Language*. Oxford: Clarendon, 1989.

Trenery, David. *Alasdair MacIntyre, George Lindbeck, and the Nature of Tradition*. Eugene, OR: Pickwick, 2014.

Trigg, Roger. *Reason and Commitment*. Cambridge: Cambridge University Press, 1973.

———. "Wittgenstein and Social Science." In *Wittgenstein Centenary Essays*, edited by A. P. Griffiths, 209–22. Cambridge: Cambridge University Press, 1991.

Turner, Denys. *Faith, Reason and the Existence of God*. Cambridge: Cambridge University Press, 2004.

Urban, Wilbur M. *Language and Reality: The Philosophy of Language and the Principles of Symbolism*. London: George Allen & Unwin, 1939.

Vanhoozer, Kevin J. *The Drama of Doctrine: A Canonical Linguistic Approach to Christian Theology.* Louisville, KY: Westminster John Knox, 2005.

———. *Is There a Meaning in This Text? The Bible, the Reader, and the Morality of Literary Knowledge.* Grand Rapids, MI: Zondervan, 2009.

Vettiyolil, Abraham. "Wittgenstein on the Grammar of Religious Beliefs." *International Journal of Philosophy and Theology* 2.2 (2014) 1–12.

Vial, Theodore. *Schleiermacher: A Guide for the Perplexed.* London: Bloomsbury T&T Clark, 2013.

Vidu, Adonis. *Postliberal Theological Method: A Critical Study.* Milton Keynes: Paternoster, 2005.

Vroom, Hendrik M. *Religion and the Truth: Philosophical Reflections and Perspectives.* Translated by J. W. Rebel. Grand Rapids, MI: Eerdmans, 1989.

Wainwright, Geoffrey. "Ecumenical Dimensions of Lindbeck's 'Nature of Doctrine.'" *Modern Theology* 4.2 (1988) 121–32.

Waismann, Friedrich. "Notes on Talks with Wittgenstein." *Philosophical Review* 74.1 (1965) 12–16.

———. *The Principles of Linguistic Philosophy.* Edited by R. Harre. London: Macmillan, 1965.

———. *Wittgenstein and the Vienna Circle: Conversations.* Translated by Brian McGuinness and Joachim Schulte. Oxford: Blackwell, 1979.

Wallace, Mark I. "The New Yale Theology: Liberalism, Realism and the Problem of Truth." *Christian Scholar's Review* 17.2 (1987) 154–70.

Ward, Keith. "*Theology after Wittgenstein* (Book Review)." *Religious Studies* 24.2 (1988) 267–69.

Ware, Ben. *Dialectic of the Ladder: Wittgenstein, the Tractatus and Modernism.* London: Bloomsbury Academic, 2015.

Webster, John, and George P. Schner, eds. *Theology after Liberalism: A Reader.* Oxford: Blackwell, 2000.

White, Roger M. *Talking about God: The Concept of Analogy and the Problem of Religious Language.* Farnham: Ashgate, 2010.

———. *Wittgenstein's Tractatus Logico-Philosophicus: Reader's Guide.* London: Continuum, 2006.

Wiles, Maurice. *Faith and the Mystery of God.* London: SCM, 1982.

Williams, Rowan. *The Edge of Words: God and the Habits of Language.* London: Bloomsbury, 2014.

———. "God." In *Fields of Faith: Theology and Religious Studies for the Twenty-First Century,* edited by Janet Martin Soskice et al., 75–89. Cambridge: Cambridge University Press, 2005.

———. "The Literal Sense of Scripture." *Modern Theology* 7.2 (1991) 121–34.

———. "Response to Kerr, Hedley, Pickstock, Ward and Soskice." *Modern Theology* 31.4 (2015) 630–36.

Williams, Stephen. "Lindbeck's Regulative Christology." *Modern Theology* 4.2 (1988) 173–86.

Wilson, Brendan. *Wittgenstein's Philosophical Investigations: A Guide.* Edinburgh: Edinburgh University Press, 1998.

Wilson, Kenneth. *Making Sense of It: An Essay in Philosophical Theology.* London: Epworth, 1973.

Winch, Peter. "Meaning and Religious Language." In *Reason and Religion*, edited by
    Stuart C. Brown, 193–221. Ithaca, NY: Cornell University Press, 1977.
Winters, Andrew Michael. "Hume's Naturalism and Logical Positivism: Epistemological
    Reliance upon Intuition." MA thesis, California Institute of Integral Studies, 2007.
Wittgenstein, Ludwig. *The Blue and Brown Books*. Oxford: Blackwell, 1958.
————. *Culture and Value: A Selection from the Posthumous Remains*. Rev. ed. Edited
    by Georg Henrik von Wright. Translated by Peter Winch. Oxford: Blackwell, 1998.
————. "Lecture on Ethics." *Philosophical Review* 74.1 (1965) 3–12.
————. *Lectures & Conversations on Aesthetics, Psychology and Religious Belief*. Edited
    by Cyril Barrett. Oxford: Blackwell, 1966.
————. *Lectures, Cambridge 1930–1932: From the Notes of John King and Desmond Lee*.
    Edited by Desmond Lee. Oxford: Blackwell, 1980.
————. *Lectures, Cambridge 1930–1933: From the Notes of G. E. Moore*. Edited by David
    G. Stern et al. Cambridge: Cambridge University Press, 2016.
————. *Letters to C. K. Ogden*. Edited by G. H. von Wright. Oxford: Blackwell, 1973.
————. *Notebooks 1914–1916*. Edited by G. H. von Wright and G. E. M. Anscombe.
    Translated by G. E. M. Anscombe. Oxford: Blackwell, 1961.
————. *On Certainty*. Edited by G. E. M. Anscombe and G. H. von Wright. Translated
    by Denis Paul and G. E. M. Anscombe. New York: Harper & Row, 1972.
————. *Philosophical Grammar*. Translated by Anthony Kenny. Edited by Rush Rhees.
    Oxford: Blackwell, 1974.
————. *Philosophical Investigations*. 3rd ed. Translated by G. E. M. Anscombe. Oxford:
    Blackwell, 2001.
————. *Remarks on Colour*. Edited by G. E. M. Anscombe. Translated by Linda L.
    McAlister and Margarete Schättle. Oxford: Blackwell, 1958.
————. *Remarks on Frazer's Golden Bough*. Edited by Rush Rhees. Translated by A. C.
    Miles. Atlantic Highlands, NJ: Humanities, 1978.
————. *Remarks on the Philosophy of Psychology*. Translated by G. E. M. Anscombe and
    G. H. von Wright. Oxford: Blackwell, 1980.
————. *Tractatus Logico-Philosophicus*. Translated by D. F. Pears and B. F. McGuinness.
    London: Routledge & Kegan Paul, 1961.
————. *Zettel*. Translated by G. E. M. Anscombe. Oxford: Blackwell, 1967.
Wood, Charles M. "Review of *The Nature of Doctrine: Religion and Theology in a
    Postliberal Age* by George A. Lindbeck." *Religious Studies Review* 11.3 (1985) 235–
    40.
Wynn, Mark. "Religious Language." In *Companion Encyclopedia of Theology*, edited by
    Peter Bryne and Leslie Houlden, 413–26. London: Routledge, 1995.
Yorke, Christopher. "The Mystic and the Ineffable: Some Epistemological, Political, and
    Metaphilosophical Concerns." MA thesis, Concordia University, 2004.
Zahl, Simeon. "On the Affective Salience of Doctrines." *Modern Theology* 31.3 (2015)
    428–44.
Zemach, Eddy. "Wittgenstein's Philosophy of the Mystical." *The Review of Metaphysics*
    18.1 (1964) 38–57.
Zorn, Hans. "Grammar, Doctrines, and Practice." *Journal of Religion* 75.4 (1995) 509–
    20.
Zuurdeeg, Willem F. "The Nature of Theological Language." *Journal of Religion* 40.1
    (1960) 1–8.

Name/Subject Index